A Peaceful
Superpower

A Peaceful Superpower

Lessons from the World's Largest Antiwar Movement

David Cortright

New Village Press • New York

All rights reserved. Except for brief portions quoted for
purposes of review, no part of this book may be reprinted,
Except for brief portions quoted for purposes of review, no
part of this book may be reprinted, reproduced, or utilized
in any medium now known or hereafter invented without
prior permission in writing from the publisher.

Published in the United States by New Village Press

bookorders@newvillagepress.net
www.newvillagepress.org

New Village Press is a public-benefit, nonprofit publisher

Distributed by NYU Press

Paperback ISBN: 978-1-61332-203-1
Hardcover ISBN: 978-1-61332-204-8
EBook ISBN: 978-1-61332-205-5
Institutional EBook ISBN: 978-1-61332-206-2

Publication Date: February 2023

First Edition

Library of Congress Control Number: 2022950157

Cover design: Kevin Stone

Contents

Foreword

They Were Right

David S. Meyer

Critics and citizens were dubious about George W. Bush's plans to invade Iraq ostensibly to punish Saddam Hussein and stop nuclear proliferation and to promote peace and democracy. They thought the administration was misrepresenting facts about the threat and even about their own intentions in threatening war.

They were right.

The clerics who marched and gave sermons; the doctrinaire leftists who challenged racism and imperialism; the environmentalists who saw no cause for an oil war; the veterans who recalled the futility and stupidity of war; the military families who knew they would pay the ultimate price of war; the resisters in the military who volunteered to serve their country and the Constitution but could not accept a war of aggression; the balance-of-power scholars who warned about unleashing countries and leaders even more malevolent and disruptive than Iraq and Saddam Hussein; the voters determined to threaten and then punish politicians who led their nations into wars; the teachers frantically trying to bone up on geography and the Middle East; the citizen lobbyists who called and emailed their representatives opposing an invasion and then demanding the withdrawal of troops; and the millions of people in the United States and around the world who showed up at mass demonstrations to try to prevent a war they did not think had to be fought.

They were right.

They had different reasons for their opposition. Radical pacifists didn't see any good coming out of massive military spending, while defense scholars saw enormous waste and risk in deploying those valuable assets—and the sacrifice of service men and women—in a war with vague and unrealistic objectives. Opponents of nuclear proliferation cautioned that inspections provided better assurance against the development of new nuclear weapons, while an invasion would incentivize dictators around the world to grab for their own nuclear forces as quickly as possible. But they all agreed on one demand: don't go to war against Iraq when there are other alternatives.

Yet, despite organizing the largest, most diverse, most internationally coordinated movement against a war that hadn't yet started, they couldn't stop the attack. Determined to punish Saddam Hussein, President George W. Bush pushed ahead with a brutal bombing campaign followed by an invasion and maintained a substantial military presence in Iraq for years. President Barack Obama withdrew the troops by 2011, fulfilling his pledge to the voters who elected him, only to return to combat three years later, this time against ISIS, a new enemy that grew up as a direct result of the invasion and its aftermath. The war cost trillions of dollars, thousands of American lives, and hundreds of thousands of Iraqi lives. It did not make the region more pacific or even more stable, nor did it usher in a new era of democratic governance in the Middle East—or even in Iraq.

But "I told you so" doesn't do much for global peace or democracy either. We must do better, and David Cortright offers a way forward.

Cortright was right in the middle of this organizing effort, brokering alliances with a broad variety of groups with different ideas and aims, arguing about tactics, and choreographing demands. He had been doing this kind of peace work for decades, beginning as a soldier organizing military opposition to the war in Vietnam. He's been enmeshed in antiwar and antinuclear weapons organizing since, spanning a half-century. He knows the difficulties of organizing, the risks and rewards of coalition building, and the very long, slow road to a more peaceful world.

Here, Cortright shows how a massive international peace movement was organized, and how it flourished but was unable to prevent the invasion. He details the successes, and then reviews the disappointments—in organizing and in efficacy. He shows that while the movement didn't stop this war, it might help to stop the next one, educating millions of citizens about the costs and dangers of war in general—and this one in particular—and showing politicians just what those citizen activists could do. Cortright identifies and claims the (always) partial victories the movement won, and how it changed the politics of peace and war . . . for a while. He shows a route to a broader movement, more powerful and pragmatic, more vital and long-lived, and more effective.

This is not an easy road, but it's far better than any imagined alternatives. *A Peaceful Superpower* is an honest and analytical examination of a campaign that had some success, but left much undone, and a sketch of the efforts that must follow.

Preface

As I was finalizing this book on historic opposition to the U.S. war in Iraq, Russia launched its unprovoked military assault on Ukraine. War suddenly returned to the global agenda, seeming to overshadow the legacy of the antiwar movement that I document in this volume.

It was clear from the initial response in Washington, however, that while Americans deeply sympathize with and support Ukraine, there would be no U.S. boots on the ground. This reflects an aversion in American politics to participation in war, the result of military failures in Afghanistan, Iraq, and Vietnam, which validates the antiwar message.

There can be no justification for Putin's savage attack against the Ukrainian people, but it is important to see parallels when states commit acts of military aggression against sovereign nations in violation of international law.

George W. Bush himself inadvertently admitted the parallel in a May 2022 speech criticizing Putin's aggression. The former president said we must condemn the "wholly unjustified and brutal invasion of Iraq." He paused and quickly corrected himself, "I mean Ukraine," then under his breadth "Iraq, too."

In both cases, government propaganda claimed that military action would be quick and low-cost, and that invading forces would be greeted as liberators. In both countries, public opinion initially favored the use of force, but as the costs of war mounted, public doubts increased. In the U.S. political demands rose for the withdrawal of troops. In Russia, hundreds of thousands of military-aged men fled the country, and low morale and acts of resistance emerged within the military.

Many activists in the U.S. and Europe oppose Putin's aggression. They have responded by aiding Ukrainian victims, supporting Russian war resisters and calling for diplomacy to end the bloodshed. Whether antiwar arguments will prevail against Russia's war is uncertain, but the lessons of past wars and the movements against them remain relevant.

November, 2022

Introduction

On February 15, 2003, in hundreds of cities across the world, an estimated ten million people demonstrated against war on Iraq. It was the largest single day of antiwar protest in human history. More than a million people jammed the center of London, and huge throngs marched in Rome, Barcelona, Madrid, Berlin, Paris, Sydney, and hundreds of other cities. Hundreds of thousands braved bitter cold in New York and demonstrated in San Francisco.[1] The people of the globe spoke out as never before in one unified voice against the planned invasion of Iraq. "The world says no to war" was the slogan and the reality.

The February 15 demonstrations were the high point of an unprecedented mobilization of public opposition to the invasion. Scholar Barbara Epstein described the Iraq campaign as "the largest transnational antiwar movement that has ever taken place."[2] In Britain, the Stop the War campaign formed in the fall of 2001 and organized a series of mass marches over the following year and half that culminated in the massive gathering in London on February 15.[3] In the United States, the movement grew rapidly in the fall of 2002 and early 2003, reaching levels of participation that

1

took years to develop during the Vietnam era. The Iraq movement was more international in character than previous antiwar campaigns, as protests were coordinated throughout the world and activists understood themselves to be part of a truly global struggle. The movement represented a convergence of antiwar and global justice efforts in a common campaign against an unjust war and military-corporate domination.[4] It was an expression of what scholar Stephen Gill called "new . . . forms of global political agency."[5] The movement emerged from traditional peace and justice networks and relied extensively on the knowledge and resources of progressive research centers and organizations and individuals with previous experience in antiwar action. The roots of the Iraq antiwar movement reached back to the Nuclear Weapons Freeze Campaign, the Central America solidarity movement, the antiapartheid struggle, and the Vietnam antiwar movement.

I was an active participant in the Iraq antiwar movement, and in many of those previous campaigns. I write as a scholar-activist, presenting lived history from one who was engaged in some of the activities described here. Mine is not a detached, ivory-tower stance. I strive to uphold rigorous standards of academic accuracy and documentation, but I bring a perspective to my analysis and a commitment to praxis. I focus on history from the bottom up, emphasizing the social and cultural forces that influence policymaking.[6] Social movements have at times played a significant role in shaping political agendas on issues from women's rights to the environment and peace. This book examines the debate about the Iraq War from a civil society perspective and explores how activists altered government decision-making.

My personal history tracks the evolution of the US peace movement over the decades and its re-emergence in the Iraq mobilization. As a reluctant soldier during the Vietnam War, I spoke out against the war and joined the GI peace movement, organizing petitions and protests among active-duty troops, and filing a lawsuit against the army over the right to dissent. I wrote about that movement in *Soldiers in Revolt* and *Waging Peace in Vietnam.*[7] In the late 1970s and 80s, I was executive director of SANE, the Committee for a Sane Nuclear Policy, and was deeply involved in the nuclear freeze campaign and the Central America solidarity movement. I wrote about those experiences in *Peace Works: The Citizen's Role in Ending the Cold War.*[8]

When the Bush administration threatened war against Iraq in 2002, I connected with old and new colleagues to attend the founding meeting of United for Peace and Justice (UFPJ) and helped create the Win Without War coalition. I also worked with partners at the Fourth Freedom Forum and the Kroc Institute for International Peace Studies at the University of Notre Dame to produce a series of policy reports rebutting the case for war and presenting alternative options for countering the potential threat posed by Saddam Hussein. For months, as the buildup to war intensified, I was engaged in coordinating coalitions, planning actions, raising money, writing articles, publishing reports, participating in protests, and speaking to the media. Millions of others were similarly immersed in antiwar activity. This is our story, offered as both a testament to history and an assessment of the movement's impact and relevance.

A Movement Profile

The Iraq antiwar movement was a continuation of multigenerational struggles for peace that emerged from networks dating back to the Vietnam era, utilizing new digital forms of mobilization and modernizing the peace movement and the landscape of political activism more generally. Drawing on these roots, the Iraq antiwar movement was able to learn lessons and sidestep pitfalls that had beset earlier movements to achieve a level of support for antiwar activism rarely seen before. Relationships developed in earlier campaigns allowed activists to build coalitions more rapidly and to mobilize larger protests on shorter timelines. Many opponents of the war sought to turn protest into policy, and after the invasion they worked for the withdrawal of troops through legislative lobbying and electoral campaigns. Themes of continuity and development in the evolution of the movement are a core subject of this volume.

The movement involved religious communities, trade unions, students, women's organizations, people of color, environmentalists, academics, business executives, members of the military, artists, actors, musicians, and many others. Networks were built largely through the internet, which served as the primary tool for communicating and disseminating strategies and actions and made it possible to mobilize huge numbers of people on short notice with limited resources. Opponents of the war also utilized conventional media. The war and the international opposition to it were a major news story, and antiwar activists found themselves in the unaccustomed position of attracting positive media attention. For the first time in history, observed writer Rebecca Solnit, the peace movement was portrayed in the media as "diverse, legitimate and representative," which she called a "watershed victory" for the movement's long-term prospects.[9] This was in sharp contrast with the news media's often negative portrayal of the Vietnam antiwar movement.[10]

The Iraq movement was relatively free of sectarian acrimony among factions on the left. Differences existed, to be sure, as several coalitions emerged in the US to reflect varying political perspectives and organizing strategies, but the sharp political divisions that split the Vietnam antiwar movement did not appear. It was a "global movement without leaders," Solnit wrote.[11] Many brilliant spokespersons and organizers emerged, as people stepped forward on their own to oppose the war in countless creative ways. The movement attracted people of "every age and every social background," wrote disarmament organizer Kate Hudson of the protests in London. It had "a mass and spontaneous character the like of which none of us had experienced before."[12] Activists felt a common sense of urgency in attempting to prevent the invasion. Many saw an unprovoked attack against Iraq without UN authorization as a breach of international law and violation of widely accepted ethical principles for the use of force, such as just cause, legitimate authority, and last resort.[13] Most also shared a common analysis of the drive for war as a dangerous manifestation of US militarism. Defenders of the Bush administration's policy talked openly of empire, which helped antiwar critics understand and portray the war as imperialist—a US attempt to gain geopolitical control over vital Iraqi oil supplies, and part of a neoconservative and Israeli right-wing agenda to make the region safe for US and Israeli interests and impose political-military domination. The stark political realities of this policy of aggression brought together a wide range of constituencies in a concerted campaign to prevent war. The administration's bellicose agenda alarmed many mainstream Americans, who found themselves for the first time listening to and agreeing with the concerns of the peace movement. Similar feelings of alarm and concern motivated protests in every part of the world.

In opposing war, activists also articulated constructive alternatives. They urged greater reliance on policing and international cooperation as nonmilitary means of countering terrorism. They called for diplomacy and peacebuilding to resolve disputes with Iraq and other countries and demanded respect for international law and the United Nations. They also called for honesty and transparency in government and a greater voice for civil society in shaping policy decisions.

Most of all, the movement was motivated by a desire to save lives, to prevent the death and destruction that inevitably accompany war. We had seen in Vietnam and learned from history that innocent civilians are often the primary victims of military conflict. We feared that the occupation of Iraq would arouse armed resistance and lead to more terrorist violence, not less, as many security experts warned at the time. We wanted to prevent further killing and human suffering.

Failure or Success?

A few days after the February 15 demonstrations, *New York Times* reporter Patrick Tyler conferred "superpower" status on the movement. The huge antiwar demonstrations were indications, wrote Tyler, of "two superpowers on the planet: the United States and world public opinion." The White House faced a "tenacious new adversary" that was generating massive opposition to the administration's war policy and had left the world's greatest military power virtually alone on the international stage.[14] Antiwar commentators quickly adopted the phrase and proclaimed their movement "the other superpower." Author Jonathan Schell wrote in *The Nation* of the movement's "immense power" in winning the hearts and minds of the majority of the world's people.[15] Even UN Secretary-General Kofi Annan reportedly used the superpower phrase in referring to antiwar public opinion.[16] A new form of global social movement had emerged, an unprecedented expression of collective consciousness and action bound together through the internet. Yet this vast mobilization of civil resistance and political opposition was unable to stop the march to war. The unavoidable fact, Schell poignantly observed, was that "candles in windows did not stop the cruise missiles."[17] The military juggernaut pushed ahead, undeterred by widespread political opposition in the United States and around the globe.

When the war began, many activists were grief-stricken. How could such a vast, worldwide mobilization fail to stop the invasion? Why did a movement that was dubbed a "superpower" seem so powerless? What could have been done differently that might have made a difference in stopping the war? These are valid questions, but as I argue in this book, the assumption of failure is too pessimistic. The movement did not prevent the attack, but antiwar pressures significantly influenced international politics and White House decision-making in ways that undermined US objectives in Iraq. Global opposition to the invasion led to US isolation and political defeat at the United Nations, which prevented the Bush administration from internationalizing the conflict. This left US and British troops to fight on their own, without allies, weakening the military effort. Antiwar protest in the US was a factor in prompting the administration's decisions to minimize the invasion force and eschew postwar planning, which contributed to US military failure. Peace activism continued after the invasion and entered the political arena, helping to elect antiwar candidates to Congress and a president who campaigned on a platform of withdrawing troops from Iraq. The consequences of the widespread political opposition to the war are greater than most observers and even many participants have acknowledged.

Through the many twists and turns of policy, amidst failure and success, it is difficult to determine the impacts of antiwar opposition, especially on the central question of how or if protesters could have prevented the invasion. I examine these issues from multiple perspectives, addressing core themes that are of interest to the theory and practice of social resistance and to the study of social movements more generally. The book reviews the core strategic challenges the movement faced, including the uphill battle for public opinion and the task of countering White House propaganda. I analyze the political and institutional obstacles all peace movements encounter in attempting to change military policy. I consider internal movement dynamics, including the need to build participation and forge broader coalitions with key constituencies, and tactical and strategic debates about the relationship between protest and engagement in lobbying and electoral activities. Throughout the volume I draw comparisons with the Vietnam antiwar movement and other peace struggles to provide historical context.

In the first section of the book, I look at the Bush administration's post-9/11 buildup to war and movement attempts to influence an administration obsessed with overthrowing the government of Saddam Hussein through armed regime change. I link this challenge with the broader question of structural weaknesses in American democracy that impede public influence on matters of war and peace. I examine the administration's manipulation of public opinion amidst the widespread anger and fear that followed 9/11, with polls showing majority support for the use of force against those responsible for the terrorist attacks.

The movement was up against a massive media onslaught from the White House, which constantly stoked public fears with false claims of Saddam Hussein having weapons of mass destruction for use by terrorists. The Iraq antiwar movement attempted to respond by placing greater emphasis on media communications than past peace campaigns, but it was unable in the short time available to turn the tide of opinion against the war. Did antiwar organizations have an effective strategy for countering the White House media blitz and influencing public opinion? Did they communicate effectively and frequently enough, with the right messages and messengers? In Chapter Three and elsewhere I look at these questions and examine the movement's communication strategies and media efforts.

I devote considerable attention to the development of the antiwar movement in the United States as it emerged from the global justice movement and from the networks and experiences of previous peace campaigns. I review the Iraq movement's pioneering use of the internet to mobilize large numbers of people, and its reliance on traditional methods of community-based organizing and movement building. Looming over the war debate was the urgency of time, as the White House rushed ahead with a rapid timeline for invasion to short-circuit the public debate and the growing power of global opposition. Activists were able to mobilize with greater speed and effectiveness than past peace movements, but it was not enough to halt the momentum towards war.

The book also reviews the extraordinary scale of transnational protest, describing the vast mobilizations that took place in Europe and around the world, particularly in countries that either refused to join or quickly left the US-led "coalition of the willing." In Germany, Spain, and other countries, popular opposition to the war determined national elections and shaped government policies.

The second section of the book looks at the multiple faces of the movement in the United States. The antiwar coalition was broad, reaching many key constituencies, especially in the religious community, but the engagement was not deep enough in some sectors. In addition to the role of faith communities, I examine the participation of organized labor, business executives, and the women's movement, while providing a glimpse of protest action at the grassroots level. I also address the persistent challenge of achieving greater racial diversity within antiwar movements. In Chapter Five I devote special attention to dissent among military service members and their families, drawing comparisons and contrasts with similar movements during the Vietnam War.

In the final section, I evaluate the impact of the movement globally and in the US, identifying a number of important but often unrecognized ways in which the movement influenced policy. The Bush administration deceived the public about the purposes of the war, using scare tactics and exaggerated threats, and it intentionally underestimated the scale and likely costs of invading and occupying Iraq. It did so to maintain public opinion in favor of the use of force and as a response to widespread public skepticism and opposition to war. Those politically motivated decisions undermined the US military mission and were a factor in the resulting strategic failure, to cite the conclusion of the US Army's official history of the war.[18]

In the United States, many within the antiwar movement pivoted toward greater involvement in conventional politics, especially during the electoral campaigns of 2006 and 2008, which led to a policy shift within the Democratic Party and in Congress toward supporting a timetable for the withdrawal of troops. These political efforts had visible effects and laid the groundwork for the Obama candidacy. Some movement analysts contend that Obama's election spelled doom for the movement, but I emphasize the role of antiwar activists in propelling him to the White House. Obama was no peace candidate, and never claimed to be, but he won the presidency with an unequivocal pledge to end the war in Iraq and eventually fulfilled that promise.

The antiwar movement had significant influence internationally. Germany, Turkey, Canada, and many other countries refused to cooperate with or participate in the US invasion. Others joined the war effort initially but withdrew under political pressure. Only the UK made a meaningful military contribution. In Spain the conservative government supported the war and joined the US-led invasion, but the ruling party was voted out of office in the March 2004 elections, in part because of its backing for the war. The new socialist-led government promptly withdrew Spanish troops, followed by other states in 2005 and later years.

Washington and London twice sought authority to use force from the UN Security Council, but they were decisively rebuffed, an unprecedented act of defiance by the world organization that both reflected and reinforced global opposition to the war. The lack of UN authorization undermined the legitimacy of the US mission and contributed to its failure. In the concluding chapter, I review and summarize these political impacts, both short and long term, and discuss the perennial challenge of recognizing unintended impacts and partial successes in assessing social movement effectiveness. I close with some reflections on the lessons of the Iraq antiwar movement for social theory and political practice, and for the strategy of resisting war and militarized policy in the future.

One

A War Predetermined

Peace supporters faced enormous obstacles in trying to halt the march to war. They sought to stop or delay the invasion, and in the process bought some time for diplomacy by pressuring the administration to spend frustrating months seeking authorization from the United Nations, but they could not deflect the White House from the chosen path of using military force in Iraq. The inability to prevent the invasion reflected not the weakness of the movement, but the institutional failings of liberal democracy, especially the lack of accountability in matters of foreign and military policy. In the United States the militarization of society from the Cold War to the present has led to the rise of a powerful national security state, what historian Arthur Schlesinger Jr. termed the "imperial presidency."[1] War-making authority has become concentrated in the executive branch of government, with national security decision making insulated from critical debate and unconstrained by checks and balances. When matters of war and peace are at stake, presidential authority is paramount, and congressional oversight and democratic participation are limited or nonexistent. The Bush administration benefitted from and further expanded presidential authority and used this power to push through its policy of regime change in Iraq, dismissing the rising chorus of opposition in the United States and around the world. In retrospect, it seems that no movement, however massive, could have dissuaded the president and his advisers from their obsession with attacking Iraq.[2]

The movement in the US faced particular challenges in the political climate following 9/11. The trauma of the terrorist attacks powerfully shaped social consciousness and public opinion. The mood of the country was vengeful and belligerent, with American flags flying everywhere and many Americans in favor of a forceful response. People were angry and fearful of further attacks, and they rallied behind the nation's leaders. Indicators of public trust in government, which had eroded after the Vietnam War, rose sharply. Bush's approval ratings jumped to 86 percent, including three-quarters of Democrats. When he declared a global war on terror amidst the smoldering ruins of the World Trade Center, many cheered. Opinion surveys showed most Americans supporting military action against those responsible for the terrorist attacks. The short military campaign to overthrow the Taliban in Afghanistan was deceptively simple and seemingly successful, and the machinery of the national security state was gearing up for more. Many believed the administration when it claimed that Iraq was involved in the 9/11 assault. As late as October 2002, 66 percent of Americans thought Saddam Hussein had helped the Al Qaida attackers.[3] Countering this misinformation and attempting to turn public opinion against war in such a bellicose political climate was a herculean challenge, one that would have taken much more time and effort than was available to the movement.

In this chapter, I examine initial efforts by peace activists and faith leaders to urge a more restrained response to the threat of terrorism and caution against military action in Iraq. I trace the origins of the Bush administration's policy of armed regime change and explain how the White House was bent on attacking Saddam Hussein from the very first hours after 9/11. The administration mounted a relentless media manipulation campaign to build the case for military action. Congress could have stopped or slowed the march to war, but most members of the Senate and the House of Representatives followed the prevailing pattern of deferring to executive authority on national security issues. Many Democrats joined Republicans in granting authority to the White House to use "all necessary means" to disarm Iraq. The White House pushed ahead, ignoring the many voices of caution and opposition, and even disregarding the advice of senior military leaders and experienced diplomats. It was a juggernaut that seemed unstoppable.

Precursors

In the wake of 9/11, many peace, human rights, and religious activists worried that Bush's rhetoric of a war on terror would become a reality. Religious leaders began to call for a different kind of response to the terrorist strikes. An open-ended war against terror was a formula for more violence and terrorism, they warned, and would cause additional loss of innocent life. Jim Wallis, founder of the progressive, religiously based organization Sojourners, and Bob Edgar, general secretary of the National Council of Churches, began to circulate a statement appealing for sober restraint and a "just and effective response," which became the name of a website established by a coalition of groups. "Let us deny [the terrorists] their victory by refusing to submit to a world created in their image," read the declaration, which was signed by more than four thousand religious leaders and published in the *New York Times* on November 19, 2001.

The Fourth Freedom Forum worked with these religious groups to develop an alternative US counterterrorism strategy based on cooperative law enforcement rather than military action. The 9/11 attackers were murderers, not soldiers. They committed a crime, not an act of war. The proper response, we argued, is vigorous multilateral police work to apprehend perpetrators and prevent future attacks. Containing and capturing terrorists is by definition a function of police and legal networks, wrote the esteemed Catholic ethicist Rev. H. Bryan Hehir: "War is an indiscriminate tool for this highly discriminating task."[4]

Experts also called for greater attention to the root causes of political extremism—not to excuse terrorism, but to understand and address the factors that motivate such violence. They urged greater efforts to heed the voice of the powerless and resolve the grievances of the oppressed, and to recognize that military occupation often generates armed resistance. They recommended alternative policies such as reducing the US military footprint in the Middle East, supporting a just peace between Israel and the Palestinians, and funding equitable development and poverty reduction programs in the region.

Many social justice activists feared the government would use the new powers acquired through the so-called Patriot Act, adopted a month after 9/11, to crack down on immigrants and people of color in the name of countering terrorism. Their worries were justified, as a wave of Islamophobia and hate crimes swept the country, directed not only at Muslim Americans but also Sikhs, South-Asian Americans, Arab-Americans, and others thought to be of Middle Eastern origin. The Civil Rights Division of the Justice Department and other government offices investigated over 800 such incidents in the decade following 9/11, involving vandalism, shootings, arson, and bombings directed at homes, businesses, and places of worship.[5]

In response to this racialized war hysteria, social justice groups in the San Francisco Bay area created a new publication, *War Times*. They hoped it would serve as an outreach and consciousness-raising vehicle for a new kind of peace and justice movement. The organizers decided to test the public response to their concept by producing a pilot issue in January 2002. Bob Wing, managing editor of the new paper, described what happened:

> We put the prospectus up on the Internet and within a week we had seventy thousand orders. We had decided to jump off a cliff and see if anyone would give us a parachute. The response was overwhelming. It blew it open for us. We gave the paper away free, but donations kept coming in to keep the presses running.[6]

The monthly distribution soon reached 130,000. From the outset *War Times* was published in English and Spanish. The paper focused not only on the buildup toward war, but on the increasing harassment and pressures faced by immigrants and racial minorities. The paper became an important organizing tool for broadening the antiwar movement. Wing became a key player in the leadership of United for Peace and Justice.

On the day after the September 11 attacks, Eli Pariser, a recent college graduate living near Boston, sent an email message to a group of friends urging them to call for multilateral police action rather than war in response to the terrorist attacks. Friends forwarded his message to others, and it began to spread exponentially. In the vernacular of the internet, it went viral. At the same time, a recent graduate of the University of Chicago, David Pickering, posted a similar message on a campus website. When Pariser saw it, he contacted Pickering, and the two joined forces on a new website, 9-11peace.org. Within a week, 120,000 people from 190 countries had signed their petition against war. By the first week of October, more than half a million signed. Thus began the age of mass digital activism. Pariser and his colleagues had discovered what a *New York Times* reporter later called "an organizing tool of dazzling power,"[7] the dawn of internet-based mobilization on a mass scale. A few months later Pariser teamed up with Wes Boyd and Joan Blades, software entrepreneurs in California, who had created MoveOn in 1998 to stop the impeachment of Bill Clinton. With Pariser spearheading its international campaigns, MoveOn quickly emerged as a major organizational and financial power in the fledgling antiwar movement.

These initial responses to the terrorist attacks occurred in the midst of an unprecedented global justice movement. The struggle against the harmful social and environmental effects of corporate globalization had burst dramatically onto the political stage with the huge protests that disrupted World Trade Organization executive committee meetings in Seattle in November 1999. Tens of thousands of labor, environmental, and student demonstrators gathered for the largest global trade protest in US history up to that time.[8] The "Battle in Seattle" was followed by similar actions in Washington, Prague, Quebec, and Genoa. Another major action had been planned for September 2001 in Washington but was cancelled after the terrorist strikes. The social trauma that followed in the immediate aftermath of the attacks was not conducive to continued protests. For a time, the global justice movement suffered from a loss of direction and was unable to recapture its previous momentum. Ironically, the Bush administration's war drive gave the movement a new sense of urgency and purpose. Thousands of activists in the United States and around the world began to see, as one activist leader put it, that "militarization was just the other arm of the corporate agenda."[9] Many suspected, as events would later prove, that a US takeover of Baghdad would lead to the privatization of Iraq's economy and would open the door to corporate profiteering by politically connected US firms. Global justice activists began to pour their energy and creativity into the emerging antiwar movement. These and other currents of opposition to the impending attack flowed together to form the new antiwar movement, as I document in the coming chapters.

Premonitions

The strategy for a preemptive attack against Iraq that would guide White House policy was percolating in Washington well before Bush's election and the 9/11 attacks. Neoconservatives argued for war against Iraq throughout the 1990s. In the last days of the first Bush administration, Paul Wolfowitz, then undersecretary of defense for policy, circulated a classified draft of a defense guidance document asserting that the United States must be "postured to act independently when collective action cannot be orchestrated."[10] In the document, Wolfowitz outlined plans for military intervention in Iraq as an action necessary to assure "access to vital raw material, primarily Persian Gulf oil."[11] When excerpts of the draft document were published in the *New York Times* in March 1992, it embarrassed the administration as being too hawkish and was shelved. Support for war against Iraq did not die, however, as military hard-liners continued to urge the overthrow of Saddam Hussein and a more assertive US military strategy to reshape Iraq and the Middle East. An influential group known as the Project for a New American Century (PNAC) emerged in 1997 to give voice to these sentiments. It was led by William Kristol, publisher of the *Weekly Standard*, and included among its supporters Dick Cheney, Donald Rumsfeld, and other future leaders of the Bush administration. In January 1998, the group sent a letter to President Clinton that urged "removing Saddam Hussein and his regime from power." Among the signers were Rumsfeld, Wolfowitz, and future Assistant Secretary of State John Bolton.[12] In September 2000, the group published *Rebuilding America's Defenses*, a detailed plan for an American strategy of global dominance and military preemption. Wolfowitz, Cheney, and other Iraq hawks returned to power as part of the Bush administration in 2001. The terror attacks later that year and the collective fear that followed created the permissive political climate that allowed the neoconservatives to pursue their vision of overthrowing Saddam Hussein.

Concrete discussion of war against Iraq began within hours of the 9/11 attacks. *Washington Post* reporter Bob Woodward describes in *Bush at War* how the president was transformed into a war leader by the tragedy and almost immediately began to think of Iraq as a potential target of attack. "I believe Iraq was involved," Bush said a few days after the terrorist attacks. He decided against striking then but told the Pentagon to get ready.[13] Secretary of Defense Rumsfeld needed no encouragement. Within hours of the attack, he instructed aides to develop justifications for invading Iraq. CBS News quoted notes from an aide who participated in a Pentagon meeting the afternoon of September 11 in which Rumsfeld ordered his staff: "Best info fast. Judge whether good enough hit SH [Saddam Hussein] at same time. Not only UBL [Usama bin Laden]. Go massive. Sweep it all up. Things related and not."[14] Rumsfeld raised the question of attacking Iraq at a White House meeting of the National Security Council on September 12.[15]

Bruce Riedel was a National Security Council staffer at the time and was present at many of these meetings. On the twentieth anniversary of those events, he wrote a recollection of the conversations. When making his first call to British Prime Minister Tony Blair three days after 9/11, Bush immediately said he was planning to "hit" Saddam Hussein. Blair was "audibly taken aback," Riedel observed. A few days later the president told Saudi Ambassador Prince Bandar bin Sultan that Iraq was behind the 9/11 attacks, which left the prince "visibly perplexed." Bush "deliberately misled the American people about who was responsible for the 9/11 attack," Riedel concluded. He ignored the "unequivocal conclusion" of the intelligence community that Iraq had nothing to do with either 9/11 or Al Qaida.[16]

Preparations for the attack on Iraq began in earnest with the overthrow of the Taliban regime in Afghanistan. On November 21,

Bush instructed Rumsfeld to start updating the war plan for Iraq. On this day, Woodward wrote, "Bush formally set in motion the chain of events that would lead to the invasion of Iraq sixteen months later."[17] An initial wave of articles about possible war in Iraq appeared at the end of 2001, and the public discussion intensified throughout 2002 as the Bush administration finalized its invasion plans. In July British officials met with senior US officials and reported secretly to Prime Minister Tony Blair in the famous Downing Street Memo that Bush was intent on removing Saddam Hussein. Military action "was seen as inevitable" and "intelligence and facts were being fixed around the policy."[18]

As military planning began, so did political efforts to mobilize public support. Senate Minority Leader Trent Lott worried that the administration was not doing enough to win popular backing. He called Cheney on a Sunday in August 2002 with a warning: "I think you may have a big problem here with the public perceptions of a possible Iraq war." He advised stronger efforts to make the case for military action.[19] The first public saber rattling came that month with Cheney's speech to the American Legion, which described the Iraqi regime as an imminent menace requiring a military response. President Bush formally kicked off the public campaign for war with his September 2002 address at the United Nations, which came on the first anniversary of the terrorist attacks.

Scholar Ole R. Holsti described the White House media operation as a "relentless overt and covert public relations campaign" to include Iraq within the war on terror.[20] The Bush administration's manipulation of public opinion was not an anomaly, but part of a persistent pattern in national security decision-making over the decades. Government officials have long sought to generate support for war and military buildups through public relations campaigns and the exaggeration or fabrication of foreign threats, supposedly based on secret intelligence. Democracy depends on open debate and access to accurate information, but both become impossible when political decisions are shrouded in secrecy and misleading claims. The pattern was established at the dawn of the Cold War, when Dean Acheson famously wrote that matters must be made "clearer than the truth."[21] At that time Americans were being warned of nonexistent missile gaps with the Soviet Union. In the 1960s, we were told that the Vietnamese struggle for national independence was communist aggression that had to be defeated by American arms. In the case of Iraq, the Bush administration conjured up images of nuclear mushroom clouds and false links to Al Qaida to justify an unnecessary war of choice.

Congress Caves

During early antiwar strategy meetings, several people suggested that demanding a congressional vote might be a way of preventing or delaying the onset of war. The assumption, naïve in retrospect, was that members of Congress would object to such an obviously unjustified attack. Be careful what you wish for, other activists cautioned. Don't count on Congress to challenge the president's war authority or stand in the way of military action. Congress might simply roll over and give the president whatever he wanted.

The history of congressional oversight of the military, or the lack thereof, is not encouraging. Congress long ago abdicated its constitutional authority to declare war, instead approving resolutions that give presidents the authority to use force. In 1964, Congress passed the infamous Gulf of Tonkin resolution, based on a nonexistent attack against US naval forces, providing the president virtually unlimited authority to wage war in Indochina. Even as the American people decisively turned against the Vietnam War, Congress was unable to muster the political will to cut off funding for the conflict until near its end. The Cooper-Church amendment was approved in 1970 to end US ground force operations in Cambodia, but it was not until 1973, after American troops had left Vietnam, that Congress finally prohibited funding for "combat in or over or from off the shores of North Vietnam, South Vietnam, Laos or Cambodia."[22]

Congress adopted the War Powers Act in 1973 to restore a degree of legislative control over the use of force and limit executive war making. The law requires the White House to notify Congress when US forces are used in foreign "hostilities" and mandates the withdrawal of forces within sixty days unless Congress authorizes or extends their deployment. Congress had to override a veto from President Nixon to adopt the measure, but legislators need not have bothered. The law has had little effect in constraining executive war making over the past 50 years. The continuous growth of the national-security bureaucracy and enlargement of presidential war-making authority over the decades have weakened the intended safeguards in the legislation. Presidents have consistently argued that as commanders in chief they have the authority to use force whenever they deem necessary. Presidential war making has become the accepted pattern, with few in Congress objecting.

In the case of Iraq, Congress was as bellicose as the White House in its zeal for regime change. In 1998 Congress passed the so-called Iraq Liberation Act, which made it the policy of the United States to support efforts to remove Saddam Hussein from office. That same year Congress urged the president to take "appropriate action . . . to bring Iraq into compliance" with its UN obligations.[23]

As the White House prepared its public campaign for war in the summer of 2002, the administration initially claimed that congressional approval was not necessary for an invasion of Iraq. White House lawyers drafted a legal brief asserting that the president could go to war without further endorsement from Congress or the United Nations.[24] Congressional leaders objected to this interpretation. Republicans as well as Democrats expressed anxiety that Bush was leading the country to war without consulting allies or thinking through the ramifications. As pressures mounted, the White House yielded in early September and announced that it would seek congressional approval.

This touched off an intensive period of debate and political jockeying as the administration sought wide freedom of action to use force while Democrats and some moderate Republicans attempted to place limits on the president's war-making authority. Senators Joseph Biden (D-DE) and Richard Lugar (R-IN), leaders of the Senate Foreign Relations Committee, introduced legislation specifying that military force could be used only to disarm Iraqi weapons of mass destruction. Their measure would have required the president to win the approval of the UN Security Council before using force, or issue a determination that the threat to security was so grave that he needed to act without UN authorization. Senator Carl Levin (D-MI), chair of the Senate Armed Services Committee, proposed a resolution requiring the administration to seek authorization from the UN Security Council before requesting congressional approval for the use of force. These and other efforts to limit the president's authority were undermined when House Minority Leader Richard Gephardt (D-MO) cut a deal with the White House and Republican congressional leaders in early October. The Bush-Gephardt compromise gave the president virtually unchecked authority to use military force, while offering the fig leaf of further consultations with Congress and the requirement of a presidential determination that diplomacy was no longer working.[25] Gephardt's action undercut Democratic efforts to restrain the president's war-making authority and handed the White House a major political victory. On October 10, Congress approved a joint resolution authorizing the president "to use the armed forces of the United States as he determines to be necessary and appropriate . . .

against the continuing threat posed by Iraq." The vote in the Senate was 77-23, and in the House, 296-133.[26]

Antiwar groups attempted to mobilize against the war resolution. MoveOn organized hundreds of antiwar meetings with members of Congress in local districts in August. The Friends Committee on National Legislation joined with Education for Peace in Iraq and other Washington-based groups to form an Iraq Working Group that lobbied members of Congress and coordinated grassroots constituency pressure. Members of Congress reported substantial voter unease about the prospect of war, and constituent messages reportedly ran four to one against the use of force.[27] A major demonstration in Washington might have helped to pressure Congress, but a previously announced rally occurred on October 26, two weeks after the congressional vote. The inability of the antiwar movement to prevent the White House from winning congressional authorization was a major blow to the prospects of stopping the invasion. The movement was not yet sufficiently large or well organized to wield the level of political clout that would have been necessary to block congressional approval.

As expected, most Republicans voted for the president's war authorization, but so did many Democrats, much to the disappointment of antiwar activists. Even liberals such as John Kerry of Massachusetts and Hillary Rodham Clinton of New York voted for the final resolution. As their constituents were mobilizing for peace, these senators were scrambling for political cover. They were swayed by the atmosphere of militarized patriotism that spread in the wake of 9/11 and fearful of being labelled weak on terrorism.[28] The senators claimed they were voting for diplomacy, not war, pointing to Bush's statement in August that he was "patient" and that all options were on the table, including diplomacy.[29] Kerry attempted to rationalize his vote by saying that it was not an explicit authorization for war but simply an endorsement of tough diplomacy.[30] As a leader of Vietnam Veterans Against the War (VVAW) during the early 1970s, Kerry should have known better. Clinton's vote for the authorization was a fatal political error that came back to haunt her in the 2008 presidential primaries, when many progressive Democrats turned against her and voted for Barack Obama, as discussed in Chapter Six.

The Democrats who voted for the war resolution in October fell victim to a trap set by White House political adviser Karl Rove. The White House strategy for the November 2002 midterm elections was to focus on Iraq and the threat of terrorism, as a way of rallying voter support behind a wartime president and taking advantage of higher Republican approval ratings on national security issues. The war debate was useful to Republicans as a distraction from domestic economic issues and corporate malfeasance, where their party was politically vulnerable. Democrats hoped to get the war vote out of the way early in the campaign, so that the focus of public attention could swing back to Bush's unpopular domestic policies. The White House easily trumped that strategy, and Republicans won control of the Senate, in a rare case of the incumbent president's party making gains in midterm elections. By standing aside on the vital issue of war, Democrats lost credibility and political standing. They handed Bush a political victory and validation for his war policy, making him even less willing to listen to reason.[31] Analyst Michael Mazarr describes the failure of senior members of Congress to inhibit the rush toward war as "one of the signal failures of legislative oversight in the modern era."[32]

The vote on the congressional war resolution revealed important cleavages in American political life. White male members of Congress from both parties voted overwhelmingly to endorse war, and African American, Latino, and female legislators voted against the use of military force. Among the thirty-three voting members of the Congressional Black Caucus, thirty voted against the resolution. Every one of the sixteen members of the Hispanic

Congressional Caucus who voted that day opposed the measure. Among the seventy female members of the Senate and House who participated in the vote, thirty-eight decided against the resolution. These votes in Congress reflected the greater skepticism about war among Blacks, Latinos, and women in the general population, as discussed in Chapter Four.

Denying Reality

The members of Congress who voted to authorize the use of force ignored warnings from senior military commanders, many of whom opposed war in Iraq. Among the most distinguished of these military voices was Brent Scowcroft, former general and national security adviser to presidents Gerald Ford and George H. W. Bush. In August 2002, Scowcroft wrote an extraordinary article, "Don't Attack Saddam," in the *Wall Street Journal*.[33] There is "scant evidence to tie Saddam to terrorist organizations," he wrote, "and even less to the Sept. 11 attacks." He warned that an invasion "would seriously jeopardize, if not destroy, the global counterterrorist campaign." There is "a virtual consensus in the world against an attack on Iraq," which would require a "go-it-alone strategy." War against Iraq could destabilize Arab regimes, Scowcroft warned, generating a worldwide "explosion of outrage against us."

Other experienced military officers also spoke out. One of the most adamant was Lieutenant General William Odum, former chief of army intelligence and retired director of the National Security Agency. Odum was unstinting in his criticism of the war and spoke frequently in public, condemning the invasion as "the worst strategic mistake in the history of the United States."[34] Also urging caution was General Anthony Zinni, former commandant of the Marine Corps and an experienced Middle East negotiator, who told a Washington audience in October, "I'm not convinced we need to do this now . . . I believe that [Saddam] can be deterred and is containable at this moment."[35] He described the Iraq operation as "a war the generals didn't want."[36] General Norman Schwarzkopf, hero of the first Gulf War, also expressed concern about the rush to invade. In an interview with the *Washington Post* in January 2003 he said, "I think it is very important for us to wait and see what inspectors come up with."[37]

Senior active-duty commanders were also skeptical of war, none more so than Lieutenant General Gregory Newbold, director of operations for the Joint Chiefs of Staff (JCS), who offered to resign over the issue. A few other JCS commanders agreed with his concerns, including General Mark Hertling, chief of war plans, but only Newbold was willing to put his "stars on the table," as he said, quietly retiring in protest over a war he considered unnecessary.[38]

The advocates of war fancied themselves military realists, but many of the most distinguished scholars of political realism spoke out against the war. In September 2002, thirty-three eminent political scientists and national security experts published an ad in the *New York Times* with the headline "War with Iraq is Not in America's National Interest."[39] The statement declared, "no one has provided credible evidence that Iraq is cooperating with Al Qaida" and warned that invading Iraq would jeopardize and divert resources from the campaign against terrorism and "increase anti-Americanism around the globe." Scientists also raised their voices. In January, forty-one US Nobel laureates in science and economics, including eighteen National Medal of Science winners, issued a statement opposing "a preventive war against Iraq without broad international support."[40] Congress and the administration refused to listen.

The White House also rebuked diplomatic advice. When Assistant Secretary of State for Near Asian Affairs William J. Burns argued at a White House meeting in September that working through the UN would enhance the legitimacy of US diplomacy, Vice President Dick Cheney scoffed, "The only legitimacy we really need comes on the back of an M1A1 tank."[41] Burns and his colleagues submitted a "Perfect Storm" memo outlining the many things that could go wrong and warning of the profound risks of an ill-prepared and ill-considered war. A State Department task force of experts produced the "Future of Iraq" study detailing the high costs and many challenges that would be involved in taking over and attempting to rule Iraq. These and other warnings and recommendations were ignored in the buildup to war.

The disregard of diplomatic and military advice and the congressional vote to authorize the use of force were major blows to those who tried to prevent war. It was already sadly obvious that Bush had made an irrevocable decision and nothing anyone wrote or said was going to change his mind. Activists knew there was little chance of stopping the invasion, but they felt compelled to speak out regardless, to register their disagreement with a war that was so obviously unnecessary and unjust. "Not in Our Name" was the name of one of the antiwar groups, a phrase that spoke directly to the sentiments and motivations of many protesters. Not just in the US and the UK but across the world, people felt they had to say no. They poured into the streets in unprecedented numbers to cry out against the madness of an unprovoked invasion into the turbulent Middle East. The next two chapters describe that extraordinary global mobilization, beginning with the emergence of the antiwar movement in the United States.

Two

Building the Movement

As the Bush administration made its military intentions clear in August and September 2002, the need for more effective antiwar leadership intensified. A growing number of activists began to call for a more broadly based national effort to oppose war in Iraq. In August I wrote an article for *The Progressive* magazine, "Stop the War Before It Starts," arguing for a mainstream movement that could "capture the patriotic wave" and build broad public opposition to war. During the summer, several experienced peace and justice activists organized a series of discussions with the specific goal of forming a new coalition that would provide a base for the increasing number of people who were speaking out against the threat of war. National organizations and local groups throughout the country began to educate themselves about Iraq and the Middle East and sponsored teach-ins and public programs to warn against the imminent danger of war.

This chapter recounts how the Iraq antiwar movement emerged in the United States. I review the initial demonstrations organized by leftist groups and recount the process that led to the founding of the largest coalition, United For Peace and Justice, and the parallel network, Win Without War. I draw from first-hand experience and interviews with many of those involved to provide an inside account of how these coalitions evolved, what purposes they served, and why some of us thought it useful to have two parallel efforts, one committed to protest action and rooted in a vast network of grassroots and national peace and justice groups, the other more oriented to media communications and digital activism and committed to engaging in legislative and political action in conjunction with progressive members of the Democratic Party. The chapter also examines the rise of digital activism and the crucial role of MoveOn, which grew rapidly during the antiwar mobilization to become an effective network of online activists—and a fundraising powerhouse that helped to support national and local activism and later raised funds for antiwar political candidates, including former Vermont Governor Howard Dean and then-Senator Barack Obama. In the final section of the chapter, I examine the Pledge of Resistance and the role of disruption and mass civil disobedience, assessing whether it was effective and appropriate in trying to prevent the war.

To the Streets

As the Bush administration's militarized policies took shape, activist groups began to organize street protests. Demonstrations and rallies are a natural social response to government policies that endanger or offend the public interest. They are an essential means of drawing media attention to a movement's grievances and demands, as discussed in Chapter Three. They help to build solidarity and commitment among activists. Antiwar movements tend to attract left fringe groups, however, which can create divisiveness within the larger movement. This was a major dilemma during the Vietnam era, as the Socialist Workers Party and other groups competed with liberal, pacifist, and radical activist groups in the Vietnam Mobilization Committee and sponsored their own coalition and separate mass rallies. As author and activist Tom Hayden wrote, many activists of the 1960s New Left were devoured "in versions of old left ideology" just as the core demands of the antiwar movement were gaining mainstream acceptance.[1] Similar though less severe problems emerged during the Iraq campaign, as small leftist factions took the initiative in organizing street protests.

The first group to respond to the war buildup was ANSWER (Act Now to Stop War and End Racism), a coalition formed by the splinter Marxist-Leninist group, Workers World Party. ANSWER called for a demonstration in Washington on September 29, 2001, to oppose the Bush administration's war on terror and the imminent military attack against Afghanistan. The initial rally was relatively small, attracting about ten thousand demonstrators. As the threat of war in Iraq increased in 2002, ANSWER organized much larger rallies in Washington on April 20 and October 26, and again on January 18, 2003. Other groups cosponsored these demonstrations, but ANSWER usually determined the program. Many activists, myself included, attended the ANSWER rallies because we wanted to be counted in opposition to the Bush administration's policies, but we were turned off by the coalition's rhetoric. Veteran activist Todd Gitlin wrote a commentary for *Mother Jones* magazine in October 2002 decrying the "old left" tenor of the antiwar movement to date, and calling for an "extensive, inclusive popular movement" against the policies of the Bush administration.[2] "We don't like the Workers' World Party," said an activist at the October 2002 rally, "but they're the only game in town."[3] Many of us wanted to see a new game, and we yearned for a more diverse, broadly based antiwar movement. We did not want to see fringe groups try to dominate the movement as they had in the Vietnam era.

Another coalition formed by leftist groups at the time was Not in Our Name, which was connected to the Revolutionary

Communist Party, a Maoist faction.[4] The coalition raised three broad demands: stop the war on the people of the world; stop the disappearances and vicious attacks on Arab, Muslim, and South Asian people in the US; and stop the destruction of civil, legal, and political rights, including the very right to dissent. These were reasonable demands that many people supported. Not in Our Name circulated a statement of conscience against the war signed by many prominent progressives and placed a full-page ad in the *New York Times* on September 11, 2002, one year after the 9/11 attacks. The statement read:

> Not in our name will you wage endless war. . . . Let it not be said that people in the US did nothing when their government declared a war without limit and instituted stark new measures of repression. The signers of this statement call on the people of the US to resist the policies and overall political direction that have emerged since September 11, 2001, and which pose grave dangers to the people of the world.[5]

Not in Our Name cooperated with ANSWER in sponsoring anti-war demonstrations in dozens of US cities on the weekend of October 6, 2002, including protests of approximately twenty-five thousand people in New York's Central Park and rallies in San Francisco, Los Angeles, and Seattle.[6] It became one of the groups within United for Peace and Justice and supported the Pledge of Resistance campaign.

Uniting for Peace and Justice

On October 25, 2002, the day before the ANSWER-sponsored rally in Washington, representatives of more than fifty peace, religious, and social justice organizations gathered in Washington to address the threat of war. By then it was clear that Bush was deadly serious about attacking Iraq. The meeting was co-chaired by Bill Fletcher, president of TransAfrica Forum, a veteran of twenty-five years in the labor movement, and former education director and assistant to the president of the AFL-CIO, and Leslie Cagan, a veteran organizer widely respected throughout the peace movement.[7] Also helping to build the meeting was Van Gosse, professor of history at Franklin and Marshall College and former organizing director for Peace Action. The breadth of participation in the discussion reflected the wide recognition that an effective antiwar coalition was urgently needed. Cagan later described the thinking that led to the meeting:

> The Bush administration's push toward war, and the growing opposition to it . . . led a number of people to feel that we should try to put together something that would have a broader reach, that would not just mobilize the most obvious layer of discontent, but would try to bring into play much broader forces. So people who knew each other from previous antiwar, anti-intervention, nuclear disarmament, and general foreign policy activism started talking to each other.[8]

Participants in the October 25 meeting included traditional peace organizations from previous antiwar efforts (Peace Action, American Friends Service Committee [AFSC], Women's Action for New Directions [WAND], Sojourners, War Resisters League, Fellowship of Reconciliation); representatives of the new Internet-based groups (MoveOn and True Majority, an activist network founded by ice-cream entrepreneur Ben Cohen); Working Assets, a network of long distance, wireless, and credit card users supporting progressive causes; global justice groups such as Global Exchange; and major constituency organizations (National Organization for Women [NOW], the Rainbow/PUSH Coalition, and the Center for Community Change). The meeting lasted all day, as nearly every one of the approximately ninety participants took a turn at speaking and debating a wide range of issues and action strategies. At the end of the session, participants agreed to create a new antiwar coalition, taking its name, "United for Peace," from a website of the same name created by Global Exchange. Cagan and Fletcher were asked to chair the new coalition, and an ad hoc committee was selected to work out the details of process and program that were left unresolved.

The new coalition faced multiple challenges as it struggled to take shape: an imminent war threat, a lack of financial and organizational resources, and an unwieldy process that complicated the task of deciding structure and strategy. One of the coalition's early decisions was to change its name to United for Peace and Justice (UFPJ), which reflected a desire to link the cause of peace to the struggle for racial and economic justice. For the first two months the coalition operated without staff or office space. Cagan served as an indispensable unpaid coordinator, while participating groups—Global Exchange, Institute for Policy Studies, Peace Action, Democracy Rising, and others—contributed staff and resources. Office space was finally secured in January, donated by 1199 SEIU United Healthcare Workers East, New York's healthcare union.

UFPJ's first action was a call for nationally coordinated local actions on December 10, Human Rights Day, commemorating the date in 1948 when the UN adopted the groundbreaking Universal Declaration of Human Rights. More than 130 events took place that day all over the United States, generating substantial local and regional press coverage for the growing antiwar movement. At the University of Michigan, demonstrators created a symbolic graveyard at the main walkway through campus. In Providence, Rhode Island, a hundred people staged a die-in at the downtown federal building. Demonstrations took place at federal buildings in Oakland and Sacramento. At the US mission to the United Nations in New York, more than one hundred protesters were arrested—including Daniel Ellsberg, Ben Cohen, and Rev. Herbert Daughtry of the House of the Lord Church in Brooklyn. None of the protests were huge, but this first wave of coordinated local action represented an important beginning for the new antiwar coalition. The December 10 actions were significant, according to Cagan, and "spoke to the real breadth of opposition to what the Bush administration was doing."[9] The demonstrations highlighted the costs and risks of war and were intended to generate antiwar sentiment that could influence public opinion. They were only a modest initial step, however, and it was obvious to many that much larger protests and more sustained pressure and effective messaging would be needed to counter the buildup to war.

The core political demand in all the protests against the looming invasion was "no to war"—a simple, clear, and broadly supported appeal. Many groups linked this demand to the lack of UN approval for military action in Iraq. "No to war without UN approval" became a subtheme in the political messaging of the movement. Most activists opposed war in Iraq unconditionally, with or without UN authorization or the support of allies, but linking the antiwar message to the lack of UN approval was important politically and analytically. It helped to broaden the base of antiwar opposition, which was particularly important in the United States, where opinion polls showed support for military action against Saddam Hussein, but not if it meant fighting the war alone. Every survey conducted before the war showed majority support for removing Saddam Hussein from power, but in none of the surveys did the option of "going it alone" gain majority approval.[10] As noted in other chapters, the lack of UN approval became a major political and operational liability for the Bush administration, undermining international support for its policy and leaving the United States alone to bear the enormous human and financial costs of the war.

The insistence on Security Council approval was also important as a matter of principle for international peace. It affirmed the role of the United Nations and the provisions of the UN Charter. Article 2 of the Charter outlaws the use of military force against other countries, with two exceptions: when force is used in self-defense against an armed attack (Article 51), manifestly not the case in the unprovoked invasion of Iraq, or when authorized by the UN Security Council (Article 42), which was blocked by political and diplomatic opposition. The fact that states often violate the principles of the Charter does not alter their status as foundations of international law or diminish their importance in establishing the moral and political legitimacy of movements against unjust war.

UFPJ played a major role in organizing national protest demonstrations, often in uneasy partnership with ANSWER. On January 18, 2003, the weekend of the Martin Luther King Jr. national holiday, ANSWER sponsored a major antiwar rally in Washington that attracted upwards of 200,000 people. Rather than attempt to compete with the ANSWER rally in Washington, UFPJ called for demonstrations on the weekend of February 15 in New York and San Francisco. The February 15 date was selected to coincide with the global antiwar protests proposed by activists at the November 2002 European Social Forum in Florence. The largest of the regional networks in the global justice movement, the European Social Forum was a leading force in mobilizing opposition to corporate globalization and support for human rights, peace, and democracy. The UFPJ call for a mass demonstration in New York in the middle of winter was risky. No one knew if the protest would be successful. Organizing for the rally did not even begin until the second week in January. The mobilizing effort combined traditional methods of activist recruitment with the innovative potential of the internet. Hundreds of thousands of leaflets were distributed in New York and in nearby states, and announcements were sent via the internet. Visits to the United for Peace and Justice website soon reached two million a day. In fact, the UFPJ website became a central bulletin board for the antiwar movement, offering action plans, contact information, news updates, and organizing tips.

The outreach effort for February 15 benefited from decades of experience among veterans like Cagan and her team of volunteers, and drew energy from a new, younger activist movement that had emerged in response to globalization challenges and the aftermath of September 11.[11] The gathering momentum of the planned rallies around the world added excitement and energy to the organizing effort in the US. Planning for the protest intensified amidst a rising sense of urgency and fear, as popular alarm over the Bush administration's war policies peaked in the United States and throughout the world, producing the historic mass demonstrations of February 15, 2003.

UFPJ remained at the center of antiwar mobilizing before the invasion and afterwards. One of the biggest US actions against the war occurred in New York on March 22, 2003. The demonstration had been announced a couple of weeks before but came just as the

Protesters gather on First Avenue in New York, February 15, 2003.
MARIO TAMA/GETTY IMAGES.

war was beginning. The crowd that day rivaled the turnout on February 15. An estimated three hundred thousand people streamed onto Broadway north of 34th Street and marched down to Washington Square Park. At one point the crowd filled Broadway for the entire two-mile length of the march. It was an overwhelming turnout that stunned even the organizers. Cagan recalled thinking, "Where are all these people coming from? We're not that good." For many New Yorkers like herself, this demonstration and the February 15 rally were a reaction to 9/11, and the Bush administration's manipulation of the city's suffering. "For those of us who lived through 9/11, there was a sense that we never wanted to see that kind of horror visited on other people, whether by a small group of terrorists or by the state terrorism of a military invasion."[12] The massive turnout at these rallies reflected the fear of many people that Bush was taking advantage of the anguish of 9/11 to start a war that would lead to even greater disaster and violence in the Middle East.

Despite its extensive grassroots network and its ability to organize massive national rallies, UFPJ was a fragile coalition. It had to broker tensions among its far-flung political factions, from strongly progressive radical groups on the left to more moderate elements that included supporters of the Democratic Party and liberal groups. It also had to deal with competition for public support from ANSWER and internal political debates over contentious issues that went beyond the question of the war. Shared hostility among all factions to the Bush administration and the invasion and occupation of Iraq kept the coalition together, as scholars Michael T. Heaney and Fabio Rojas note, but after the Democratic Party won control of Congress and Obama was elected president in 2009, support from moderate elements dwindled and the coalition faded.[13]

Notwithstanding these challenges, UFPJ grew to a massive scale and was able to mobilize large-scale opposition to war and occupation for several years. At its peak, the coalition included

1,624 affiliated local, state, regional, national, and international organizations.[14] From 2002 through 2007 there were eight demonstrations in the United States that attracted estimated crowds of 100,000 or more participants, ranking the Iraq movement among the largest peace campaigns in US history.[15] One can question whether all of the demonstrations were as large as claimed, given the limitations until recently of crowd-counting methodology, but there is no doubt that massive organized opposition to the war continued right up to the time of the Obama candidacy.[16] Below is a listing of the major actions:

Major antiwar protests before and during the Iraq War[17]

- October 26, 2002, Washington DC, 100,000 plus
- January 18, 2003, Washington DC, 200,000
- February 15, 2003, New York, 375,000
- March 23, 2003, New York, 300,000
- March 20, 2004, New York, 100,000
- August 29, 2004, New York, 500,000
- September 24, 2005, Washington DC, 300,000
- January 27, 2007, Washington DC, 100,000 plus

Street protests against the Iraq war were comparable in number and scale to the demonstrations organized during the Vietnam antiwar movement. The major protests that took place in 2002 and 2003 prior to the invasion had no precedent in the Vietnam movement, when large protests began only in 1965 after a substantial number of US ground troops were already in Vietnam. As Noam Chomsky observed in 2007, "protests against the Iraq war, throughout, have been at a far higher level than they were with regard to Vietnam at comparable stages of the invasions."[18] On the other hand, there were no protests during the Iraq war comparable in scale to the vast Vietnam Moratorium of October 1969, in which millions of people protested against the war in their local communities, or the nationwide strike of millions of students in the wake of the Cambodia invasion and the killing of four students at Kent State University in May 1970.[19] The demonstrations and protests around the Iraq war were nonetheless massive, against a war much smaller in scale and with far fewer American casualties than the Vietnam debacle.

As Tom Hayden wrote, the movement against the war in Iraq was partly a reflection of the "Vietnam Syndrome," the public revulsion against war and American militarism that emerged in the wake of the humiliating defeat in Vietnam and the massive upheaval in society against the war. In the aftermath of their failure in Southeast Asia, US policymakers lamented the collapse of popular support for the use of military power abroad and were hoping to rally public support for new imperial ventures. In 1991, after the success of the 1991 Gulf War, the first President Bush exulted: "By God, we've kicked the Vietnam Syndrome once and for all."[20] His son was determined to finish the job by overthrowing the despised Saddam Hussein, but his ill-fated invasion and occupation prompted a new wave of protest and public revulsion against intervention, an "Iraq Syndrome," Hayden called it, with people in the United States and around the world once again mobilizing in massive numbers against American imperialism.[21]

Win Without War

The October 25, 2002, meeting in Washington that resulted in the formation of United for Peace and Justice also spurred the creation of Win Without War. Several of us who attended the larger meeting were impatient with the tedious process and lack of focus during the all-day session. We had experienced and wanted to avoid the laborious and often acrimonious debates of the Vietnam antiwar coalitions, and we saw the need for greater emphasis on media communications to influence mainstream opinion. We decided to meet for dinner that evening at a nearby Chinese restaurant. I had prepared a concept paper outlining the idea of creating a more structured and focused coalition of mainstream national organizations with a streamlined decision-making process and a greater focus on strategic messaging. The others around the table—Alistair Millar from the Fourth Freedom Forum, Susan Shaer of WAND, Eli Pariser of MoveOn, Duane Peterson of True Majority, Melissa Daar of Working Assets—had been thinking similarly, and we agreed to begin working together to create such a committee. Our goal was to build a coalition that could attract major constituency organizations, not just traditional peace groups. We wanted a quick and efficient decision-making process. We believed that the political message of the activist movement should emphasize containing and disarming Saddam Hussein without war. We also saw the need for an effective public relations and communications campaign to reach mainstream audiences and influence public opinion. Other groups that agreed to come together on this basis included the National Council of Churches, Sojourners, the United Methodist Church, Physicians for Social Responsibility, the Sierra Club, NOW, and the National Association for the Advancement of Colored People (NAACP). The presence of these mainstream groups extended the reach of the movement to political circles within the Democratic Party and facilitated subsequent engagement in congressional and electoral politics.[22] Forty organizations eventually joined the coalition, which was officially launched at a press conference in Washington on December 11.

The development of the new group and of the antiwar movement benefited enormously from a planning and strategy retreat the weekend of November 15–17, 2002, at Blue Mountain Retreat Center in the Adirondack mountains of upstate New York. The session was hosted by Harriet Barlow, director of the center, who played an indispensable role in organizing financial support for the emerging movement. It was during a creative brainstorming session at Blue Mountain that the name "Win Without War" emerged. Participants agreed on a proactive and positive political message: the United States and the United Nations can disarm Iraq and enhance security through vigorous weapons inspections and continued containment. Many acknowledged the need for a sophisticated and large-scale public relations effort to communicate a patriotic antiwar message. Participants also recognized the need for close cooperation between Win Without War and UFPJ. The two coalitions would have different emphases—grassroots demonstrations for UFPJ, media communications for Win Without War—but they would strive to share information and coordinate their efforts.

In practice, the coordination between UFPJ and Win Without War was limited. Concerns were raised within UFPJ about the development of Win Without War. UFPJ co-chair Bill Fletcher noted that some activists were "perplexed" by the creation of a parallel coalition.[23] At the first Win Without War meeting in December, Medea Benjamin, cofounder of the women's organization Code Pink, questioned the need for a new group. Bob Edgar of the National Council of Churches and others explained that the founders saw the need for a coalition with a speedier and more efficient decision-making process, a greater emphasis on public relations, and a narrower political agenda focused on stopping the war. Some activist leaders, such as Peace Action Director Kevin Martin, saw value in having two coalitions so that the movement could reach out both to the left and the center.[24] The two groups maintained friendly relations, and there was some overlap in membership, with AFSC, Peace Action, Global Exchange, and other groups participating in both coalitions. A de facto division of labor developed, with UFPJ focusing on the mobilization of grassroots protest, while Win Without War emphasized internet organizing and media communications.

One of the first decisions of the new Win Without War coalition was to create an effective leadership structure. We chose two national co-chairs, Susan Shaer and Bob Edgar, and began the search for a national director/spokesperson. By this time, public alarm about war was spreading rapidly, and money to support our cause was pouring in. We were in the rare and fortunate position of having the resources to hire a professional. The first person we approached was former member of Congress Tom Andrews. Andrews had represented the first district of Maine for six years and served as a member of the powerful House Armed Services Committee. He was known and respected as one of the most effective progressive leaders in Congress, with a stellar voting record on issues of peace and arms control. Prior to being elected to Congress, Andrews had been a community organizer and progressive leader in Maine for a variety of causes. Following his congressional service, Andrews created his own media advocacy firm, New Economy Communications, and worked on a range of human rights campaigns. As the threat of war loomed, Andrews served as an adviser for the antiwar project created by the public interest media company Fenton Communications, where he shared office space. Andrews was thoroughly familiar with the issues and arguments against war, and he shared our shock and dismay at the prospect of the United States invading Iraq. He agreed to become national director and served as chief strategist and spokesperson for the coalition. His extensive political experience and creative organizing and speaking abilities were an enormous asset for the movement. Andrews appeared on numerous national talk shows and was respected by the national media as an articulate and reasoned opponent of war. Later, as the struggle shifted to lobbying Congress and urging electoral candidates to support an end to the occupation, his political acumen and connections proved invaluable. Andrews became the media voice of the antiwar movement.

Virtual organizing became the métier of the Win Without War coalition, as it mobilized the vast membership networks of its internet-based groups and constituency organizations for coordinated lobbying and action campaigns. Its most ambitious effort was the "virtual march on Washington" on February 26, 2003. Citizens all over the United States phoned, faxed, or emailed their elected representatives to oppose the invasion. Andrews conceived the plan as a way of harnessing the grassroots networking and organizing power of MoveOn, True Majority, and other coalition member groups to apply focused political pressure on Congress. The point was not to back any specific congressional legislation but to demonstrate the organized clout of the antiwar movement, in the hope that legislators would redirect pressure for military restraint onto the White House. Win Without War mounted a huge

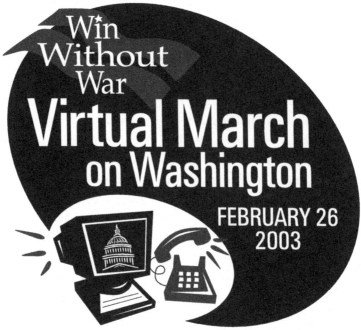

The virtual march, March 2003. MOVEON AND WIN WITHOUT WAR.

outreach effort, mobilizing networks of churches, women's groups, campus committees, environmentalists, and a wide range of constituencies. All across Capitol Hill on February 26, the phones and fax machines were jammed. Members of Congress reported receiving hundreds and even thousands of messages by early afternoon that day. It was impossible to calculate the exact number of messages, but Andrews estimated that the appeal generated more than a million calls, faxes, and email messages. Coming just eleven days after the massive street demonstrations of February 15, the virtual march was further evidence of the vast scale of the movement against war.

In the final weeks before the invasion, the Win Without War coalition maintained a frenetic pace of activity in a desperate attempt to prevent an increasingly inevitable military attack. Relying primarily on the rapidly expanding membership networks of MoveOn and True Majority, Win Without War launched an international online petition to the UN Security Council urging rejection of a US and British draft resolution authorizing war. The response was overwhelming. Within days, more than one million people signed the petition to the Security Council. It was delivered to UN representatives in New York at a Win Without War/MoveOn press conference on March 10. At the same time the coalition issued an international call for antiwar vigils the following weekend, March 15–16. Once again, the response was overwhelming, as thousands of groups all over the world announced plans to hold candlelight and prayer vigils in their communities. More than six thousand vigils took place in more than one hundred countries that weekend. Once again, the world said no to war, this time in a prayerful plea at the last hour before the onset of military hostilities. It was the most diverse and widespread international wave of local peace action ever organized, another powerful indication of the unprecedented scale of the global movement against war.

The World Speaks

Of the many extraordinary features of the antiwar movement, none was more remarkable than its international dimension. Organized opposition to US policy emerged in every part of the world, expressed in countless statements, petitions, and demonstrations. The protests of February 15, 2003, were literally a global phenomenon, with reports of antiwar actions that weekend in more than six hundred cities. The film *We Are Many* found that protests occurred in 789 cities or towns in 72 countries.[25] Opinion polls in many nations showed solid and sometimes overwhelming majorities against US-led military action in Iraq. In some countries, people considered George W. Bush more of a threat to international security than Saddam Hussein.[26] In the United States, the global movement was a source of inspiration for those of us who spoke out. We gained confidence and strength in knowing that we were standing with the vast majority of the world's people. For a few incredible months, the human family joined together as seldom before, united in a fervent plea for peace.

The five-day gathering of the European Social Forum in November 2002 concluded with a march through Florence and a rally of hundreds of thousands of people protesting the impending war against Iraq. Posters read "No War," "Not in my name," and "Bush, Blair, Berlusconi—assassins," among many other messages.[27] The initial call from the Social Forum for coordinated international actions on February 15 urged groups and individuals in Europe and beyond to organize massive opposition to the US attack through antiwar demonstrations in the capital of every nation. Further preparations took place a month later in Copenhagen, with representatives of United for Peace and Justice also in attendance. The final plans were laid at the World Social Forum in January in Porte Alegre, Brazil. Thousands of global justice organizers participated in these forums and helped to spread the call throughout the world. In dozens of countries national coalitions were created, encompassing a wide range of movements and organizations. The UK had the Stop the War Coalition; Italy, Fermiamo la Guerra all'Iraq; Germany, Netzwerk Friedenskooperative; Spain, No al la Guerra. All the national coalitions set up websites and linked to each other. Many adopted the same slogan and graphic symbol, a missile crossed out with the words "stop the war."

Waves of protest were already coursing through Europe and the United States prior to the scheduled February demonstrations. Coordinated protests occurred across the UK on October 31, 2002, and in Canada the weekend of November 16–17, 2002. Major demonstrations occurred on January 16 and January 18 in Tokyo, Moscow, Paris, London, Dublin, Montreal, Ottawa, Toronto, Cologne, Bonn, Gothenburg, Florence, Oslo, Rotterdam, Istanbul, and Cairo, as well as large rallies in the United States in Washington DC and San Francisco.[28] All the protests rose in a crescendo to the historic February events.

The February 15 demonstration in London was the largest in the history of that city. It was a typically gray February day, but the rain held off, and it was not bitterly cold. The crowd embarked from two separate assembly sites, pouring into and filling much of Hyde Park. More than one million people overflowed the city's center.[29] March organizer Kate Hudson put the number of demonstrators at two million.[30] One of the speakers that day was Rev. Jesse Jackson Sr. He traveled to London as the guest of the city's Mayor Ken Livingstone, who feted him at a peace reception at City Hall. Jackson gamely joined the march despite having a cast on his foot after recent surgery. When Jackson was introduced on stage, according to longtime aide Steve Cobble, "the response from the crowd was electrifying. A roar started up, similar to the 'wave' at a football game, rolling from front to back, a huge greeting of welcome. The goose bumps stood up on my arms."[31] Jackson's speech was one of the highlights of the day.

The London march was sponsored by a broad coalition of groups, including the Muslim Association of Britain and the Campaign for Nuclear Disarmament, all part of the Stop the War coalition, which was founded in September 2001 by organizations on the left, but also drew support from trade unions, green activists, Liberal Democrats, and even some nationalists. The march and the Stop the War coalition were endorsed by many celebrities from all sectors of cultural life. The most significant feature of the coalition, according to Hudson, was the creation of a strong relationship between the antiwar movement and the Muslim community. This was a "groundbreaking achievement," she wrote, marking the first

Antiwar march in London, February 15, 2003. IAN WALDIE/GETTY IMAGES.

time the Muslim community in Britain "worked in this way within British campaigning and political life."[32]

Much of the media coverage of the London demonstration was favorable, noting that the participants were not the "usual suspects" at protest rallies. They were "middle-class, middle-aged, politically mannered and jolly angry," wrote the *Sunday Mirror*.[33] The demonstrators were "quiet, decent people," wrote the *Daily Mail*, reasonably affluent and politically centrist, the type of people who usually don't demonstrate but were brought into the streets by the urgency of trying to stop an unnecessary war.[34] Journalists and MPs also joined the march, as did the family members of many government officials, including some of Blair's closest colleagues.[35]

The massive protest in London reflected profound public doubts about the argument for war. A comprehensive, integrated analysis of public opinion by scholar James Strong found that the British people broadly opposed the prospect of war in Iraq. Strong's examination of opinion polls, parliamentary debates, and press coverage confirmed that the massive outpouring of antiwar sentiment in London accurately reflected British public opinion. There were a few brief moments prior to the start of war when support slightly outweighed opposition, but the dominant sentiment in the fourteen months leading up to the invasion was opposition to the use of force.[36] Blair ignored the demands of the protesters, of course, but he paid a political price for his obsequiousness to Bush and was widely lampooned as the president's "poodle."[37] His reputation suffered enormously over the subsequent years, as noted below.[38]

Rivaling the London march on February 15 was the massive protest of more than a million people in Rome. Dozens of special trains and over 2,000 buses from all over Italy ferried protesters to Rome that day. The historic heart of the city, between the Colosseum and Piazza San Giovanni in Laterano, was packed for hours by a slow-moving procession of protesters. The *Guinness Book of*

Records claims that three million people participated in the demonstration, making it the largest antiwar rally in history.[39] The
demonstration was a carnival of protest with music and dancing
and omnipresent rainbow flags of peace. Participants included
workers, students, grassroots Catholic activists, and, as in London,
even supporters of nationalist parties. Sizeable protests were also
reported in other Italian cities that day, including Milan, Palermo,
Cagliari, and Bergamo. All over Italy, people spoke out in unprecedented numbers against Bush's war.

Major demonstrations occurred in dozens of other cities all
over the world. Tens of thousands marched in Glasgow, Dublin,
and Belfast. Half a million people assembled in Madrid, while the
crowd in Barcelona was estimated at one million. Smaller protests
occurred in the Spanish cities of Valencia, Seville, Los Palmas, and
Cadiz. Half a million marched in Berlin, and crowds of one hundred thousand or more gathered in Brussels, Paris, and Athens,
with smaller protests in more than a hundred other European
cities. More than a hundred thousand demonstrated in Montreal,
Toronto, Vancouver, and other Canadian cities. Indeed, the February 15 protests in Canada would be followed by even larger
antiwar rallies a month later. On March 15, more than 200,000
marched in Montreal as the Quebec Federation of Labor mobilized
its members to participate, with protests also taking place that day
in Toronto, Ottawa, and elsewhere in Canada. The demonstrations
reflected strong Canadian public opinion against the war and came
just two days before Prime Minister Jean Chrétien confirmed to
Parliament that Canada would not participate in the US war effort,
an announcement that brought loud cheers and an ovation from
ministers and back benchers alike.[40]

The February 15 mobilizations went far beyond Europe and
North America. Tens of thousands turned out in Mexico City, Rio
de Janeiro, Montevideo, and Buenos Aires. Several hundred thousand gathered in Sydney and Melbourne. In New Zealand, protests

took place in Auckland, Wellington, and more than a dozen other cities. Thousands marched in Tokyo, Seoul, Bangkok, Manila, Kuala Lumpur, Jakarta (the week before), Lahore, New Delhi, Calcutta, and other Asian cities. Approximately twenty thousand people marched in Johannesburg, Cape Town, and Durban. In Damascus, some two hundred thousand demonstrated at the People's Assembly. Tens of thousands rallied in Cairo, Beirut, and Amman. Several thousand people, Jews and Palestinians together, marched in Tel Aviv. A few dozen hearty souls even demonstrated at McMurdo Station in Antarctica, forming a giant peace sign in the snow with their bundled-up bodies.

Protests continued after the invasion in the United States and around the world. Another round of demonstrations occurred on the first weekend of the war, March 22–23, with major marches and rallies in New York, London, Barcelona, several cities in Germany, and many other locations across the planet. Large protests also took place on the second, third, and fourth anniversaries of the invasion, although the numbers gradually diminished over the years. In many countries the energy of antiwar protests not only drew citizens into the streets but generated action within established political institutions. The leaders who supported Bush's war paid a political price, and antiwar politics became a winning formula for elective office, not only in the US, as described in Chapter Six, but also in such countries as Germany, Spain, Turkey, and the UK, as recounted in Chapter Seven.

Digital Activism

Much of the success of Win Without War and the antiwar movement in general can be ascribed to the powerful impact of internet organizing and the specific role of MoveOn. The internet emerged as a tool of mass political mobilization in the campaign against the impeachment of President Bill Clinton in 1998 and in the broader global justice movement that emerged in 1999. MoveOn was created as a means of lobbying Congress to halt the Clinton impeachment proceedings. Its message then: censure and "move on" to other more important legislative business. It was not until the Iraq antiwar movement, however, that the full range of possibilities for utilizing the internet for social change organizing became evident. Global justice organizers used the internet effectively as a means of communication, coordination, and education among decentralized networks in multiple countries. To these functions antiwar activists added new dimensions of internet mobilization: the development of organized "membership" networks, the creation of "meeting tools" to facilitate coordinated local action, and online fundraising. The result was an unprecedented capacity to raise consciousness and organize political action, a development that has come to define political activism and social mobilization on virtually every issue since.

MoveOn was the pioneer and leading force in this internet revolution. It was the lead group within Win Without War and served as the backbone of the movement's most extensive organizing and communication efforts. In August 2002, as antiwar actions were beginning to emerge, MoveOn organized hundreds of local meetings in which constituents urged their members of Congress to oppose war. Prior to the congressional vote in October, MoveOn circulated an antiwar petition to Congress signed by hundreds of thousands of people. After the vote, in a tribute to the twenty-three senators who stood against the resolution, MoveOn launched a campaign to "reward the heroes." It appealed for online contributions to antiwar members of Congress who faced difficult reelection campaigns, most importantly Minnesota Senator Paul Wellstone. The response was overwhelming and set an early record for online fundraising. In a matter of days, MoveOn raised more than $2 million, including $700,000 for the Wellstone campaign.

Tragically, the senator died in a plane crash a few days later. When the news of Wellstone's death arrived during the United for Peace and Justice founding meeting in Washington on October 25, there was stunned shock. Several people wept openly, and the meeting was suspended for a time. The loss of Wellstone was a crushing blow to many antiwar activists. We had taken encouragement from his principled vote against war and were hoping that his reelection could send a message to other Democrats: that standing up for peace is good politics.

MoveOn played a central role in building support for major antiwar actions, including the February 15 rallies, the virtual march on Washington, the petition to the UN Security Council, and the worldwide antiwar vigils in March 2003. All of this action flowed from an organization with a tiny staff of seven people working from their homes—an organization with a powerful computer and sophisticated software system, but no office and none of the usual accoutrements of traditional membership groups.[41] In the six months leading up to the outbreak of war in March 2003, MoveOn's online network, US and international, jumped from approximately seven hundred thousand to nearly two million participants. Win Without War contributed to this membership growth by feeding contacts to MoveOn in its outreach efforts and by using the network as a central repository for capturing new names. The relationship between MoveOn and Win Without War was symbiotic. MoveOn helped to found, lead, and sustain Win Without War and played a leading role in the antiwar movement.[42]

Other electronically based networks also experienced extraordinary growth and activity during the antiwar movement. The True Majority network founded by Ben Cohen expanded rapidly, reaching 350,000 members in the fall of 2003.[43] Working in close partnership with Business Leaders for Sensible Priorities, True Majority specialized in producing bold, visually appealing newspaper ads and internet messages that helped to attract new supporters. True Majority also developed a partnership with the National Council of Churches, helping to reach and mobilize religious leaders and faith-based activists throughout the country. Working Assets represented a different kind of electronic activist network. Founded in 1985 as a progressive telecommunications company, Working Assets developed a customer/subscriber base of several hundred thousand households. It donated a portion of its revenues to support organizations working for peace, human rights, social equality, education, and the environment. Over the years it contributed millions of dollars to these causes. Working Assets also mobilized its customers to engage in progressive action through notices that were included with monthly subscriber bills. As the antiwar movement grew, Working Assets developed web-based organizing tools, and during the pre-war Iraq debate, it generated more than 430,000 online actions, letters, and calls in opposition to Bush administration policy. The organization also raised over $465,000 for antiwar and humanitarian relief/democracy-building activities.[44]

Existing organizations with more traditional membership structures also developed email networks and increased their fundraising potential. Sojourners saw its newly created "Sojo" list expand from twenty thousand in the summer of 2002 to more than seventy thousand in March 2003. Peace Action, Code Pink, the Council for a Livable World, WAND, Physicians for Social Responsibility, and other peace organizations also developed email listservs and experienced growth in membership and electronic participation.[45] All of them participated in Win Without War and UFPJ and were able to multiply their influence by working in concert with MoveOn and other online groups and with dozens of other organizations. The internet emerged as an effective mechanism for political communication and fundraising and as a vehicle for building coalitions and mobilizing collective action.

When internet organizing began, some skeptics questioned the value of a tool that kept activists glued to their computer screens. A new word entered the lexicon: "clicktivism," defined as a form of social action that uses the internet to influence politics but involves minimal effort or physical commitment.[46] The very ease with which one could click and send off a message, sometimes to hundreds or thousands of recipients, seemed to cheapen the value of the effort. Lobbyists reported that the impact of an email message as a form of political communication paled in comparison with other types of messages, such as a letter, phone call, or personal visit. MoveOn and the other internet-based activist groups recognized these limitations early on and devised methods of mobilization that significantly broadened the impact of email activism. One significant innovation was the use of the internet

Eli Pariser, Washington DC, 2007. TOM MATZZIE/MOVE ON.

to organize coordinated local meetings. Activists were encouraged to get up from their computer screens and go out to meetings where they could connect with other activists in their communities. MoveOn developed a meeting tool that Pariser termed "action in a box." Campaigns were programmed so that respondents could be led easily through a series of prompts offering venues and functions for action. An email message from MoveOn would contain the call to action, and by clicking the appropriate icons, the respondent could connect to other activists and volunteer for various tasks, from attending a meeting or sending an email to Congress, to more ambitious activities, such as coordinating a meeting, speaking in public, or contacting the media. Working Assets developed a similar meeting tool, which gave subscribers options for participating in local activities. By segmenting lists according to location and interest, internet organizers could use their membership bases to sponsor highly particularized forms of action.

As scholar David Karpf explains, the political significance of MoveOn was the introduction of a new model of political advocacy that combined online and in-person activities. The network organizers not only mobilized people to sign petitions, but also persuaded them to make contributions, engage in legislative lobbying with their elected representatives, and participate in or organize local meetings with like-minded people in their communities.[47] In important respects, MoveOn unlocked the secret of how to harness the internet for political action.[48] The antiwar movement was the laboratory in which these tools were developed.

One of the most significant aspects of translating internet communications into political power was the development and use of online fundraising. Just as online marketing had become increasingly significant in the commercial economy, internet-based fundraising rapidly became a vital source of income for social movements, nonprofit groups, and political campaigns. Now an essential element of every electoral campaign, social action movement, and public interest group, online fundraising got its start in the Iraq antiwar movement, with MoveOn leading the way. The network's first foray into antiwar fundraising was its "reward the heroes" campaign of October 2002. This was followed by many subsequent appeals for donations to finance organizing campaigns and paid advertising and public relations efforts. In the months preceding the war, MoveOn raised more than $1 million for newspaper and television ads and associated public relations activities, turning its vast internet network into a crucial source of financial support for the antiwar movement. MoveOn remained a fundraising source after the invasion as well, fueling the initial presidential drive of Howard Dean and generating millions of dollars for advertising and public relations efforts to support the withdrawal of troops.

Social movement theory emphasizes the importance of resource mobilization as a means of exerting political influence. Movements are linked to social change organizations, which depend upon formal dues-paying membership networks. These structures provide a sustained and predictable base of income and activism. Traditional membership networks also offer opportunities for participatory decision making, with individual members or chapters playing a role in determining organizational priorities and selecting leaders. The internet-based networks MoveOn developed are less formal and more loosely structured, with no annual dues or membership requirements, no chapters or affiliates, indeed no fixed organizational structure at all. The "members" of MoveOn participate only to the extent that they are motivated to respond to particular email action alerts. This is an approach, said writer Andrew Boyd, that "embraces the permission-based culture of the internet, and consumer culture itself." Pariser described this as a "postmodern organizing model."[49]

This new form of organizing raises important questions about traditional models of social change. The classic theory, following Gandhi, King, Chavez, and other nonviolent leaders, is that political impact depends on organizational strength. This was the approach that many of us learned in the Vietnam antiwar movement: to create the power for confronting the war system we needed organizational strength. Many activists were trained in the methods of the legendary community organizer Saul Alinsky, who emphasized the connection between building organizations and achieving political results. As Alinsky wrote in his 1971 guidebook *Rules for Radicals,* "power and organization are one and the same thing."[50] Scholars Peter Ackerman and Christopher Kruegler similarly emphasized the importance of "efficient, fighting organizations" as crucial elements of successful social action.[51]

Internet-based groups such as MoveOn only partly follow the classic model. They provide networks for fundraising and coordinated action, but do not create long-term institutional structures. The memberships of these groups consist of atomized individuals rather than networks of organized affiliates. There are no formalized mechanisms for grassroots decision making or structured feedback on group priorities. Marshall Ganz, who helped Chavez and the United Farm Workers union in the 1960s, observed that MoveOn engages in marketing more than organizing. "It's important to distinguish between sharing information and forming relationships. . . . Participation in democratic organizations is not just an individual act. It's an act of affiliation with others."[52] Internet organizing and the tools of digital messaging offer valuable means of mobilizing for social change, but they are not a substitute for community-based contact and the creation of sustainable organizations. Both forms of mobilization, digital and organizational, are necessary to build political power for change.

Resistance and Disruption

On the opposite side of the social action spectrum from clicktivism is disruptive civil disobedience, often involving direct action to create disorder and prevent the functioning of targeted institutions. Individuals and groups make a commitment of maximum participation, putting their bodies on the line to risk arrest or even injury for the sake of the cause. The Iraq antiwar movement featured a substantial Pledge of Resistance campaign, in which tens of thousands of people and a network of more than fifty organizations agreed to engage in nationally coordinated civil disobedience. Its purpose was to deter US aggression by creating a credible threat of massive social disruption in the event of war. The hope was that this commitment would convince decision makers to reconsider the costs of military action. The campaign was modeled on the Central America Pledge of Resistance, which sponsored civil disobedience during the 1980s to prevent direct US military intervention in Nicaragua and El Salvador.[53] Not in Our Name helped to initiate the pledge effort, which was supported by the Fellowship of Reconciliation, Global Exchange, Pax Christi, Peace Action, and the War Resisters League, among other groups. The pledge sought to emulate the nonviolent witness of Gandhi and King, while also borrowing tactics from the global justice movement.

Considerable resistance emerged, but most of the civil disobedience that occurred came in the days immediately after the outbreak of military hostilities in March 2003. Some activists engaged in civil disobedience prior to the invasion—during the demonstrations on December 10 and then again during the King Day protests in mid-January—as a way of trying to prevent war through moral persuasion, but most concentrated on organizing resistance on the "day after." Organizers threatened to disrupt downtown business areas as a form of pressure to deter the war makers. In the days after the start of the invasion, civil disobedience occurred in fifty cities, with thousands arrested. In some of these actions, protesters halted traffic and blockaded government buildings. In Seattle, demonstrators briefly blocked Interstate 5 in the center of the city. In Washington DC, protesters attempted to block the Key Bridge across the Potomac River. In New York, civil resisters shut down a two-block stretch of Broadway.

The most significant actions occurred in Chicago and San Francisco. In Chicago, more than ten thousand people gathered in Federal Plaza on Thursday night, March 21, the day after the outbreak of war. It was the largest antiwar rally in Chicago since the Vietnam era, and the crowd was in a defiant mood. After a spirited rally, the demonstrators began to move slowly toward the east, pushing the police line block by block toward Lake Shore Drive. A police officer later explained to the *Chicago Tribune* that the only way to control "a crowd of that size" was to "move with it and try to contain it, not try to stop it."[54] As the crowd neared Lake Michigan, its numbers swelling, demonstrators snaked north onto Lake Shore Drive, blocking traffic in the northbound lane. When the demonstrators passed Navy Pier, they took over the southbound lane as well. Protesters weaved in and out of stalled traffic. When part of the crowd pushed up Michigan Avenue and sat down on Chicago Avenue, the police finally moved in and began making arrests "by the busload." More than 550 protesters were arrested and held overnight. Another large rally was held in downtown Chicago the next day, but this time thousands of police in two lines surrounded the crowd. When the protesters headed up Dearborn Avenue, police lined the streets and refused to allow anyone to enter or leave the march. A smaller demonstration took place on Saturday, concluding three days of protest.

In San Francisco, as many as 20,000 antiwar resisters converged on the city center on March 21, shutting down thirty intersections and blockading a dozen buildings in the downtown financial district. The demonstrators used innovative hit and run tactics "to an extent never before seen in the Bay Area."[55] Small groups of activists armed with cell phones flitted from block to block, closing down intersections and then quickly dispersing as police arrived to make arrests. Some demonstrators chained themselves together, forcing police to use saws to separate them. The combination of mobile tactics and constant police action caused widespread chaos. The disruption was so severe that police issued public notices urging motorists not to enter the downtown area. The police arrested 1,400 people during the disturbances on Thursday.[56] A smaller but still angry crowd assembled the next day, but police kept a tighter rein on the demonstrators. Approximately 200 were arrested on Friday. Total arrests were more than 2,000.[57]

The methods of urban lockdown and hit and run tactics are a far cry from the approaches of Gandhi and King, who encouraged their followers to engage in disciplined civil disobedience and accept police arrest openly and even joyfully. They embedded their resistance tactics within a larger political strategy designed to win the sympathy and support of third parties and build broad public support for specific policy objectives. Writer/activist Barbara Deming was a proponent of nonviolent disruptive action, but she cautioned that such action must be done in a way "that the general population understands, that encourages more and more people to join us."[58] Scholars Erica Chenoweth and Maria Stephan have shown that the success of civil resistance is directly related to the scale of public participation.[59] To influence policy, movements need to win as many people as possible to their side. It is hard to see how actions that disrupted the lives of tens of thousands of people in liberal cities such as Chicago and San Francisco helped to win support for the antiwar cause.

The Iraq antiwar emerged from the anti-Vietnam War movement and other previous peace campaigns as well as the more recent global justice movement. It built upon the experience of these movements and adopted the tools of the internet to develop innovative methods of mobilization that modernized the peace movement and social resistance campaigns generally. The scale and breadth of the movement were unprecedented, more genuinely global than any previous peace movement. To create all of this protest activity over the course of just a few months was a significant accomplishment, although it was not sufficient to turn public opinion against the war.

Once the war began and troops were committed to battle, a "rally 'round the flag" effect kicked in, as is often the case when soldiers are sent to war.[60] Public opinion turned sharply in favor of Bush's policy, and the rising wave of protest faded. Few saw any point in opposing an invasion that was already underway. Some small protests and vigils continued, however, and the movement regained momentum over the coming months and years. Bush's bump in the polls did not last long as Iraq descended into violence and chaos, and prewar claims of weapons of mass destruction (WMDs) and a quick and easy war proved false. Antiwar opposition persisted and grew within society and began to emerge within the ranks of the military. Activists worked within the political system to end the occupation and force the withdrawal of US troops.

There are many reasons why the movement fell short of stopping the invasion, including the government's enormous advantages in political power and communications capacity, and the Bush administration's iron determination to overthrow the Iraqi government no matter what. But the movement could have done more. The major coalitions UFPJ and Win Without War could have formed earlier and organized larger and more frequent protests. Activists could have acted more decisively to influence the October 2002 vote in Congress. Planning for civil disobedience could have focused on stopping the war before it started rather than the day after. Activists could have done more to organize in their communities and apply pressure on local elected leaders. There are always what ifs.

Changing public opinion was the movement's biggest challenge. Demonstrations helped to attract public attention to the antiwar cause, but they were not enough. The movement needed a larger media effort and more effective communications strategy. Opponents of the war were successful in avoiding the negative press coverage that shadowed the Vietnam peace movement, and Win Without War, MoveOn, and other groups sponsored an array of significant media activities that communicated the antiwar message to large audiences. These efforts were cut short by the start of the war, however, and were not able to shift public opinion decisively in the short time available. We delve into this part of the story in the next chapter.

Three

Communicating for Peace

The mobilizations against war in Iraq featured the largest and most sophisticated media communications effort in the history of the peace movement. That's not saying much given the paltry record of media relations in previous antiwar campaigns. As Todd Gitlin and others have observed, peace activists have been slow to recognize the significance of strategic communications in working for social change. During the Vietnam era, press coverage of the peace movement often conveyed images of a motley rabble, with opinion surveys showing low approval ratings for antiwar protesters.[1] The major coalitions at the time were more interested in street protest than media communications, and little effort was made to hire professional media consultants or sponsor public relations and advertising campaigns. In recent decades, activists have become more media savvy.[2] They have recognized the power and influence of the media, and the importance of communications in shaping political discourse and swaying public opinion. When the debate over war in Iraq began, many activists were determined to overcome the limitations of the past and devoted greater attention to media communications.

In this chapter, I review some of these efforts and examine the struggle over the war as a contest of contending narratives and media framing strategies. I begin with a glimpse into the massive media operations of the White House as it sought to manufacture consent for its policies, and the obsequiousness and gullibility of the national press corps in reporting the fabricated justifications for war. I follow with an overview of social movement theory on the centrality of communications, a discussion of attempts by anti-war groups to counter the White House media onslaught, and an examination of some of the movement's specific media framing strategies and messaging activities, including an assessment of anti-war advertising efforts. I give significant attention to the involvement of artists and celebrities in communicating for peace. The chapter concludes with a consideration of lessons learned from these efforts and the inherent challenges of contesting dominant media frames amidst a militarized culture and media landscape.

Selling Their "Product"

The Bush administration launched a sophisticated media operation to convince Americans of the need to take military action against Saddam Hussein. As examined in Chapter One, planning for military action began right after the 9/11 attacks and was well underway by the summer of 2002. In July of that year, senior communications officials began forming the White House Iraq Group, which mounted an elaborate media rollout to convince people of the case for war. Bush speechwriter Scott McClellan described the process as developing a "strategy for carefully orchestrating the coming campaign to aggressively sell the war."[3] The administration waited until early September to launch the campaign. As White House chief of staff Andrew Card cynically explained at the time, "From a marketing point of view, you don't introduce new products in August."[4]

The sales pitch began with President Bush's nationally televised speech on the anniversary of September 11. Using the Statue of Liberty as dramatic backdrop, the president spoke ominously of the terrorist threat and the menace of weapons of mass destruction in the hands of a ruthless tyrant. He followed up the next day with a bellicose speech at the United Nations General Assembly. In the following weeks and months, Bush and senior officials Dick Cheney, Condoleezza Rice, Paul Wolfowitz, and others relentlessly beat the drums for military action and issued constant warnings of the supposed imminent threat of Iraqi weapons. Their core message was captured in a frequently repeated, powerfully evocative, but thoroughly misleading sound bite: "the first sign of a 'smoking gun' may be a nuclear mushroom cloud."[5] The claims of WMD and connections to Al Qaida were groundless, as some contemporary reports and subsequent documentation confirmed,[6] but facts mattered less than the constant barrage of threat warnings and a steady stream of sensationalist disclosures of information that proved to be false: Saddam Hussein supporting Al Qaida, 9/11 bomber Mohamed Atta meeting Iraqi officials in Prague, an International Atomic Energy Agency report that Iraq was close to having the bomb, purchases of uranium from Niger, the use of aluminum tubes for centrifuges, defectors claiming renovated nuclear facilities, mobile biological weapons labs.

With the PR campaign at full throttle, the national press corps swallowed the deceit whole cloth. Newspapers and television broadcasts endlessly parroted the administration line. A study of on-camera sources for the major US television networks in the weeks prior to the invasion found that 75 percent of the American experts interviewed were either current or former government officials and military officers. Only one of nearly 200 experts expressed skepticism about the impending attack.[7] A follow-up report of on-camera sources for the first three weeks of the war confirmed a continuing pattern of pro-war sources on major news talk shows.[8]

A study of media coverage in the UK found similar patterns, with only 6.7 percent of media reports presenting antiwar voices.[9]

The *Washington Post* featured 140 front-page articles reporting the claims of Bush, Cheney, and other officials in the pre-war period, but published only one front-page story raising doubts. Scholar Ole R. Holsti described the press as quiescent and complacent. He and others cite the example of *New York Times* writer Judith Miller, whose byline appeared on sixty-four articles, reporting stories of Iraqi WMDs that were "later shown to be totally false."[10]

The framing of the issues and the images presented on television reinforced the White House narrative and the expectation of war. As PBS *News Hour* reporter Jim Lehrer observed, the conversation was always about the "liberation" of Iraq. The word occupation was never mentioned. In October, MSNBC launched a new program, *Countdown: Iraq*. A few months later, the network cancelled the Phil Donahue show, one of the few programs seriously questioning the prospect of war.[11] Television news broadcasters spoke in front of an image showing the map of Iraq superimposed on a target, with Baghdad in the crosshairs. No wonder so many Americans told pollsters they supported military action in Iraq.

White House media manipulation continued during the occupation. When the US invasion triggered a powerful insurgency of armed resistance, American readers and television viewers were shielded from the harsh realities. When the costs of the war for US taxpayers soared to tens of billions of dollars a year, contrary to absurdist pre-war claims that Iraq would pay for the war itself,[12] the costs were partially shielded in a separate budgetary account known as "Overseas Contingency Operations." Reporters were barred from access to Dover, Delaware, and Ramstein, Germany, where the bodies of dead American troops returned. Coverage of soldier funerals in local communities was restricted.[13] The Pentagon continued the policy of embedded journalism that began during the 1991 Gulf War, when restrictions were imposed on the ability of reporters to travel and investigate freely.[14] To cover the war, reporters had to apply for a limited number of spots in a press pool controlled by military officers. Under constant escort, the reporters could go only to locations approved by their military handlers. When this system was imposed back in 1991, Walter Cronkite and other veteran reporters lamented the lack of independent reporting. Pulitzer Prize winner Malcom W. Browne of the *New York Times* said the system turned reporters into "essentially unpaid employees of the Defense Department."[15]

Gaining Coverage

Overwhelmed by the media power of the government and beset by a supine press corps, the antiwar movement faced an uphill struggle in trying to counter White House propaganda and expose the false assumptions that led to war. Social movements in all settings face challenges in gaining positive news coverage and countering the narratives of their opponents. As Charlotte Ryan and other analysts have observed, challenger groups seldom have the resources to match the communications power of governments or major corporations. Activists also must contend with the inherent media bias in favor of those in power—a tendency that is particularly pronounced on national security issues.[16] The options available to social movements for overcoming these obstacles are limited. They can organize events that attract media coverage, they can place advertisements that communicate their message directly, or they can use celebrities and "famous faces" to attract publicity to their cause. They can write articles and reports that counter official lies, although these seldom reach mainstream audiences or decision makers. The Iraq antiwar movement used all of these methods, with varying degrees of effectiveness.

Facebook and other social media platforms did not exist for the Iraq antiwar movement. Social media methods have many advantages and have become powerful tools for movements today in framing messages and mobilizing mass participation. Conventional broadcast media are also important, however, and reach wider and more diverse audiences and have an aura of credibility and official authority that social media lacks. Although Facebook and other platforms now outpace print newspapers as sources of information, most Americans still get their news from broadcast television and radio.[17] Conventional and social media are both important for movements seeking to shape policy agendas.

Demonstrations are the classic means for attracting attention and delivering activist messages. They can be highly effective as communicative events. As noted in earlier chapters, the February 15, 2003, rallies in the US and around the world were enormously successful in gaining media coverage. The demonstrations that day were a lead story in practically every broadcast and print news outlet in the United States and in much of the world. Never before had the peace movement attracted such favorable attention globally. The legitimacy and image of the Iraq antiwar movement as a "second superpower" were the direct result of those demonstrations and the resulting media coverage. The demonstrations were dramatic "real-world events" that generated significant news coverage and helped to influence public opinion and policy.[18] They were planned with media communications in mind and gave credibility and legitimacy to the antiwar cause. There were many other demonstrations against the war that occurred in the United States and other countries in the following years. These also attracted press attention, especially in the cities and regions where they occurred, but never with the impact of the February events.

Protest actions at the community level are often effective at gaining local press coverage and can deliver targeted messages to local representatives.

Scholar Ian Taylor's examination of press coverage in the UK found that local press outlets were often more favorable to antiwar messages than the national media. A majority of the activists he surveyed felt they had more positive coverage from local media than regional or national media. This was partly the result of the closer connection between the local papers and their readership. According to Taylor, "as far as the local press was concerned, such legitimacy as the antiwar movement had, and the reason why they merited being taken seriously, derived from the widespread support their cause has among the general public."[19]

Frames and Messages

One of the most important dimensions of media strategy is the framing of messages. Every political contest is at its core a struggle over the meaning of words and ideas. As William Gamson observed, the images and metaphors activists convey are central to their prospects for political success.[20] Ideas such as justice or peace do not exist in a vacuum, in some rarified form that everyone automatically accepts. Their meaning is shaped by the social and political context in which they are communicated. Organizers seek to shape that context and offer compelling images, symbols, and metaphors that resonate with and capture public imagination. The contest over symbolic expression is a central element of social movement strategy and was crucial to the struggle against the war.

Win Without War was specifically created as a vehicle for media communications. The coalition placed a great deal of emphasis on framing its messages and maintaining a sustained and disciplined press operation. From the outset, Win Without War sought to portray itself as mainstream and patriotic. Its press releases and newspaper ads featured an American flag, and the mission statement began: "We are patriotic Americans . . . ." By framing messages in these terms, Win Without War sought to capture the flag for the cause of peace and thereby inoculate itself against charges of aiding the enemy or disrespecting the troops. The coalition explicitly

condemned Saddam Hussein's rule and supported vigorous inspections and containment as alternative means of countering the
Iraqi threat. The coalition expressed full support for international
efforts to counter terrorism, although it was careful to avoid any
specific reference to the administration's "war on terror" language,
so as not to reinforce Bush's militarized metaphor. Through the
framing and delivery of these messages, Win Without War sought
to reach the political mainstream and contest the administration's
case for war.

The Win Without War name was itself a form of message framing. The phrase was alliterative and easy to express. It conveyed a
positive theme—everyone wants to "win"—without the negativ-
ity of being "against" war or the military. Yet it was specific about
seeking a solution "without war," thus marking a clear break with
White House policy. The title implied support for constructive
alternatives to war, such as vigorous UN weapons inspections and
continued containment. It conveyed a desire to counter the per-
ceived threat from Saddam Hussein through diplomatic rather
than military means. It also implied a strategy for winning the
struggle against Al Qaida through the force of law rather than the
law of force. The name avoided the ambiguity and negative con-
notation that some people, still influenced by Cold War miscon-
ceptions, associate with the traditional "peace" movement. Win
Without War projected a new, proactive image for the movement.
It was both message and sound bite, a brand that was among the
most widely communicated messages of the antiwar movement.[21]

The Win Without War coalition worked closely with Fenton
Communications in sponsoring public relations and media advertising efforts. Fenton created a special "antiwar room," which provided sustained professional public relations services, helped to
frame messages, and developed media communications strategies.
They were in contact with hundreds of reporters and editors on a
regular basis. They organized numerous press events, tried to book

spokespersons on national and regional interview programs, and placed paid newspaper and television advertising in targeted media markets. Other movement media firms also played an important role in communicating the antiwar message, including Mainstream Media in California, and Avenging Angels in New York. These efforts were substantial, but they paled in comparison to the White House media operation.

The Win Without War media strategy sought to raise doubts about invading Iraq among "persuadables"—those who might be persuaded to change their views. Opinion polls showed a third of the population strongly opposed to war but 60 percent or more favoring military action. Support for war depended greatly on how the question was asked and whether the U.S. had backing from the United Nations and allies. Opinion surveys showed a public preference for seeking the approval of the UN and acting with the support of allies.[22] A poll by the Chicago Council on Foreign Relations in June 2002 showed only 20 percent of respondents believing "we should invade Iraq even if we have to go it alone," with 65 percent agreeing the United States "should only invade Iraq with UN approval and the support of its allies."[23] A February 2003 poll found similar sentiments, with 64 percent agreeing that "the US needs to wait for approval of the United Nations before taking action against Iraq," and 62 percent favoring "[giving] the United Nations inspectors more time."[24] An *LA Times* poll and analysis at the time found similar results, with many respondents agreeing that the US should take military action only with the support of the UN Security Council.[25] These polling results suggested the existence of a sizeable constituency that could be persuaded to oppose a costly war fought without allies or UN authority.

The political debate about the war was a struggle to influence that persuadable population by focusing on these issues. The movement's "inspections, not war" messages and its support for UN Security Council authorization were calibrated to address that critical element of public opinion. The focus on alternatives was strategically selected to undermine support for Bush's unilateral war policy. The messaging of the movement also warned that attacking Iraq would stoke anti-American hatred in the region and generate greater support for terrorist violence. The prediction proved accurate, as the occupation fostered growing insurgency. This argument became the basis for later advocating the withdrawal of troops.

Patriotism, Militarized and Peaceful

There was considerable, sometimes heated debate within the movement about the use of patriotic symbols and language. Some activists expressed discomfort with this approach because the flag and patriotic themes have been so often used to justify militarism. As the cognitive linguist George Lakoff and other communications experts have noted, right wing groups have "commandeered patriotic language" and appropriated the meaning of the flag and other national emblems in support of war.[26] Scholar Jane Cramer argued that militarized patriotism was a major factor in explaining the Bush administration's ability to override rational objections and win congressional approval for the use of military force.[27] Politicians of national stature, especially those with presidential ambitions, such as Kerry, Clinton, and Biden, were fearful of being labelled unpatriotic. They were captives of Cold War cultural norms that valorized military approaches and deferral to presidential authority on national security issues.

Those of us who argued for a patriotic framing of the antiwar message contested this bellicose interpretation. We did so not only to win the support of persuadable Americans, but also as a matter of principle. The peace movement should not concede patriotism to militarism, we insisted, but should struggle to redefine the concept of loving one's country, to separate patriotism from militarized nationalism. Patriotism implies positive values of sacrifice, duty, honor, selflessness, and generosity toward others. Nationalism, by contrast, often evokes images of domination, militarism, xenophobia, and imperialism. The challenge is to emphasize the former over the latter. This means engaging in message-framing contests, struggling to reshape the meaning of commonly used words and images. For the antiwar movement this meant presenting a positive interpretation of patriotism: the greatness of America lies in its core values—freedom, equality, democracy, and the right to dissent—not in war and militarism. Martin Luther King Jr. famously declared, "I oppose the war in Vietnam because I love America." He cited the values of freedom and human rights enunciated in the Constitution and Declaration of Independence as the basis for opposing militarism.[28] Activists sought to capture that positive spirit through a cosmopolitan vision of striving for international cooperation and justice rather than war. They conveyed a "peace is patriotic" message by displaying the flag and other patriotic symbols as part of the movement's visual imagery.

Working Assets president Michael Kieschnick was one of those who sought to reclaim patriotic themes. "We are trying to take back the language," said Kieschnick.[29] Working Assets sought to reframe the "support the troops" message. The organization placed

Working Assets billboard, 2003. WORKING ASSETS/CREDO.

hundreds of billboards and advertising signs in San Francisco, Washington DC, New York, and other cities with the message "Support Our Troops. Bring Them Home Now." Working Assets also attempted to link patriotism and energy conservation, emphasizing the national interest in weaning the US economy from dependence on Middle Eastern oil. On the day of the January 18, 2003, rally in San Francisco, more than five thousand Working Assets customers and friends attended an "Environmentalists Against the War" protest cosponsored by the Sierra Club outside Grace Cathedral. Afterwards, an eco-caravan of one hundred hybrid and electric vehicles proceeded down to the main protest rally. Bumper stickers on the vehicles read "Go Solar, Not Ballistic" and "Real Patriots Drive Hybrids." These were among the many creative attempts within the movement to redefine patriotism and link love for country and the earth with opposition to war.

During the Vietnam War activists were falsely accused of disrespecting the troops, a pernicious myth that was used to discredit the peace movement.[30] Opponents of the Iraq War were careful to avoid even the hint of disdain for people in the military. The message for many became "support the warrior, not the war." Groups such as Win Without War endorsed proposals to improve conditions for service members and to increase GI Bill educational benefits for veterans. When active-duty service members and their families began to speak out against the war, as examined in Chapter Five, the antiwar movement gained greater legitimacy. The soldiers, veterans, and family members who urged an end to the war embodied patriotic messaging and were effective spokespersons for peace.

Advertising

Both antiwar groups and individuals spent substantial funds for the placement of full-page newspaper ads and television advertising in the months leading up to the US attack. The ads were an effective means of delivering antiwar messages. They assured that the movement's words and images would be communicated directly as intended, without mediation or interpretation. At times the advertising efforts themselves became a news story and helped to generate "earned media" through the novelty and sharply worded focus of the message. One of the boldest examples was a full-page advertisement produced by Fenton Communications that appeared in the *New York Times* on September 25, 2002, under the banner "Uncle oSama Wants You to Invade Iraq." The ad featured Osama bin Laden in the traditional Uncle Sam pose urging Washington to: "Go ahead. Send me a new generation of recruits. Your bombs will fuel hatred of America and their desire for revenge. Please attack Iraq. Distract yourself from attacking Al Qaida. Go ahead. . . . Make my day." Widely reproduced around the world, the powerful ad generated dozens of news stories and was read on the floor of the US Senate.

Another controversial and innovative ad was a thirty-second television spot produced by MoveOn in January 2003. The spot reproduced the famous "Daisy" ad from Lyndon Johnson's 1964 presidential campaign: a girl innocently picking petals from a daisy as a voice ominously counts down to zero, and the screen dissolves into a nuclear mushroom cloud. The 1964 ad was meant to raise fears about the extremist leanings of Republican candidate Senator Barry Goldwater. Its use in 2003 was an attempt to counter the Bush administration's disingenuous use of the mushroom cloud image. The MoveOn ad aimed to carry the message that if Saddam Hussein actually had such weapons, the war itself could lead to their use. The ad stirred controversy and attracted media attention to the antiwar campaign of MoveOn and other groups.

In October 2002 a group of corporate executives in Business Leaders for Sensible Priorities placed a full-page ad in the *New York Times* under the banner "They're selling war. We're not buying."

I Want You print ad, September 2022. DAVID FENTON/FENTON
COMMUNICATIONS.

The statement used the language of business in repudiating Bush's sales pitch. It illustrated the diversity of antiwar sentiment, showing that many business executives were also concerned about the risks and costs of war. In December 2002, Business Leaders joined with religious leaders in appealing to Bush's declared religious beliefs with a *New York Times* ad that read: "Jesus changed your heart. Let him change your mind." In January 2003, the group placed a full-page ad in the *Wall Street Journal* signed by Republican Party supporters and donors. Written and paid for by Edward H. Hamm, a member of the Republican Regents, a committee of donors who contribute six figures or more to the party, the ad declared "A Republican Dissent on Iraq" and proclaimed in bold print, "a billion bitter enemies will rise out of this war."

The organization True Majority, which had also come out of the business community, via Ben and Jerry's, sponsored a number of communications efforts. They produced a series of television ads that paired foreign policy experts with Hollywood artists and popular musicians. One ad featured actress Susan Sarandon and retired admiral Jack Shanahan. The television spots were placed nationally and in targeted local markets. Other organizations that placed full-page ads in the *New York Times* in the months preceding the invasion included Not in Our Name, the Center for Community Change, and 1199 SEIU United Healthcare Workers East, New York's healthcare union. Actor Sean Penn placed a personal full-page ad in the *Washington Post* in October. As noted in Chapter Four, Sojourners announced a six-point plan for preventing war with full-page ads in all the major London dailies in March 2003.

Advertising efforts continued after the invasion with the goal of ending the occupation and withdrawing US troops. MoveOn sponsored many of these messages and was generally effective in producing full-page newspaper ads with a sharp edge. One of the most hard-hitting ads featured on the left side of the page a stark image of tiny print listing thousands of names of US soldiers who died in Iraq. On the other side of the page were photos of Bush, Cheney, Rumsfeld, and Rice. In bold type under the names were the words "They Died." Under the photos "They Lied."

MoveOn committed a political error, however, when they mounted an attack against General David Petraeus, the senior commander in Iraq. In September 2007, in the midst of the Bush administration's escalation of the war and as congressional leaders sought to impose a timeline for the withdrawal of troops, Petraeus returned to Washington to claim success for Bush's surge policy and testify against troop withdrawal. On the day before Petraeus's appearance in Congress, MoveOn ran a full-page ad in the *New York Times* with the provocative headline "General Petraeus or General Betray Us?" accusing the general of "cooking the books" to support claims of reduced violence in Iraq.

MoveOn asked Win Without War if we wished to cosponsor the ad, but we demurred, fearing the ad might backfire, which it did. Howls of protest greeted the ad, and the Senate took the extraordinary step of adopting a resolution condemning MoveOn and the statement. The vote was 72–25, as many Democrats joined in repudiating the ad.[31] The factual analysis of MoveOn's message may have been correct—civilian casualties remained very high in Iraq and many Baghdad neighborhoods were suffering brutal ethnic killings—but the wisdom of directly challenging the commanding general was questionable, to say the least. Win Without War and other groups had always maintained a careful distinction between the war and those who fought it, knowing that many rank-and-file troops and even senior officers opposed Bush's policy. The agreed-upon message, "oppose the war, not the warrior," was an important element of patriotic framing compatible with American cultural norms. The MoveOn ad clearly went off script. Despite the controversy, however, opinion polls showed continued and growing support for withdrawing the troops. MoveOn quickly regained its footing and played an important role in mobilizing antiwar voters in the 2008 presidential primaries.

Artists

Many in the arts community participated in the antiwar movement. Actors, musicians, performers, writers, and other creative workers spoke out and contributed their time and talent to the cause. In Hollywood, the initiative for forming an antiwar artists' group came from actor Mike Farrell and producer/director Robert Greenwald. In July 2002 I received a call from Farrell about inviting former UN weapons inspector Scott Ritter to Los Angeles for an event in early October. Artists are becoming increasingly concerned about the threat of war, Farrell said, but we need to be briefed on the details. Was Iraq really a threat? Is military action necessary? "We're not foreign policy experts," he said. "We want to be sure of our information before speaking out. Our careers depend on it."

The briefing took place on October 2 at a reception in the home of Stanley and Betty Sheinbaum, longtime progressive philanthropists and supporters of civil rights and peace. Dozens of artists and Los Angeles community leaders attended the event that evening, including Warren Beatty, Annette Bening, Barbra Streisand, James Brolin, and James Cromwell. Ritter gave a riveting presentation, based on his personal experience as a Marine Corps officer during the first Gulf War and seven years as a senior UN weapons inspector in Iraq. He and Gulf War vet Erik Gustafson confirmed that Iraq posed no military threat to the United States and had been systematically disarmed by UN inspectors. It was exactly the kind of informed reassurance the artists were seeking. After the session we huddled, and Ritter suggested asking artists to sign a public statement as a way of attracting press attention.

Greenwald was skeptical: "no one will sign, the press won't cover it," but the presentations that evening were powerful and convincing, and they agreed to give it a try.

As they contacted colleagues, Farrell and Greenwald were "surprised and thrilled" at the positive response. More than a hundred artists and entertainers signed the statement. They called themselves Artists United to Win Without War and officially launched the group on December 10, 2002, with a full-page ad in the *New York Times* and a press event in Los Angeles. More than two dozen artists came to the launch, including Anjelica Huston, Tony Shalhoub, Loretta Swit, and Martin Sheen. Retired admiral Eugene Carroll, former deputy director of the Center for Defense Information, was on hand to provide expert commentary and validation of the artists' concerns. After the press conference, Artists United hired a staff director, former film producer Kate McArdle, who worked with Farrell and Greenwald to recruit additional artists and arrange interviews on news and entertainment programs. Through these efforts, Artists United reached an estimated 125 million viewers with the antiwar message.[32]

A related group, Musicians United to Win Without War, took shape a few weeks later. Former Talking Heads star David Byrne and a few other musicians had signed the artists' statement in December. As the likelihood of war increased, Byrne and other musicians decided to issue their own statement. Byrne contacted David Fenton to help produce an ad and arrange a press event announcing the group's creation. In February 2003 Fenton and Win Without War Director Tom Andrews met in New York with Byrne, producer Russell Simmons, and others to make plans.[33] The musicians went public a few days later with a full-page ad in the *New York Times* on February 27 and a press event attended by Byrne, Simmons, and other performers. The musicians' statement was signed by fifty rap, hip-hop, and rock stars, including Rosanne

Cash, Sheryl Crow, Jay-Z, Dave Matthews, Mobb Deep, REM, and Suzanne Vega. Their newspaper ad said simply: "War on Iraq is Wrong and We Know It." The announcements of the artists' and musicians' committees generated widespread broadcast and print news coverage. Stories appeared not only in hard news sections of papers and broadcasts, but also in entertainment and style programs. Youth-oriented outlets like MTV aired stories about the celebrities and musicians, helping to generate widespread sympathy and support for the antiwar cause.

Some of the artists and entertainers who spoke out against the war faced backlash. Susan Sarandon was disinvited from a United Way event in Florida, and she and Tim Robbins were barred from a Baseball Hall of Fame event to celebrate the fifteenth anniversary of their hit film *Bull Durham*. Sarandon and Robbins were unbowed and used the resulting publicity to reiterate their criticism of war and defend their right to dissent. So many sportswriters and fans criticized the Hall of Fame cancellation that its president, Dale Petroskey, had to admit his mistake.[34] In a speech to the National Press Club, Robbins expressed gratitude for the support he had received, which he acknowledged was "not about my views but my right to express them."[35] The controversy brought the debate over war into the sports pages.

The strongest right-wing reaction was reserved for the Dixie Chicks (now renamed the Chicks). During a March 10, 2003, concert in London, lead singer Natalie Maines told the audience, "We're on the good side with y'all. We do not want this war . . . we're ashamed the president of the United States is from Texas."[36] The comment touched off a storm of controversy in the world of country music. Maines quickly apologized for her comment about the president, but she did not back off from questioning the war. "We support our troops," the group said, but "there is nothing more frightening than the notion of going to war with Iraq and

the prospect of all the innocent lives that will be lost."[37] The Clear
Channel radio network, with some 1,200 stations, ordered Dixie
Chicks music off the air. Some hate groups sponsored bonfires to
burn the group's CDs. The trio refused to be intimidated, however,
and strongly defended both their right to speak out and their concerns about the war. Many artists came to their defense, including
Bruce Springsteen, who wrote on his website that banishing the
group from radio networks was "un-American."[38] When Maines
received the VH1 "big quote of the year" award in November 2003,
she jokingly thanked "all the haters because you make me strong,
empowered, involved, and proud." One of the messages Maines
received was a death threat, warning her to "shut up and sing or
your life will be over." She and the band used that line in their hit
song "I'm Not ready to Make Nice," which won the Grammy Song
of the Year award for 2006. Academy award–winning filmmaker
Barbara Kopple and Cecilia Peck produced a documentary film
about the episode, *Shut Up and Sing.*

The participation of celebrities helped the antiwar cause by
bringing public recognition and validation to the widespread
opposition to the war, especially among those who pay little attention to national policy issues. The movement message was entering
mainstream culture and had the potential to reach the moveable
middle of American public opinion. The mobilization of artists for
peace was gathering momentum on the eve of the war. Musicians
United discussed plans for a major antiwar concert, and other
media communications projects were in the works, but the bombs
started falling before the events could be organized. Additional
time would have made a real difference in mobilizing and communicating greater opposition to the pending invasion. Activist
pressures and plans for further mass mobilizations were in the
works, and public protest was spreading across the country and
around the world. All of this vast effort was cut short by the start

of war. Further organizing and media efforts continued, as activists demanded an end to the occupation and the withdrawal of troops, but the upsurge that was building prior to the invasion dissipated.

The movement's media efforts were nonetheless significant and more extensive than in previous antiwar campaigns. Through use of the internet, professional public relations services, paid newspaper and television advertising, and the participation of famous artists and musicians, the movement utilized the tools of mass communications to an unprecedented degree. More than a dozen full-page ads in the *New York Times*, hundreds of ads in local newspapers and on local radio stations, hundreds of national and regional television ad placements, thousands of national and local television and radio interviews, and thousands of articles in national and local newspapers—all brought visibility and credibility to the antiwar message. The combined media efforts of Move On, Win Without War, Business Leaders for Sensible Priorities, Working Assets, and many other antiwar groups generated hundreds of millions of reader and viewer impressions. This vast media communications campaign both reflected and shaped public opinion and had a significant impact on the political climate in which the Bush administration went to war. It was not enough to stop a predetermined war, but it gave the peace movement visibility and credibility and greatly amplified the voice of antiwar dissent.

In the next section of the book, we turn to an examination of the various social sectors and constituencies that comprised the antiwar movement within the United States. In Chapter Four, a closer look at mobilization within specific communities helps to illuminate the breadth of the movement and the extraordinary extent of opposition to the war in many parts of society. The analysis highlights strengths but also weaknesses in movement coalition building and identifies some of the challenges activists face in creating more diverse and politically effective movements for peace. In Chapter Five, I review the growth of antiwar sentiment within the military, emphasizing lessons from the Vietnam era on the role of service members, veterans, and military family members in speaking with authenticity against unjust war.

Four

Faces of the Movement

The Iraq antiwar movement was a vast and diverse worldwide mobilization of social resistance, protest, and political engagement. People of all classes, ethnic origins, and political tendencies participated in the movement. The spark for organizing protests and building coalitions came from peace organizations and the political left, but once the movement took off it attracted support from all sectors of society and from organizations and parties across the political spectrum. That's the magic of a social movement, the ability of people in particular historical moments to transcend existing political and social identities to voice a collective outcry against egregious instances of injustice.

This chapter examines the social composition of the movement within the United States, focusing on the faith community, organized labor, business executives, people of color, and women, while also providing glimpses of activism at the grassroots level. Many social sectors were part of the movement, but I focus on these because of the contributions they made singularly and in concert to building political opposition to the war. I begin with an analysis of the pervasive condemnation of the war that emerged especially within the church community, with a focus on the moral debate about preemptive attack and the challenge of countering the tyranny of Saddam Hussein. This is followed by a discussion of the labor movement, where opposition to war was more pervasive than in previous peace movements, and the important role of business leaders in warning against the costs of war. African Americans and Latinos widely rejected the Iraq War, although they were less likely than whites to participate in peace demonstrations, reflecting a historic racial pattern within peace movements. Women spoke out for peace actively and utilized distinct forms of leadership to help turn public opinion in favor of bringing the troops home. In the last section of the chapter, I give a sense of grassroots activism to provide a flavor of antiwar action at the local level.

Faith

The church community has considerable influence on US public opinion and historically has engaged in policy debates on a range of issues. Not surprisingly, faith groups played an important role in the debate about military action in Iraq. Many Christian denominations issued public statements opposing war and expressing deep concerns about the doctrine of preemption. At the local level, many religious leaders and members of congregations participated in antiwar activities. Church-based opposition to war was broader in the case of Iraq than in any previous conflict in modern US history. Religious leaders were important players in the United for Peace and Justice and Win Without War coalitions. Ordained ministers Bob Edgar and Jim Wallis helped to mobilize the religious community and were among the founders of Win Without War. In January 2003, Wallis and Edgar joined John Chane, Episcopal Bishop of Washington, to organize a Martin Luther King Jr. Day gathering of more than 3,500 religious leaders and other concerned citizens at Washington National Cathedral. That evening they led a dramatic candlelight procession from the cathedral to the White House. In early March, Edgar spoke at an interfaith service at Grace Cathedral in San Francisco, cosponsored by Working Assets, where more than two thousand people overflowed the sanctuary. Traditional religious peace groups—including the Catholic pacifist organization Pax Christi and groups within the Friends, Mennonite, and Brethren communities—also played a leading role in raising awareness and organizing expressions of antiwar concern.

The US Conference of Catholic Bishops made concerted efforts to prevent the invasion. The international committee of the bishops met with national security adviser Condoleezza Rice in May 2002 to express their concerns. This was followed by a letter to the White House in September from the president of the bishops' conference, and then a major policy statement on Iraq by the full conference of bishops in November. In the final weeks before the war, senior cardinals from New York, Washington, Baltimore, and Philadelphia met with Rice again. Two days later, papal envoy Cardinal Pio Laghi delivered a letter from Pope John Paul II to Bush at the White House. As he left the meeting, the Cardinal was not permitted to speak with the press on White House grounds, an unprecedented snub and a break from the typical pattern when dignitaries meet with the president.[1] The Catholic Church also organized local activities on a scale not seen since the 1980s nuclear debate, when the bishops issued their famous pastoral letter, *The Challenge of Peace*.

The November 2002 statement by the Catholic bishops was unusually clear and forceful. In some parishes, excerpts from the document were read aloud from the pulpit. The bishops expressed concern that in the given circumstances and with the information available, the resort to war "would not meet the strict conditions in Catholic teaching for overriding the strong presumption against the use of military force." In remarks that proved sadly prescient, the bishops warned that the use of force "might provoke the very kind of attacks that it is intended to prevent, could impose terrible new burdens on an already long-suffering civilian population [in Iraq], and could lead to wider conflict and instability in the region."[2] The deliberative bodies of Protestant denominations in the US and many other religious communities around the world joined in urging alternatives to war and opposing the planned invasion. The American Baptist Churches USA urged greater efforts to resolve the crisis through the United Nations. The United Church of Christ and the Disciples of Christ issued a joint statement calling for peace and reconciliation. The Standing Conference of the Canonical Orthodox Bishops in the Americas urged peaceful resolution of the crisis. The presiding bishop of the Episcopal Church, Frank Griswold, asked the White House to exhaust all diplomatic options and work through the United Nations. The Lutheran World Federation denounced a preemptive war for regime change. The National Association of Evangelicals urged the exploration of alternatives to war. The leaders of the National Baptist Convention issued a statement opposing war. The president of the Council of Bishops of the United Methodist Church, Bishop Sharon Brown Christopher, urged the pursuit of every possible means to prevent war. The World Council of Churches said a war with Iraq would be "immoral, unwise and in breach of the principles of the United Nations Charter." Archbishop of Canterbury Rowan Williams reiterated the Church of England's opposition to war.

Within the Jewish community, opposition to war was less extensive, although some progressive Jewish groups actively participated in the antiwar movement. Leading voices against the war included the Tikkun Community founded by Rabbi Michael Lerner, and the Shalom Center in Philadelphia led by Rabbi Arthur Waskow, a veteran of antiwar resistance during the Vietnam War and former senior fellow of the Institute for Policy Studies. Opponents of the war were minority voices in the organized rabbinical community, however. The lack of a substantial Jewish presence in the Iraq antiwar movement contrasted sharply with earlier anti-war movements, in which Jewish activists, intellectuals, and artists played important leadership roles. Even Reform constituencies such as the Union of American Hebrew Congregations (now known as the Union for Reform Judaism) remained mostly silent in the face of the buildup to war, while more Conservative and Orthodox communities supported the administration's policies. This pro-war stance reflected a right-wing, pro-Likud political tendency among some influential American Jewish leaders. It was also the result of Saddam Hussein's virulent hostility toward the state of Israel and his government's support of anti-Israeli terrorist groups, policies that deeply troubled many in the Jewish community and beyond.

Arab Americans and Muslims in the United States were not highly visible in the antiwar movement, but many were opposed to the war. Several leading Muslim American organizations issued public statements. The Council on American-Islamic Relations warned that war in Iraq would destabilize the region, fuel anti-American sentiment, and harm America's image in the Middle East and among Muslims worldwide. The Muslim American Society released a statement calling upon on "our government and all peace-loving people and nations to do everything in their power to avoid war, and resolve all pending issues through peaceful means." On the basis of Islamic teaching, the organization argued, an attack on Iraq could not be considered a just war.[3]

In May 2003 the Islamic Society of North America joined with the Religious Action Center of Reform Judaism for a two-day interfaith summit that expressed concern about the war and occupation of Iraq. The groups issued a statement signed by seventy-five mostly Christian, Jewish, and Muslim leaders urging the United States to "draw back from the use and threat of first strike war" and to "bring the US occupation of Iraq to an end." Kareem Irfan, chair of the Council of Islamic Organizations of Greater Chicago, told a reporter that the war and American policies in the Middle East were turning the United States into a global "pariah."[4]

The opposition to war among Muslims in the United States paralleled the anger and animosity toward the United States that existed globally in Muslim-majority nations. The invasion and occupation of Iraq generated what political scientist Francis Fukuyama termed a "frenzy of anti-Americanism" around the world.[5] Negative views of the US were widespread in the Middle East and among Muslim populations in Turkey, Pakistan, Indonesia, Morocco, Nigeria, and other countries. Favorability ratings for the US in Indonesia fell from 61 percent in 2002 to 15 percent in June 2003. Majorities in seven of the eight Muslim populations surveyed by the Pew Research Center viewed the US as a military threat. In Pakistan and some countries, opinion polls showed the public had a more favorable opinion of Osama bin Laden than George W. Bush.[6]

Arab Americans are not a large political constituency in the United States, and their electoral choices generally do not influence national politics, but it is interesting to note how they turned against the Republican Party over the war issue. They expressed their opposition to the war as many Americans did in the years after the invasion by voting for political candidates who promised to end US involvement. A June 2007 opinion poll by James Zogby, president of the Arab American Institute, found that Arab Americans were abandoning the Republican Party in droves. In the 2000 elections, 38 percent of Arab Americans identified themselves as Republicans, but in the lead-up to the 2008 elections, only 14 percent said they intended to vote Republican.[7] At the time, only 10 percent of those surveyed wanted the United States to remain in Iraq.

Just as the overall antiwar movement became internationalized to an unprecedented extent, so did the religious opposition to war. Never before did so many religious leaders and organizations around the world speak so forcefully against war. The Catholic voice was strongest, especially that of Pope John Paul II, who pleaded with world leaders to pursue diplomatic rather than military solutions. "War is always a defeat for humanity," the pope told assembled diplomats during his New Year's address in January 2003. "War cannot be decided upon," he declared, "except as the very last option."[8] As hostilities began in March, he urged people to continue standing against war. "It is ever more urgent to proclaim that only peace is the road to follow to construct a more just and united society."[9]

Senior Vatican officials also spoke out. Archbishop Renato Martino, head of the Pontifical Council for Justice and Peace, condemned unilateral or preventive military action as a "war of aggression."[10] An intense debate was underway at that point over the doctrine of preemption. Some supporters of military action in Iraq suggested that armed regime change against a repressive dictator would be compatible with Just War teaching, which allows for the use of force to protect innocent civilians from imminent threats of mass violence. The Vatican and most Catholic ethicists rejected this analysis. They pointed to the lack of convincing evidence of the existence of weapons of mass destruction in Iraq, and the absence of apparent intention or preparation by the Baghdad regime to commit aggression, as it had done in the past. Even Cardinal Joseph Ratzinger, the conservative Prefect of the Congregation for the Doctrine of the Faith, who later became Pope Benedict XVI, spoke out against the doctrine of preemption. He declared in September 2002: "The concept of 'preventive war' does not appear in the Catechism of the Catholic Church."[11] National conferences of Catholic bishops in North America, Europe, Asia, and Africa joined the Vatican in issuing statements against the impending war.

To help harness the international religious voice for peace, the US National Council of Churches (NCC) organized a series of religious delegation meetings with world leaders. In early February Bob Edgar led a delegation that met with senior religious leaders in Germany and then joined with these leaders in a one-hour session with German Chancellor Gerhard Schröder. The following week, an NCC delegation visited Paris to confer with colleagues in the European Council of Churches and meet with aides to French President Jacques Chirac. The following weeks included similar visits to London for a fifty-minute meeting with Prime Minister Tony Blair, to Rome for meetings with Italian and Vatican officials, and to Moscow for sessions with Orthodox Church leaders and aides to President Vladimir Putin.[12]

Jim Wallis led the religious delegation that met with Blair in London in mid-February. That session focused on the development of an alternative to the invasion in the form of a six-point plan for preventing war. The plan called for the indictment of Saddam Hussein on war-crime charges and urged a vigorous multinational effort for the "coercive disarmament" of Iraq. Sojourners published the six-point plan in full-page advertisements in all of the major London newspapers as Parliament debated whether to support the war. A last-minute attempt to dissuade Blair and Bush from invading Iraq, the plan was also an attempt to influence public opinion by addressing ethical concerns about the crimes of the dictator and his Baathist government. The plan reflected Wallis's conviction that the antiwar movement needed to answer the "what about Saddam?" question. For both ethical and practical reasons, Wallis believed, the movement had to take a tough stance toward Saddam. It was not enough simply to point to US and UK complicity in previously supporting Saddam. That may have been true, but it was insufficient as a moral and political argument. It was also necessary to acknowledge and condemn Saddam's brutal regime. The call for his indictment by an international criminal tribunal was a concrete way of undermining the Iraqi leader's legitimacy and paving the way for his removal from office. The indictment of Serbian leader Slobodan Milošević by a UN tribunal in June 1999 had been followed by a popular resistance movement that forced him from office in October 2000. The proponents of indicting Saddam hoped that a similar fate might befall the Iraqi dictator.

The attempt to develop an alternative to war did not convince Blair or Bush, of course, and it's clear in retrospect that the six-point plan had serious flaws. Any coercive attempt at disarmament without the Baghdad government's cooperation would have required armed confrontation with Iraqi forces and could have quickly escalated into war. The proposal for unarmed regime change was naïve in the absence of an organized mass resistance movement within Iraqi society of the kind that brought down Milosevic in Serbia. The emergence of such a movement in Iraq was impossible in Saddam Hussein's murderous police state. Thus, the plan's attempt to address the potential threat from the Iraqi regime while remaining true to peace principles came up short on both counts. This is not to suggest that nonmilitary, alternative means of containing the regime were unavailable. In fact, they were already in place. Reports published at the time confirmed that UN sanctions and weapons inspections had been successful in eliminating Iraq's capacity for developing weapons of mass destruction and had significantly degraded its military capabilities. The problem of the regime's gross human rights violations and abuses of its own citizens remained, but there is little that external actors can do to force a regime to respect the rights of its citizens, short of war, which is itself a gross violation of human rights. This is the unavoidable conundrum in the human rights debate about war.

The antiwar movement nonetheless could have done more to address public concerns about the Iraqi dictator.[13] Such a discussion might have helped to attract greater participation from the Jewish community and would have acknowledged the widespread perception of Saddam as evil incarnate. Sojourners and the Tikkun community called for the dictator's indictment, while simultaneously opposing a US invasion, but most peace groups were silent on the issue. Some worried that a critique of the oppressive nature of the Iraq regime and other authoritarian regimes in the region would feed into Bush's claim that overthrowing Saddam would be a way of "democratizing the Middle East." There are limits to a movement's ability to develop and communicate a nuanced political analysis, especially when faced with a rapid timetable for military action. Activists focused on a simple "no to war" message as the broadest theme for building and unifying the movement and communicating with the press. Perhaps with more time and reflection, the movement might have been able to follow the lead of Wallis and others in crafting a more sophisticated message, but the necessary analysis and debate never took place.

While not overtly against Saddam Hussein, the movement clearly was not for him either. The movement thus succeeded where past movements had failed. As Rebecca Solnit phrased it, the movement was able "to refuse the dichotomies. We were able to oppose a war in Iraq without endorsing Saddam Hussein."[14] The Iraq movement thus avoided the pitfalls of earlier movements, which in their solidarity for the victims of US attack sometimes seemed to support armed revolutionaries. During the Vietnam War, many activists admired and sympathized with the National Liberation Front. There was little chance of this happening in Iraq. Saddam Hussein was such an odious figure that few could find any redeeming merit in him or his regime. It was easy to avoid the trap of seeming to support the dictator. The movement thus remained true to its nonviolent principles and to the vision of a world without war, with many recognizing that while democracy and human rights are essential foundations of that vision, they cannot be imposed externally by invasion and war.

Labor

Trade unions played a major role in the Iraq antiwar movement, which was a new development for both labor and the peace movement. During the Cold War, trade union leaders in the United States often supported US military action abroad. While a progressive internationalist tradition also existed within labor—reflected by the Labor Committee to End the War in Vietnam, the participation of the machinists and food workers unions in the Nuclear Freeze campaign, and labor solidarity committees for Central America—trade unions generally were on the other side of the peace issue. AFL-CIO President George Meany was an ardent supporter of the Vietnam War, as was Peter J. Brennan, president of the Building and Construction Trades Council of Greater New York. In May 1970, hundreds of hard-hat construction workers infamously attacked peace demonstrators in lower Manhattan and rallied in support of the war, with active encouragement from the Nixon administration. In 2001, following the 9/11 attacks, most unions supported the so-called war on terror. The president of the International Association of Machinists at the time, R. Thomas Buffenbarger, openly called for a military campaign of vengeance against Iraq.

As the debate over war heated up, however, trade union members expressed increasing skepticism. A growing number of local unions and central labor councils adopted resolutions against war and began to speak out for alternative means of containing Iraq. A substantial US antiwar labor movement emerged, led by Bob Muehlenkamp, who had served as organizing director for the Teamsters Union and vice president of 1199 SEIU, New York's healthcare union, and Gene Bruskin, secretary-treasurer of the Food and Allied Service Trades division of the AFL-CIO. Muehlenkamp and Bruskin were aided by the leaders of union locals and regional councils in dozens of cities. In January 2003, antiwar labor activists came together for a meeting in Chicago at which labor veteran Bill Fletcher and I, among others, spoke. The more than one hundred delegates in attendance agreed to form a new organization, US Labor Against the War (now named US Labor Against Racism and War). An unofficial tabulation at the Chicago meeting counted forty-two local unions, thirteen district or regional bodies, five national unions, twelve central labor councils, and five state federations that had passed antiwar resolutions. Many other union bodies adopted antiwar resolutions in subsequent weeks. In total, more than three hundred local unions and committees, forty-five central labor councils, and seven national unions came out against the war.[15] The level of antiwar activity among trade unions far exceeded comparable opposition to previous US military actions.

Labor's participation in the antiwar movement flowed partly from its involvement in the Global Justice movement and benefitted from the progressive leadership of the president of the AFL-CIO, John Sweeney, former head of the Service Employees International Union (SEIU). In the late 1990s, Sweeney and other labor leaders began to work in partnership with social justice and environmental groups to demand fair labor standards in international trade agreements. Thousands of trade union members marched in the historic, union-sponsored protest in the streets of Seattle in November 1999. Sweeney spoke at that rally, famously demanding "fair trade, not just free trade." As the buildup to war accelerated in 2002, Sweeney and other labor leaders increasingly saw a link between the anti-labor and pro-business policies of the Bush administration and its plans for a war in Iraq that would primarily benefit major oil corporations and military contractors. Labor groups in Europe also participated in global justice protests and in the massive World Social Forum gathering in Florence in November 2002 that issued the call for worldwide protests against the impending war.

In February 2003, the executive council of the AFL-CIO passed a resolution in opposition to a preemptive war fought without UN support. The threat posed by Saddam Hussein "deserves multilateral resolve not unilateral action," the resolution read. If military action is considered, it should be "truly a last resort, supported by both our allies and nations united."[16] The statement was hardly a ringing indictment of war, but it was a departure from previous AFL-CIO positions on war and another sign of deepening doubts about White House policy.

In 2005, the AFL-CIO went further and took the strongest stand against war in the federation's history. At its summer convention in Chicago, the AFL-CIO overwhelmingly adopted a resolution calling for the "rapid withdrawal" of all US troops from Iraq.[17] In his speech supporting the resolution, Communications Workers of America Vice President Brooks Sunkett said that the government had lied to him when he was sent to Vietnam three decades ago. "We have to stop it from lying to a new generation now." Henry Nicholas, a hospital union leader in the American Federation of State, County and Municipal Employees, also spoke for the resolution, telling delegates that his son had served multiple tours of duty in Iraq and was facing yet another.

Passage of the resolution reflected more than two years of effort by US Labor Against the War and other activists. Organizers built support for the resolution before the convention by arranging a US tour of Iraqi union leaders. The Iraqi labor delegation traveled to more than fifty cities in sixteen days, pleading the case of Iraqi workers and speaking before hundreds of union members to demand an end to the American occupation of their country. Resolutions calling for the withdrawal of troops poured into AFL-CIO headquarters from local unions, labor councils, and state labor federations across the country. As writer David Bacon observed, passage of the resolution marked "a watershed moment in modern US labor history."[18] It was the product of grassroots action at the local level, not a directive from top leaders, and it echoed the sentiments of ordinary workers and rank-and-file union members throughout the country.

Labor opposition to the war was also reflected in worker participation in antiwar rallies and political mobilization. Surveys of participants in the rallies of February 15, 2003, in the US and several European countries found many labor movement marchers. In the United States, 44 percent of respondents identified themselves as current or former union members; in the UK the percentage was 43 percent.[19] Union members participated as well in many of the rallies against the occupation after 2003, including the huge August 2004 demonstration in New York and the January 2007 rally in Washington DC. Labor support for the antiwar movement was also reflected in the SEIU decision in 2007 to cohost and support the new Americans Against Escalation in Iraq coalition, further described in Chapter Six. In addition, union members participated in "Iraq Summer" town hall meetings that year, demanding that Congress approve a timetable for the withdrawal of troops. SEIU also provided crucial support for the Obama campaign during the early Democratic Party primaries in 2008,[20] a decision that was influenced in part by his strong stance against the war.

Business Executives

Many in the business community were skeptical of the war, although relatively few spoke out publicly against it. Those who did often joined or supported efforts by Business Leaders for Sensible Priorities (BLSP), an organization cofounded by organizer Gary Ferdman and ice cream entrepreneur Ben Cohen, who also created the online advocacy group True Majority. Ferdman and his colleagues focused on media communications and advertising. They sponsored a number of significant national newspaper ads,

They're Selling War print ad, October 2022. GENE CASE/AVENGING ANGELS AND BUSINESS LEADERS FOR SENSIBLE PRIORITIES.

including the October 2002 *New York Times* statement "They're Selling War, We're Not Buying" mentioned in Chapter Three. Dozens of business leaders signed and contributed money for the placement of the ad, which brought in more than enough money in donations to pay for itself. Local BLSP members also ran the ad in papers in Maine and in the *Philadelphia Inquirer*.

One of the supporters of BLSP who was willing to raise his voice in public was Alan Kligerman, founder and chief executive of AkPharma in New Jersey. His company created digestive aids like Lactaid, a brand of milk for people who cannot digest lactose, and Beano, an enzyme that breaks down the complex sugars that can make beans hard to digest. Earlier, Kligerman had protested the Vietnam War and was a supporter of the Anti-Defamation League, the NAACP, and other social action groups. He worried that the war would divert resources from programs to improve the economy and help people in need. He was also concerned about the likely human cost of war and the risk that unprovoked aggression against Iraq would breed more terrorism and tarnish the global image of the United States. He was a vocal and unrelenting critic of the war.[21]

Another business leader who signed the "We're Not Buying" BLSP newspaper ad was Marcel Arsenault, founder and CEO of a major real estate investment company in Colorado. Business leaders should stay focused on their companies, Arsenault told a *Rocky Mountain News* reporter, but he felt strongly about the war and decided to add his name to the ad. He was motivated by ethical concerns about war but also by worries about its effects on the fragile US economy. Several other Colorado business executives joined him in signing the ad, many of them agreeing that war and excessive military spending are bad for the economy and that their tax dollars should be spent instead on education, the environment, and job creation.[22] One of the most prominent business leaders against the war was Connecticut telecommunications executive

Ned Lamont, who ran for office on an antiwar stance in 2006 and won an upset victory in the Democratic primary against veteran incumbent Senator Joe Lieberman, as described in Chapter Six. Some executives faced backlash for supporting the antiwar movement. When Richard Abdoo, chairman and chief executive of the Wisconsin Energy Corporation, made a modest personal donation to the group Not in Our Name, he was criticized on right-wing talk shows and in an editorial in the *Milwaukee Journal Sentinel*. A senior executive in a Wall Street investment firm ran into flak for signing an earlier BLSP statement critical of Pentagon spending. When the ad appeared with the executive's name and the firm listed for identification purposes, representatives of a major arms contractor called the company and threatened to withdraw their holdings if there was any further association with such statements.[23] The stakes were high for antiwar business leaders.

I had personal experience with the business community at the Fourth Freedom Forum, whose trustees were mostly business executives, many of them Republicans. The founder and chair of the foundation was Howard S. Brembeck, an inventor and manufacturer of grain storage and poultry feeding equipment who sold his agricultural products throughout the US and in dozens of countries. He believed in the power of trade as an alternative to the use of force and supported research to refine the use of economic sanctions and incentives as tools of diplomacy. He was conservative and a lifelong Republican, but he was strongly opposed to the Iraq War and devoted the foundation's resources to trying to stop it. His business colleagues on the board were fully supportive.

Communities of Color

"The most glaring weakness of the movement against the war in Iraq," wrote Barbara Epstein, "was the limited involvement of people of color, especially African Americans."[24] People of color were more strongly opposed to the war than whites, but they were underrepresented among those who demonstrated against it. A *Time*/CNN poll of February 19–20, 2003, found 61 percent of Blacks opposed to using military force against Saddam Hussein, compared to 35 percent of whites. An ABC/*Washington Post* poll at the time found 62 percent of "nonwhites" in opposition to war, compared to 32 percent of whites.[25] Yet in most of the major national and regional protests, the demonstrators were predominantly white. In their surveys of participants in the major antiwar protests in 2004 and 2005, Heaney and Rojas found African Americans were only 7.6 percent of total respondents.[26] The main exception to the monochromatic pattern among peace groups was ANSWER, which generally did better than other antiwar coalitions in mobilizing people of color.[27] African Americans, Latinos, and Arab Americans were part of the coalition's leadership, and ANSWER's political agenda of opposing racism and advocating Palestinian rights appealed more directly to the immediate concerns of communities of color. United for Peace and Justice also took steps to include people of color in its leadership structures.

According to organizer Bob Wing, racial representation in the Iraq movement was better than in past antiwar movements.[28] African American leader Bill Fletcher agreed, noting that UFPJ responded positively to diversity concerns by reaching out to people of color.[29] The coalition made a greater programmatic commitment to justice, including support for an equitable peace settlement between Israel and Palestine. The greater involvement of people of color was also a result of the Bush administration's policies, which combined a mobilization for war abroad with passage of the so-called Patriot Act and increased repression at home. In the context of a wartime crackdown on communities of color, it was easier for many to see the links between militarism and racism. In keeping with its political agenda combining justice and peace issues, United for Peace and Justice made a concerted effort to develop a more racially diverse leadership structure. At its national conference in Chicago in June 2003, UFPJ voted to create a decision-making committee in which more than half the members were people of color. This was a major advance for the antiwar movement.

The Win Without War coalition included a number of mainstream organizations that do not normally address war and peace issues. One of the most important of these was the National Association for the Advancement of Colored People. The relationship between Win Without War and NAACP was limited, however, and involved only occasional conversations. NAACP opposed the invasion and endorsed lobbying efforts for the withdrawal of troops, but Win Without War made no effort to build a more sustained partnership with NAACP or engage its national membership and local chapter network.

African Americans may not have marched frequently in antiwar protests, but they demonstrated with their feet by rejecting the appeals of military recruiters. People of color generally have had higher army enlistment rates than whites, the result of limited social and economic opportunities within their communities and military recruitment offers of employment opportunities and educational benefits. During the Iraq War, however, the enlistment rate among Blacks dropped sharply. The percentage of African Americans among army recruits dropped from 23 percent in 2001 to 13 percent in 2007. In the Marine Corps, the proportion of Black recruits fell during the same period from 12 percent to 8 percent.[30] Many African Americans were reluctant to fight for a cause they did not support.[31] The army did a study of the reasons for the decline in enlistment and found that parents, teachers, coaches, and other influencers of Black youth were strongly against the war and were advising against joining the military. In response, the army created a new recruitment commercial showing a young Black man defying his mother and convincing her that joining the military would be the right choice for him.[32] African American recruitment rates did not return to previous levels until after the war.

The antiwar movement had only modest success in attracting the participation of Latinos. The post–September 11 crackdown on immigrants seriously affected Americans of Hispanic descent, especially the foreign born, and deterred many from public engagement and speaking out against the war. Opinion polls nonetheless showed that Latinos were less supportive of the war than Americans as a whole.[33] Opposition to war was greatest among foreign-born Latinos. National antiwar groups, however, made little effort to recruit Latinos. Other than *War Times*, few antiwar publications were in Spanish. Win Without War made a belated effort to reach out to the Latino community, but the effort was short lived. In February 2003, Angela Sanbrano of the Central American Resource Center in Los Angeles and Antonio Gonzalez of the William C. Velasquez Institute in Texas helped to organize a "Latinos to Win Without War" group. A few national and regional leaders signed the initial statement, but the effort was not sustained after the invasion. The failure to involve a significant number of Latinos was a significant weakness of the antiwar movement.

The lack of racial diversity is a recurring problem in the peace movement. The Vietnam antiwar movement, the Central America movement, the Nuclear Freeze campaign—all suffered from underrepresentation of communities of color. One of the dangers of this imbalance, Epstein noted, is that activists may attempt to address this problem by "slinging charges of racism at each other."[34] This was a problem in past movements and had a corrosive effect on activists' morale and energy. It was less of a problem in the Iraq antiwar movement, in part because United for Peace and Justice took concrete steps to create a more racially diverse leadership structure. Such attempts to broaden the racial representation of antiwar coalitions and organizations are important. Several traditional peace groups, including the American Friends Service Committee and Peace Action, have made major efforts over the years to enhance diversity, and to create more racially representative staffs and boards of directors. Within these groups, however, most of the members and local activists are white.

Although underrepresented at peace demonstrations, Latinos and other communities of color were by no means silent on the Iraq War. In Los Angeles and other California communities, Latino groups led protests against war and in opposition to the clampdown on the rights of immigrants. In October 2002, some two hundred Mexican Americans signed an open letter to members of Congress urging opposition to the resolution authorizing military action in Iraq. The letter was read aloud at a rally in San Diego and published in several Latino papers. In January 2003, hundreds of Latinos joined an antiwar crowd of twenty thousand in Los Angeles. In March, Latinos Por La Paz organized an antiwar vigil in Guadalupe Plaza in Houston.

Native Americans have the highest rate of military enlistment of any ethnic group, but indigenous people were skeptical of the war. Political activist Winona LaDuke spoke for many in 2003 when she described the invasion of Iraq as an unjust war. Anishinaabe philosophy allows for defense of the people, she wrote, but "there is no set of teachings for a pre-emptive war." The invasion of Iraq was another example of the United States violating solemn treaty obligations, including the UN Charter and the Nuremberg principles. "I say the United States should . . . abide by its own treaties, and be about the process of making peace, not making war," LaDuke said. She criticized federal budget priorities that squeeze "the lifeblood out of our families and our communities for war."[35] Tex Hall, president of the National Congress of American Indians, sounded a similar theme in his State of the Indian Nations address in 2005: "When I think of the war in Iraq, I am reminded of the basic principle that the United States cannot do good around the world unless we first do good at home." Tribal citizens must have "the opportunity to attend safe schools, drink clean water, receive quality health care, and live and work in a safe community," he declared. "America, you have to do better at home."[36]

Many Black leaders spoke out, including Representative Barbara Lee (D-CA), who cast the lone vote in Congress against the resolution authorizing the use of force after 9/11. Others who were featured at antiwar rallies included Rev. Al Sharpton of New York; representatives Charles Rangel (D-NY) and John Conyers Jr. (D-MI), who spoke at the major antiwar rallies in Washington; Rev. Jesse Jackson Sr.; and actor Danny Glover, board chair of TransAfrica Forum. African American churches such as the Church of God in Christ and the Progressive National Baptist Convention were among the first to register their opposition to war in Iraq. The grassroots network Racial Justice 9-11 organized antiwar events in nearly a dozen cities in September 2002.[37] In Brooklyn, New York, Rev. Herbert Daughtry hosted large antiwar rallies at his House of the Lord Church in the months before the invasion. In Washington DC, veteran organizer Damu Smith organized Black Voices for Peace, to help articulate African American opposition to war.

These expressions of opposition to war are consistent with a historic pattern of opposition to imperialism and military adventurism among African Americans. In a 1986 special issue of *The Black Scholar* devoted to Blacks and the struggle for peace, authors Frances Beal and Ty dePass wrote:

> A consistent thread that has been woven into black intellectual and political thought in the United States has been a pattern of ardent anti-colonial and anti-imperialist consciousness. From a historical perspective, therefore, one of the strongest voices for peace within this country has come from the black community.[38]

People of color have direct understanding and experience of institutional oppression and racism. They recognize more readily than most whites the connections between wars against people of color abroad and poverty and racism at home.[39] Dr. King saw the Vietnam War as an "enemy of the poor" and opposed it as such. He spoke often of the "triple evils" of racism, militarism, and poverty and decried the war as a "demonic destructive suction tube" drawing people, skills, and money away from needed programs of social uplift at home.[40] The African American community is a natural constituency for peace and justice movements. Greater efforts to diversify antiwar activism can strengthen the peace movement and increase the potential for preventing wars and military repression in the future.

As antiwar groups have struggled to diversify, many activists have recognized the importance of supporting the self-organization of Blacks and other communities of color. Important guidance on these issues came from Jack O'Dell, former aide to Martin Luther King Jr., member of the board of directors of SANE and other peace organizations, and international affairs director of Rev. Jackson's Rainbow Coalition.[41] O'Dell encouraged peace activists to recruit Blacks, Latinos, Native Americans and Asians into their organizations, but he also urged support for independent groups within these communities. Some people of color prefer to have their own organizations, he said, and they frame the issues in ways that are most compelling to their constituency. Diverse groups can work in parallel within the same movement, provided they strive toward common ends, and show mutual respect and support for one another.

Writer and activist Malik Miah offered a similar perspective on Blacks and the antiwar movement.[42] He recalled an incident from his youth during the Vietnam War:

> During a high school walkout in my senior year in 1969 against . . .
> a racist . . . Black judge . . . and an antiwar protest occurring the
> same day, most Black students joined the antiracist protest. Few

went to the antiwar demonstration even though most Black students opposed the war.

This was not a problem, he argued. Blacks naturally focus more on immediate threats from racism and police oppression at home than on military interventions abroad, however much they oppose such wars. The question is not why don't Blacks join the peace movement, Miah wrote, but rather, why don't white people support the struggle against racism? Where are white people when Blacks and other people of color organize against police violence and racism? It's a valid and important question that all white activists must address. To some extent, that question was answered with a resounding affirmation of solidarity in June 2020, when millions of people mobilized for Black Lives Matter following the murder of George Floyd. Some 20 million people marched in multiracial demonstrations in hundreds of cities and towns to protest police violence and demand racial equality.[43] The challenge for the anti-war movement and for all social movements is to learn from and replicate that experience, making multiracial solidarity for social justice the norm not the exception.

Women

Women traditionally have been more opposed to war than men and have been at the heart of many peace movements.[44] Studies of public attitudes have documented a substantial gender gap on war and military-related issues, with women showing a greater propensity to support peaceful, diplomatic solutions to international crises and greater reluctance to endorse the use of military force.[45] Opinion surveys during the buildup to the Iraq War confirmed these findings. A *Time*/CNN poll of February 2003 found 59 percent of men favoring the use of military force, compared to 50 percent of women.[46] A Zogby International poll around the same time found 34 percent of men opposed to war, compared to 46 percent of women.[47] According to a survey by Vietnam Veterans of America, women were also much more likely than men—54 percent compared to 34 percent—to favor giving UN weapons inspectors more time.[48] Eurobarometer surveys in several countries in Europe in 2003 found similar results.[49] The Iraq antiwar movement reflected these preferences, and in countless localities in the United States and throughout the world, women took the lead in speaking out and organizing actions for peace.

Women's groups in the US played important roles in national and local antiwar coalitions. The National Organization for Women (NOW) and Women's Action for New Directions (WAND) were leading groups within the Win Without War coalition. Eleanor Smeal, former president of NOW and founder and president of the Feminist Majority Foundation, added her voice to the movement and encouraged women leaders to speak out against the war. WAND helped to write and organize support for an extraordinary statement on the war from the National Council of Women's Organizations, a bipartisan network of more than 170 groups representing over seven million American women. The council had not previously taken a stand on war and peace issues. Its January 15, 2003, statement emphasized the importance of diplomacy and nonviolent measures as proven tools for resolving conflict and overcoming terrorism. It expressed concern about the heavy toll that war and increased military expenditures would exact on American families, especially on women and children. The statement declared that the council "opposes any preemptive military action against Iraq at this time."[50]

In November 2002, a group of veteran peace and justice organizers led by Medea Benjamin, Starhawk, and Jodie Evans created Code Pink: Women for Peace. The goal, according to Benjamin, was to introduce a new discourse into a national debate dominated by the Bush administration's "testosterone-poisoned rhetoric."[51] The

Code Pink demonstration in Washington, March 2003.
LISA NIPP/AP PHOTO.

formation of Code Pink was announced at a vigil in front of the
White House that began on November 17, 2002, and continued
daily through March 8, 2003, International Women's Day. On that
day ten thousand demonstrators marched toward the White House
to protest the impending war, and Women's Day actions occurred
in more than fifty cities in the United States. As peace activism

spread across the country, some ninety Code Pink chapters were formed.

The women's peace movement introduced a creative, at times humorous spirit into the antiwar debate. Liza Featherstone wrote in *The Nation* that Code Pink was "not an organization but a phenomenon: a sensibility reflecting feminist analysis and a campy playfulness influenced in style and philosophy both by ACT UP and the anti-globalization movement."[52] Code Pink activists specialized in high-spirited, in-your-face, and disruptive actions that directly challenged those responsible for making and promoting the Bush administration's war policies. In November 2002, they interrupted Secretary of Defense Donald Rumsfeld as he testified before Congress. In December, they disrupted a briefing by State Department public relations official Charlotte Beers, unfurling a banner that read, "Charlotte, stop selling war." One of their trademark actions was to deliver "You're fired" pink slips, presenting pink women's undergarments to officials who supported the war. Among those targeted for such treatment was Senator Hillary Clinton. The Code Pink actions were part of a rising tide of innovative feminist action against war. Code Pink and other women's groups engaged in counter-recruitment actions, some of which highlighted the prevalence of sexual assault cases in the military, hoping to discourage men and women from joining the military.[53] Early in January 2003, a group of women gathered without clothes on the Point Reyes beach in California to spell out "Peace" with their bodies. The women explained that they were protesting the Bush administration's "naked aggression."

Another creative women's initiative was the Lysistrata Project. Organized by women and men in the arts, the project sought to bring to light the powerful but mirthful message of the 2,400-year-old antiwar comedy by Aristophanes. The play tells the story of Lysistrata (literally "she who disbands armies") who organizes women of Greece to refuse to sleep with their men until they end

Lysistrata poster, 2003. MARK GREENE/LYSISTRATA PROJECT.

the Peloponnesian War. On March 3, 2003, an estimated one thousand readings of the play took place across all fifty states and fifty-nine countries.[54] In New York and Los Angeles, prominent actresses headlined star performances. In London, hundreds of British performers gathered at 11:00 a.m. in Parliament Square to read the play in what they termed a mass Greek chorus of disapproval.

Women continued to play a major role in all the protests and political mobilizations of the antiwar movement in the following years. Female voters provided a strong base of support for antiwar Democratic Party candidates who won victories in the 2006 congressional elections and for Obama's candidacy during the 2008 primaries. NOW, WAND, and other women's groups participated in legislative lobbying efforts to win congressional support for the withdrawal of troops, while Code Pink and other groups remained active in organizing street protests against the war.

Grassroots

Activists and academics tend to focus on national political actors, but the greatest impact of antiwar action is often at the local level. An overemphasis on national events may overlook the extent and significance of grassroots organizing. Scholar Daniel Q. Gillion observes in his study of racial justice protests that politicians are more likely to respond to local events than national movements, especially when protests are in their own districts.[55] During the Iraq antiwar movement, local actions generated widespread political pressure on political decision makers. In the months prior to the invasion, activists organized demonstrations and events in thousands of communities in the United States and throughout the world. In their surveys of protesters at major rallies, Heaney and Rojas identified 3,000 unique organizations that were active in one or more of the national antiwar coalitions.[56] Many of these groups were locally based. In smaller conservative localities, antiwar action emerged for the first time in many years. In communities with a history of activism, the events that occurred were larger and more frequent than in the past. Protests continued after the invasion, but many local activists shifted to greater engagement in lobbying and electoral work. A full rendering of the vast outpouring of grassroots action in the antiwar movement is beyond the scope of this volume, but a few brief examples may give a glimpse of the extent of local activism.

One of the most significant grassroots initiatives was Cities for Peace, a campaign conceived by Marcus Raskin, founder and senior fellow of the Institute for Policy Studies in Washington DC. The campaign emerged as a coalition of elected officials and citizen groups working to convince city councils to adopt local resolutions against war. The resolutions were tailored to the procedures of each town, city, county, or elected body, but all made links to common themes in opposing the war, including the likely loss of life and the potential costs of war to state and local budgets. In all, some 165 city councils, representing forty million American citizens, adopted official resolutions opposing war.[57] Most major cities, including New York, Los Angeles, and Chicago, approved resolutions, along with a host of smaller municipalities. In some localities, such as Madison, Wisconsin, convincing the city council to approve such a resolution was easy and required little community mobilization. In other instances, such as New York City, the reluctance of some officials made the task more challenging and required extensive lobbying of local city council members. Ballot initiatives were organized in some cities and towns. Voters in San Francisco approved a strongly worded antiwar measure on the ballot in November 2004. The resolution began "George W. Bush disgracefully lied to the American people to make the case for Iraq."[58] The proposition won with 63 percent of the vote.[59]

In Wisconsin local activists in dozens of towns placed antiwar referenda on the ballot in the April 2006 primary election. The call for troop withdrawal won in twenty-four of the thirty-two communities.[60] The process of placing the resolutions on the ballot required either gaining local city council approval or collecting a requisite number of valid voter petition signatures. In the conservative town of Watertown, for example, the city council objected to the proposed resolution, but activists went door-to-door and secured the nearly 1,000 signatures needed to get on the ballot.[61]

In localities around the country activists organized events that fit with the culture of their community. They instinctively understood Saul Alinsky's famous rule of tactics: "Never go outside the experience of your people."[62] In the conservative religious communities of northern Indiana near where I live, local action revolved around churches and religious schools. Immediately after 9/11, students and faculty at Goshen College, a small Mennonite college, began to circulate a statement calling for a response to the attacks based on reconciliation and justice, rather than revenge and war. They sent the statement to dozens of congregations and religious communities in Goshen, Elkhart, and South Bend, asking for signatures and contributions so that it could be placed in local newspapers. The response was overwhelming. More than eight hundred people signed the ad, contributing $14,000 for its dissemination. This was a considerable sum for so small a community and enabled the group to place full-page ads in all the local newspapers.

As the discussion of invading Iraq heated up in the fall of 2002, educational events occurred at many local colleges and universities and in high school classes. At Notre Dame, the Kroc Institute for International Peace Studies sponsored a series of faculty panels examining the security consequences and ethical implications of war. Hundreds of students and faculty attended these events, including student-sponsored conversations in dormitories led by Professor George A. Lopez, who argued that a preemptive attack without international authorization would not meet the criteria of Catholic social teaching. He expressed the same concern in a widely read article for the influential Catholic journal *Commonweal*, and in his presentation to the US Conference of Catholic Bishops as they prepared their statement on the war.[63]

The northern Indiana chapter of WAND sponsored a local radio advertising campaign. The initiative was the brainchild of

Julia King, a local writer and commentator for the Great Lakes Radio Consortium, later an elected member of the Goshen city council. The ads featured a husband and wife questioning the wisdom of war and ended with a simple plea to "think about it." King and local chapter president Karen Jacob raised money from local WAND members to purchase ads on a local pop music station, whose station manager initially questioned their content but later agreed to air them. The ads and the controversy they stirred generated coverage in local broadcast and print media.[64] WAND chapters in Detroit and Little Rock borrowed the idea and sponsored similar radio ad campaigns in their communities.

Protest demonstrations are relatively rare in northern Indiana, but they occurred frequently in the months preceding the outbreak of war. One of the first actions occurred in October, when President Bush came to South Bend to campaign for the local Republican candidate for Congress. When word of the president's visit was announced, antiwar groups and local trade unions joined together to organize a protest of more than three hundred people in downtown South Bend. In Goshen local church-based groups called for a rally at the local courthouse on December 10, in conjunction with the nationally coordinated actions sponsored by United for Peace and Justice. Initially the county commissioners denied the local group a permit, but this only helped build interest in the protest.[65] More than 150 people turned out for the courthouse rally, while local church groups collected contributions and relief items for humanitarian aid to Iraqi families.[66] Demonstrations also occurred on Martin Luther King Jr. Day and then again on February 15, when hundreds of demonstrators turned out for rallies in South Bend, Elkhart, and Goshen. On March 8, nearly one hundred people gathered at the public library in South Bend for an International Women's Day event.

The protests continued after the invasion. WAND activists used inventive tactics to mock Vice President Dick Cheney when he came to Notre Dame in October 2003. Cheney was known as the chief architect of the war, one who had brazenly and repeatedly lied about the Iraqi weapons threat. Borrowing an idea from the Atlanta chapter of WAND, the local members volunteered to conduct a search for weapons of mass destruction. As more than 150 people gathered to protest Cheney, thirty members of the local WAND group marched to the rally donning yellow hazmat suits emblazoned with "hunt for WMD" in fluorescent orange lettering. "We're here to help the vice president find those elusive weapons of mass destruction," they declared. It was a clever bit of political ridicule that brought laughs from the crowd and extensive news coverage from the local media, with good visuals for television. The rally sent a message to the White House that even in the conservative heartland, administration officials could not avoid antiwar protest.

WAND protest against Vice President Dick Cheney, October 2003.
TIM NAFZIGER.

Students and youth organized against the war in many communities. Teach-ins and educational events occurred on hundreds of campuses in October 2002, and again in March 2003. The March events were billed as the International Student Day of Strike and Action against War in Iraq, a "books, not bombs" speak out. It was initiated in the US by the Student Environmental Action Coalition, Students Against Sanctions and War in Iraq, United Students Against Sweatshops, and the National Youth and Student Peace Coalition. Student groups also participated in Canada, Mexico, the UK, France, Spain, Italy, Greece, and Australia.[67] In the US, students participated at hundreds of high schools and college campuses, skipping class to join teach-ins, mass leafleting, rallies, marches, debates, antiwar forums, and strikes. At some schools, students engaged in a walkout from classes.[68] At dozens of universities, student councils or faculty senates adopted resolutions opposing war. A faculty statement against war that began circulating in the fall was signed by more than ten thousand college and university professors. Although student and campus-based organizing did not reach the massive scale of youth protest that existed during the Vietnam era, the level of protest against the Iraq War was significant, especially so given the absence of a military draft.

The college students who protested did not have to worry about being sent to Iraq. The burden of fighting the war fell on the small percentage of the population who volunteer for the military, most of whom enlist to gain educational and employment opportunities. The all-volunteer force was created as a response to the draft resistance movement and growing dissent within the ranks during the Vietnam War. The expectation was that those who volunteered for the military would be less likely to protest. The service members who served in Iraq were not indifferent to the injustice of the war, however, and they began to speak out for peace, as examined in the next chapter.

Five

Dissent in the Ranks

During the Vietnam War, a significant antiwar movement developed among active-duty soldiers and recent veterans. I was part of that movement and worked with fellow soldiers to organize petitions and demonstrations against the war. Hundreds of underground GI newspapers were published on ships and at military bases around the world. Unauthorized absence and desertions rates reached record levels. Combat refusal and avoidance spread.[1] Nothing on the scale of the GI revolt in Vietnam occurred during the wars in Iraq and Afghanistan, but antiwar sentiment nonetheless developed within the ranks and among recent veterans. In this chapter I review the dissent that emerged in the military, paralleling the widespread opposition to war that existed in society. I examine the early doubts about the invasion that existed among service members and their families, offer brief portraits of some of those who resisted the war, and describe the antiwar organizations that emerged within the ranks and among military family members. I close with reflections on what it means to "support the troops" and the importance of antiwar voices in the military for strategies of peace.

123

Reluctant Warriors

As within American society, misgivings about the war emerged among service members even before the war started. As troops assembled in Kuwait in the early months of 2003, they brought with them the widespread skepticism about war that existed at home. A reporter for the New York *Daily News* who interviewed troops just before the invasion reported that many "would give peace a chance if they had the choice." The war was a troubling matter of conscience for many troops, said a military chaplain. "I've been surprised at how much sympathy there is with the [antiwar] position of the Pope," he told the reporter.[2] The soldiers were willing to perform their duties as ordered, but for many their hearts were not in it.

The war began ominously for the army. Just three days after the invasion started, an explosion ripped through the headquarters tent of the 101st Airborne Division at Camp Pennsylvania in central Kuwait. The deadly grenade attack and rifle fire killed two officers and wounded more than a dozen others. The perpetrator was not an Iraqi terrorist but US Army Sgt. Asan Akbar, an engineer from the 326th Engineer Battalion from Fort Campbell, Kentucky. An army spokesperson said that Sgt. Akbar had "an attitude problem" and was angry about the war.[3] The horrifying incident brought back grim memories of the "fraggings" that convulsed the army in Vietnam. More than five hundred fragging assaults occurred in the military from 1969 through 1971, resulting in more than eighty fatalities, mostly among officers and noncommissioned officers.[4] The Camp Pennsylvania fragging was an isolated incident, but it left many commanders and troops shaken.

After defeating the Iraqi army and conquering Baghdad in just three weeks, American troops hoped for a quick return to the States. They were led to believe that "the way home is through Baghdad." Instead, they were soon assigned to nation-building duty and became bogged down in a prolonged military occupation. When troops were informed during the summer of 2003 that their deployment in Iraq would be extended, there was a palpable wave of resentment through the ranks and among family members. Soldiers expressed their dissent not through petitions, as some of us had done during the Vietnam era, but through emails and comments to news reporters. Iraq was the first "wired war," and many troops had access to the internet. They communicated with family, friends, and hometown newspapers, and in some cases to media outlets and prominent public personalities. Their messages were frank and unabashed, and often expressed doubts about the mission in Iraq. Newspapers reported a flood of "war-weary emails." David Hackworth, a retired army colonel and prolific writer and media commentator, reported receiving five hundred emails a day, many from soldiers in Iraq complaining about mistreatment by officers, shoddy equipment, and a flawed mission.[5] Documentary filmmaker Michael Moore reported receiving hundreds of letters from the troops, including this message from a Marine lance corporal: "You'd be surprised at how many of the guys I talked to in my company and others believed that the president's scare about Saddam's WMD was a bunch of bullshit and that the real motivation for this war was only about money."[6] In July, a message circulated on the internet from soldiers of the Second Brigade, Third Infantry Division, based at Fallujah: "Our morale is not high or even low. Our morale is nonexistent."[7]

Military family members were especially angry when the deployments of their loved ones were extended. Family members have become an important constituency in today's volunteer armed forces and in the antiwar movement. A majority of service members are now married, a substantial change from the Vietnam era when relatively few low-ranking soldiers had families. The prolonged occupation of Iraq and multiple deployments of troops created family hardships. Some family members took the lead in demanding an end to the occupation. At Fort Stewart, Georgia, home of the Third Infantry Division, frustrations reached the boiling point. In early July 2003, the *New York Times* reported an incident in which a colonel, meeting with eight hundred "seething spouses," had to be escorted from the session. The family members were "crying, cussing, yelling, and screaming for their men to come back," according to the director of community services at the base.[8] A couple of weeks later, the Fort Stewart wives organized a gathering of nearly one hundred family members in a vacant shopping center near the base to announce a letter-writing campaign to bring the troops home. Hundreds of family members subsequently contacted their elected representatives and members of the press. News accounts told of similar discontent and anger among family members at Fort Gordon, Georgia; Fort Hood, Texas; and Fort Campbell, Kentucky. At Fort Campbell, according to one report, "frustration runs especially high in the treeless blocks of low-rent apartments where many younger soldiers live." Concern about attacks on American troops was "gnawing at support for the US mission."[9]

Some soldiers took their concerns directly to the press. In July 2003, viewers of ABC's "Good Morning America" heard remarkably blunt comments from soldiers of the Second Brigade, Third Infantry Division: "If Donald Rumsfeld was here I'd ask for his resignation," Specialist Clinton Deitz told an interviewer. "I've got my own 'most wanted' list," said a sergeant. "The aces in my deck [a reference to the cards displaying the 52 most wanted senior Iraqi officials given to US soldiers at the start of the war] are Paul Bremer, Donald Rumsfeld, George Bush, and Paul Wolfowitz." The Pentagon acted swiftly to muzzle such dissent. Commanders announced that soldiers who criticize senior officials in public would be punished. At some bases, family members received emails admonishing them to refrain from public complaints. Some Third Infantry officers feared they would lose their jobs over the ABC incident. Said one, "This thing went all the way up to President Bush and back down on top of us."[10] The army also tried to manipulate the press, launching a campaign of managed letters home to local newspapers. Identical letters to the editor from different soldiers in the Second Battalion of the 503rd Infantry Regiment appeared in eleven newspapers across the country, according to a report by Gannett News Service. The letters gave upbeat accounts of American efforts in Iraq and said that US troops were welcomed by Iraqis "with open arms."[11]

Pressure and media manipulation could not alter the deeply felt grievances of service members and their families. Angry email messages continued to pour forth. Many were sent to *Stars and Stripes*, a traditional military newspaper that receives some funding from the Pentagon but is not subject to its editorial control. After receiving scores of messages from troops in Iraq, more than half of them complaints, *Stars and Stripes* decided to conduct an in-depth investigation. In August 2003 the newspaper sent seven reporters to visit nearly fifty camps in Iraq, interviewing troops and administering an informal questionnaire. Though the findings were unscientific, drawn from 1,935 completed surveys, they showed widespread discontent. Half of those interviewed rated their unit morale as low, and more than a third did not consider their mission clearly defined. When asked if they thought the war was worthwhile, 31 percent said it was of "little value" or "no value at all." According to the paper's analysis, "last spring's good-natured grousing about lousy food and no showers has given way to edgier complaints about inequality among the forces and lack of confidence in their leaders."[12]

Problems of low morale were greatest among reservists and National Guard members. The mobilization of reserve forces that began with Afghanistan and accelerated for the war in Iraq put an enormous strain on reserve troops and their families. As of November 2003, approximately 42,000 of the 160,000 US troops in the

Iraq theatre were members of the reserves and National Guard.[13] These troops tended to be older than active-duty soldiers and even more likely to be married, and had jobs and professional commitments in their communities. When called to active service, they were separated from family and experienced a significant disruption and reduction in their quality of life. Not surprisingly, they and their families were most vocal in complaining about the mission and demanding a return home. In the *Stars and Stripes* survey, 71 percent of Reservists and Guard members rated their units' morale low or very low. The interviewers found many reservists angry and confused, unsure of their mission, and disappointed in their commanders. Family members shared these frustrations and campaigned publicly for the troops' return. In Kansas, family members of the 129th Transportation Company of the Army Reserve set up a website and gathered eight thousand signatures on a petition demanding an end to extended duty tours in Iraq. In Florida, twenty National Guard family members petitioned military commanders to bring the troops home. Some of the soldiers' wives vowed to go on hunger strikes if their demands were not met.[14]

By late 2003 the first signs of overt resistance within the ranks began to appear. In October, thirty soldiers who went home on two-week leave missed their return flight from Baltimore.[15] In Rochester, New York, more than a dozen members of the 401st Civil Affairs Battalion refused to sign waivers for their unit to redeploy to the combat zone.[16] The GI Rights Hotline, a national soldiers' support service organized by peace activists, reported receiving hundreds of calls a week to their toll-free number, many from soldiers or family members asking about the penalties associated with going absent without leave (AWOL).[17] In October 2004, reserve soldiers of the 343rd Quartermaster Company at Tallil Air Base in Iraq refused to drive a convoy of fuel. The soldiers complained about faulty equipment and the lack of protection for their vehicles, calling their assignment a "suicide mission."[18] The army initially threatened twenty-three soldiers with punishment but brought charges against five.

Resisters

Unlike GIs of the Vietnam era, soldiers opposed to the wars in Iraq and Afghanistan did not publish underground newspapers. They expressed their grievances in blogs and emails. In 2004, Garett Reppenhagen, an army sniper in Iraq, helped to start the *Fight to Survive* blog. It was described as "the mouthpiece for a group of soldiers who are fighting in a war they oppose for a president they didn't elect while the petrochemical complex turns the blood of their fallen comrades into oil." Reppenhagen's friend, Jeff Engelhardt, wrote from Baquba: "The best way to counter terrorism is not to participate in it. War is not the solution, and until we realize this, no one is safe."[19] Reppenhagen later became executive director of Veterans For Peace.

One of the first public resisters to the war was Camilo Mejía, who later wrote a compelling memoir of his experience, *The Road from ar Ramadi*. A combat infantry leader in Ramadi during the early months of the war, Mejía refused to return to Iraq after going home on leave and was subsequently court-martialed and sent to prison. Mejía was the son of prominent Sandinista revolutionaries in Nicaragua, but he and his mother lived on limited means as immigrants in Florida in the 1990s. To earn income and get college tuition benefits he enlisted in the Army National Guard. He was nearing the end of his contract and preparing to graduate from college in 2003 when the mobilization for war began. He was called up for active duty and deployed to Iraq, and then his enlistment was extended indefinitely, a policy the military termed "stop loss," and troops referred to as a "backdoor draft." He opposed the war but felt he had to go as ordered.

In his memoir Mejía recounts both the mundane and the terrifying details of life as an infantry squad leader in the early stages of battling the insurgency. He describes the killing of civilians that he witnessed and in which he participated, and the corrosive effects such incidents had on his conscience as he struggled to justify his actions. The line between right and wrong "starts to vanish in a heavy fog," he wrote, "until it disappears completely and decisions are weighed on a scale of values that is profoundly corrupt."[20] As he sought a way out of his dilemma, he agonized about whether to resist—weighing the shame at serving in an unjust war against the guilt of abandoning the soldiers he led in combat. His odyssey of self-reflection led him to become a pacifist, opposing not only the Iraq war but war in general.

During his nine months in prison, Mejía had time to think more deeply about the motivations that led him to refuse to return to the war. It was not the fear of dying, he wrote, but "the fear of putting myself in a position where to survive means to kill. There was the fear of losing my soul in the process of saving my body, the fear of being lost to my daughter, to the people who love me. . . . I was afraid of waking up one morning to realize my humanity had abandoned me."[21] In the decision to resist and sacrifice for what is right, he experienced an unexpected sense of freedom:

> Today, as I sit behind bars . . . I remain free in many important ways. What good is freedom if we are afraid to follow our conscience? What good is freedom if we are not able to live with our own actions? I am confined to a prison but I feel, today more than ever, connected to all humanity. Behind these bars I sit a free man because I listened to a higher power, the voice of my conscience.[22]

Joshua Key followed a similar path to resistance. After spending seven months in Fallujah and Ramadi as a combat engineer, he refused to return to Iraq while on home leave and fled with his family to Canada. Key's saga is told in his memoir, written with

Lawrence Hill, *The Deserter's Tale*.[23] Like many army enlistees, Key joined the military because of economic need. He was struggling without a decent job to support two young children, with a third on the way. Faced with the choice between Uncle Sam and Ronald McDonald, as he put it, he chose the former. During his tour in Iraq, Key participated in numerous house raids. His squad would burst into homes with guns raised in the middle of the night. They would awaken the household and ransack the home, searching for weapons and supposed terrorists, separating women and children, and forcefully detaining and apprehending military-age men and boys—often learning afterwards they had gone to the wrong house and detained the wrong persons. The US military's policy of conducting these raids contributed significantly to Iraqi resentment of the occupation and created greater support and sympathy for the insurgency. It also generated anger and anguish among some of the soldiers who were forced to carry out these operations, as explored further below.

Key served at traffic control points. In an interview with journalist Peter Laufer, he recounted an incident in which a car failed to stop as it approached a checkpoint. The troops shouted for the driver to stop—pointlessly, since they had no interpreters—and when the vehicle kept coming, they "totally let loose." When they examined the car after the shooting, the soldiers found a dying father and his wounded son, but no evidence of weapons or explosives. "That hit us all hard," Key said. They had killed the man and wounded the boy for no reason, simply out of confusion, fear, and an inability to communicate.[24] After eight months of this kind of duty, Key could not continue. It was not cowardice that prompted his decision to go to Canada, he said, but a voice of conscience that would not be silenced:

> I never flinched from danger. The easiest thing would have been to keep on doing what I was told to do. Ever so slowly, as the jets

raced and the illumination rounds burned and the houses fell down during the long Iraqi nights, my conscience returned. It could no longer be Army first, God second, and family third. I had to be the tiny voice inside me that would not sleep any longer. *I am not this man,* I told myself. *I cannot do these things any longer.*[25]

One of the most visible active-duty resisters was Jonathan Hutto, communications specialist and petty officer aboard the aircraft carrier USS *Roosevelt*. Hutto was a graduate of Howard University, where he had been president of the Student Association, and worked for a time with the ACLU (American Civil Liberties Union) and Amnesty International. He was an experienced human rights organizer, but nonprofit work did not pay enough to support his son and repay student loans. He was in difficult economic straits and needed a new pathway in life. When a recruiter said the Navy would cover all his debt and promised training and assignment as a communications specialist, he couldn't resist. He signed up for the military.

The Navy has a reputation for being the most racially biased of the services.[26] Hutto experienced that personally when he was assigned to the *Roosevelt*. Soon after boarding, he found himself the victim of harassment and racial abuse. The worst incident came when a co-worker pulled down a hangman's noose in front of him and joked that somebody could use a lynching. Hutto was outraged. He decided to fight back, using the skills he had acquired as a student leader and human rights advocate. He filed an equal opportunity complaint against the perpetrator and his supervisor through official Navy channels. He documented the incident thoroughly and won the case, and those responsible were punished.[27]

Hutto knew the war in Iraq was wrong and wanted to speak out against it. As the *Roosevelt* returned from deployment in the Persian Gulf in 2006, he joined with Marine Sergeant Liam Madden and others to create one of the largest organized expressions of opposition to war within the military, the Appeal for Redress. The Appeal was directed to members of Congress from individual service members. It read:

> As a patriotic American proud to serve the nation in uniform, I respectfully urge my political leaders in Congress to support the prompt withdrawal of all American military forces and bases from Iraq. Staying in Iraq will not work and is not worth the price. It is time for US troops to come home.[28]

More than 2,000 active-duty, reserve, and National Guard service members signed the Appeal. Its public release attracted widespread media coverage, including a feature with Hutto, Madden, and other signers on the CBS news program, *60 Minutes*.[29] Hutto wrote about the experience and the struggle for justice in his book *Antiwar Soldier: How to Dissent within the Ranks of the Military*.

In the fall of 2002, as the drumbeat for war quickened in Washington, Ann Wright became increasingly troubled. A retired army colonel who had spent thirteen years on active duty and sixteen years in the reserves, Wright also had served for fifteen years as a US diplomat and at the time was deputy US ambassador in Mongolia. She had not questioned military action against Al Qaida in Afghanistan in 2001, but she considered the planned invasion of Iraq unnecessary and immoral. Invading another country without provocation, she believed, was an act of aggression, a war crime. On March 19, 2003, as the attack against Iraq began, she submitted her resignation to the State Department and embarked on a new career as peace advocate and defender of those who speak truth to power. She became an active member of Veterans For Peace and worked with many antiwar groups.

With Susan Dixon, Wright later wrote *Dissent: Voices of Conscience*, which tells the story of dozens of whistleblowers and resisters within government and the military—diplomats, senior military officers, and enlisted service members—who spoke out against

Navy Petty Officer Jonathan W. Hutto, Sr., Appeal for Redress, January 2007, Norfolk, Virginia. GARRIE ROUSE/PBASE GALLERIES.

the deception and criminality of official policy.[30] Wright's book examines the statements of retired US military officers who opposed the war and the way it was conducted. She also highlighted the voices of nearly fifty retired generals and admirals who spoke out against the Bush administration's policies of torture and so-called "enhanced interrogation." The flag officers signed public letters criticizing the 2006 Military Commissions Act as a violation of the Geneva Conventions on the rights of detainees. Wright and other retired military officers demanded that US detention and interrogation policies conform to the rule of law. She and others in the veterans movement played an important role in giving credibility to the antiwar movement and building support for the withdrawal of US troops.

Families and Veterans Organize

During the years 2003–2011, approximately twenty organizations of active-duty service members, recent veterans, and military family members participated in the antiwar movement.[31] Some of the groups focused on conditions of service and military grievances (such as the lack of body armor in the early years of the war), while others were explicitly antiwar and articulated a radical critique of US foreign policy. Four groups stand out in the latter category—Veterans For Peace, Military Families Speak Out, Gold Star Families for Peace, and Iraq Veterans Against the War. These groups opposed US war policy but also addressed the grievances of veterans and returning soldiers, demanding improved conditions and services while linking these issues to the war's deceptive origins and disastrous outcomes.

Veterans For Peace was founded in 1985 by veterans of the Vietnam War and earlier conflicts. Its membership grew rapidly during the Iraq War. The organization played an important role in organizing symbolic antiwar memorials, which were displays of crosses placed in public locations, each cross bearing the name of a fallen soldier. The tactic emerged in early November 2003, when a local Veterans For Peace chapter and other antiwar groups in Santa Barbara created "Arlington West," planting 340 unpainted wooden crosses on a popular beach next to Stearns Wharf. A few months later a similar antiwar memorial was placed in the sand next to Santa Monica Pier. Over the next six years, similar memorials were established in public locations in dozens of communities across the United States, the number of crosses steadily increasing. The memorials were expressions of grief by veterans and military family members that attracted sympathy and support for ending the war. Veterans For Peace remained active throughout this period, helping to organize many national and local antiwar actions.

Military Families Speak Out was founded in November 2002 by Nancy Lessin and Charlie Richardson, parents of an army linguist. When the group sponsored a televised press conference with another veterans group in January 2003, the response was strong. More than two hundred military families joined in just forty-eight hours. Within a year the organization numbered one thousand families. Many of those who contacted the group were new to the peace movement. Typical was the comment of a wife who confided to Lessin: "Our family has been military for generations. I'm a lifelong Republican. I voted for President Bush. But we've been lied to. I want my husband home."[32] Family members often focused on the well-being of troops and demands for better protective equipment, but they also addressed the broader policy issue of ending the occupation.

The most visible military family organization was Gold Star Families for Peace, cofounded by Cindy Sheehan, whose son Casey was an army specialist killed in Iraq in 2004. Speaking with the passion and moral authority of parents who have lost a child in war, the gold star parents embodied the pain of the war's human cost. Sheehan became famous when she demanded an explanation for her loss, publicly confronting President Bush with the question: "What was the noble cause that my son died for?" In August 2005 she organized a vigil called Camp Casey outside the president's ranch near Crawford, Texas, demanding to see the President. Bush had met Sheehan and her husband Patrick briefly the year before, and he wrote in his memoir that he felt sympathy for her.[33] He decided not to see her at the ranch, however, to avoid what he considered a publicity stunt. Sheehan continued to demand an explanation from the president and traveled with antiwar veterans on a national speaking tour that concluded with a protest in front of the White House at which she and 370 others were arrested. Another leader of Gold Star Families for Peace was Celeste Zappala, whose son Sherwood Baker was killed in Iraq in April 2004, ironically while guarding the Iraq Survey Group, the mission sent to find Iraq's nonexistent weapons of mass destruction.

Sheehan, Zappala, and other gold star parents gained extensive media coverage and spoke with unique "moral authority," wrote *New York Times* columnist Maureen Dowd.[34] Their tragic experience dramatically illustrated the suffering and terrible price of the war. They spoke with a confidence inspired by decades of feminist organizing in the peace movement and the women's liberation movement of the 1970s. They employed a maternalist political narrative that attracted sympathy and personalized a war that for many people was distant and unknown. They combined their role as grieving parents with a sharp critique of the deceptions and injustices of the war to exert a significant influence on public opinion. Their demand to bring the troops home resonated widely.

In 2004 and 2005, Veterans For Peace helped to create a new organization, Iraq Veterans Against the War (IVAW), which was inspired by and named after Vietnam Veterans Against the War. Like its predecessor, IVAW emerged as an important voice within the larger antiwar movement. By fall 2008, the organization claimed more than 1,300 members, a quarter of them active duty, with fifty-eight chapters, a few of them at or near military bases.[35] One of the most significant actions organized by IVAW was the

Winter Soldier hearing of March 2008. The goal was to create a kind of truth commission that would cut through the propaganda of military and political leaders to tell Americans what was actually happening in Iraq and Afghanistan. In organizing the hearing, IVAW was reaching back to the similarly named war crimes hearings organized by VVAW in 1971.[36] The appellation "winter soldier" was derived from the famous opening lines of Thomas Paine's paean to the revolutionary war soldiers of 1776 who stood by their country not merely in easy times but in the months of darkest tribulation: "These are the times that try men's souls. The summer soldier and sunshine patriot will, in this crisis, shrink from the service of his country; but he that stands it now deserves the love and thanks of man and woman." The veterans used Paine's stirring tribute and their distinctive military identity to reframe the meaning of patriotism and uphold the right of dissent. True patriots, they asserted, are not the militarists who clamor for more weapons and military intervention but those who take risks to speak out against the abuses of power that lead to unjust war.

About two hundred recent veterans participated in the IVAW Winter Soldier hearing, including a few active-duty troops. Approximately fifty gave presentations. Over three days of often emotional, poignant testimony at a labor center near Washington DC, the veterans described the atrocities they personally committed or witnessed in Iraq and Afghanistan. They addressed themes such as: disregard for the rules of engagement, dehumanization of the enemy, the breakdown of the military, sexual abuse, and profiteering by military contractors. The record of those hearings was published by Haymarket Books as *Winter Soldier: Iraq and Afghanistan: Eyewitness Accounts of the Occupations*, which stands as a powerful testament to the war's brutality and futility.[37]

No incidents of mass atrocities were revealed during the hearing, but there were many stories of the dehumanization of Iraqis, the killing of innocent civilians, the torture and abuse of prisoners,

Veterans testifying at 2008 Winter Soldier hearing. MIKE HASTIE/
HAYMARKET BOOKS.

sexual abuse against women, the breakdown of military morale and
discipline, and the lack of adequate health services for wounded
and traumatized veterans when they returned home. Several soldiers spoke of the terror and futility of conducting nighttime
house raids, which needlessly exposed troops to the danger of
attack and generated hatred and enmity from the civilian populations they were supposedly sent to help. Participation in such missions wore on their consciences, several said, generating what
experts refer to as 'moral injury,' the emotional cost of seeing or
committing acts of moral transgression.[38]

The Winter Soldier testimonial received considerable press coverage. Pacifica Radio led the coverage, with the indomitable Amy
Goodman of *Democracy Now* reporting live from the hearing. CBS,
NPR, Fox, and other networks were also there. The *Washington Post*,
Newsday, the *Boston Globe*, and other papers covered the event, and
stories appeared in *Stars and Stripes* and in *Army Times*, *Navy Times*,
and other major military publications.

Supporting the Troops

As US troops were sent to Afghanistan in the weeks after 9/11 and then to Iraq for Bush's war in 2003, yellow ribbons and "support our troops" signs sprouted everywhere. The ubiquitous messages were intended as a humanitarian gesture for those who serve, but the slogan contained an implicit accusation against those who continued to oppose the war, "the civil equivalent of dereliction of duty," as Andrew Bacevich put it.[39] As a "rally 'round the flag" effect took hold after troops were committed to battle, the yellow ribbons for some were a call to support the war. Antiwar activists responded by emphasizing their support for the troops, while remaining critical of the war and demanding an end to the occupation. The best way to honor and support the troops, they said, is not to send them on unjust wars of aggression.

Some activists showed their support for the troops by helping soldiers who spoke out against the war. During the Vietnam era, activists provided political encouragement and material assistance for GIs like me who resisted the war. Antiwar organizers launched a Summer of Support project in 1968 to assist in establishing coffeehouses at dozens of major military bases.[40] These centers became countercultural oases for antiwar troops and hubs for organizing protests and publishing underground GI newspapers. Military counseling agencies also emerged during that era to support service members as they filed for conscientious objector status and faced repression and/or racial abuse from their commanders.

Similar though less extensive efforts developed during the Iraq War. Civilian groups provided support for the Appeal for Redress and for the organizing efforts of IVAW. The Center on Conscience and War and the Military Law Task Force of the National Lawyers Guild provided support for the increasing number of service members who sought to become conscientious objectors, or who needed legal help in response to repression or racial abuse.

A modest version of the coffeehouse movement also emerged. In 2007, attorney Tod Ensign of the organization Citizen Soldier helped to open an internet coffeehouse known as the Different Drummer in Watertown, New York, near Ft. Drum, home of the 10th Mountain Division. The coffeehouse sponsored film showings, rock bands, and photography exhibits and organized discussion groups and protest events, but it had little success in attracting the participation of local soldiers.[41] Other coffeehouse efforts emerged with the opening of Coffee Strong in 2009 near Ft. Lewis, Washington, and Under the Hood, in Killeen, Texas, adjacent to Ft. Hood. These centers provided critical support for individual soldier resisters and for local chapters of Veterans For Peace and IVAW, but they were established relatively late in the war. They emerged at a time when protest action was diminishing and the attention of many activists was turning to congressional lobbying and the election of antiwar candidates, as examined in the next chapter.

Morale problems and antiwar dissent were not supposed to happen in an all-volunteer force, but when men and women join the military, they do not sign away their consciences. They are not immune to societal trends that influence how we think. Americans were skeptical of the war before it began and became more so as the occupation continued, and this was true within the military as in society. Some service members voiced their opposition and called for an end to the war, despite the risks to them and their families. They spoke with the legitimacy of those who have served in war and in the process helped to shape public opinion and redefine the meaning of patriotism as distinct from militarism.

While soldier resistance and dissent did not undermine the US war effort in Iraq, as was the case in Vietnam, military morale was low to begin with and declined further as the occupation dragged on and troops faced multiple deployments. In 2006 Zogby International conducted a poll among troops in Iraq that found only 23 percent in support of White House policy, while 72 percent said that all US troops should be pulled out within one year.[42] Opposition to the war was especially strong among National Guard and reserve troops. In 2006 and 2007, the army had to lower entrance standards to meet recruitment quotas, in part because of the decline in enlistment rates among African Americans, as noted in Chapter Four.[43] Service members were increasingly worn down by repeated deployments to Iraq and Afghanistan and by rising rates of brain injury and post-traumatic stress disorder. Suicide rates among army soldiers began to rise in 2008 and by 2012 were increasing at an alarming rate.[44] Suicide levels within the military and among veterans reached levels significantly higher than in the civilian population.[45] At the Winter Soldier hearing, IVAW members testified to the "breakdown" of the military as they experienced it, tracing rising levels of trauma to the consequences of fighting unwinnable wars of dubious moral purpose. The stress suffered by service members was one of the most significant unacknowledged costs of the war.

Military strategists have long recognized the will to fight as an essential element of war. Napoleon considered moral factors three times more important than the material aspects of combat. The so-called "war on terror" began with patriotic fervor, as many soldiers believed their service would avenge the 9/11 attacks and defeat terrorism, but the harsh realities of serving in an occupation and battling an insurgency altered the moral equation and generated a growing sense of futility. A strategically flawed mission led to lower morale, which in turn sapped the will to fight. Troops continued to follow orders and wore the uniform with pride, but many had growing doubts. Morale was poor and there was little enthusiasm for the fight. How much this affected military effectiveness and contributed to the US failure in Iraq is unknown, but it was a factor.

In the last section of the book, we focus on the ways in which antiwar opposition influenced political decision making in the US and other countries and significantly affected the outcome of the war. Contrary to the assumptions of many observers, including antiwar activists, the protests of February 2003 and worldwide mobilizations for peace were not a failure. The Bush administration pretended to ignore the antiwar movement, but White House officials were worried about the protests and waged a relentless battle to control public opinion. The decisions they made to ease public concerns about the likely costs of the war—minimizing the invasion force and failing to plan for the occupation—contributed to strategic defeat, as noted above and explained further in Chapter Eight. Bush may have won the first round of the contest, as the invasion rolled ahead and succeeded in overthrowing Saddam Hussein, but his victory lap a few weeks later—landing in a Navy fighter on an aircraft carrier and declaring "mission accomplished"—proved hasty. A powerful insurgency soon developed in Iraq, US military casualties rose, and the country devolved into violent chaos. Antiwar opposition continued, with significant political impacts in many countries, including in the US. In the final section of the book, I explore these effects, beginning in the next chapter with an analysis of the movement's turn toward institutional politics in the United States, which led to the rise of an antiwar lobby in Congress and the election of candidates who promised to end the war, most importantly Barack Obama.

Six

Protest and Politics

Many on the left consider the embrace of conventional politics a mistake. The role of the antiwar movement, wrote activist scholar Mike Davis, is to hold politicians' feet to the fire and raise a principled criticism of US foreign policy, not to support candidates for office or lobby in Congress. Commenting on activist involvement in the 2004 presidential election, Davis lamented that the antiwar movement was "absorbed" by the campaign of former Vermont governor Howard Dean and then "dissolved" into the candidacy of Senator John Kerry.[1] Writer Anthony Arnove also criticized the left for backing Kerry and "giving up its independence and principles to support a pro-war candidate."[2]

Social movement scholars share the criticism of activist involvement in conventional politics. In their important book, *Party in the Streets*, Heaney and Rojas acknowledge the role of the antiwar movement in the 2006 congressional elections and the candidacy of Barack Obama in 2008, but they offer a gloomy assessment of these developments. They bemoan the "decline" and "demobilization" of protest activity and describe the shift toward lobbying and electoral politics as the "collapse" of the movement.

They assert that the election of Obama "spelled doom for the antiwar movement."[3]

These assessments are too pessimistic, I believe. They fail to acknowledge the significant impact of antiwar activists in turning Congress against the war and helping to elect a president who campaigned on a promise to end it and followed through on that pledge by withdrawing the troops. The critics are right that Obama and Democratic Party leaders were not pacifists or opponents of military intervention per se, but they were committed to ending the war. As elected officials, they were dependent on voters who were increasingly dissatisfied with Bush's policy in Iraq. This provided an opportunity for the movement to exert pressure for ending the conflict.

Politics is not about perfection or the purity of one's position. It is the realm of the possible, and the arena in which social movements can engage to achieve progress toward their objectives. Rather than spelling doom, I argue, the election of Obama was an indication of partial success for the peace movement. Obama hesitated and wavered about the Iraq issue, but he eventually removed US troops and fulfilled his pledge to the voters.

Those who criticize activist involvement in conventional politics have an overly narrow view of social movements. As Tom Hayden wrote, the peace movement cannot be defined solely on the basis of action in the streets.[4] Scholars David S. Meyer and Catherine Corrigall-Brown explain that movements are composed of broad coalitions that "straddle the boundaries between institutional and the extra-institutional politics."[5] They involve rallies and demonstrations, but also the mobilization of voters and citizen lobbying, action in the streets and in the suites. To evaluate movement impacts we need to widen our scope of analysis and include an assessment of political activities such as lobbying and electoral campaigning.

In this chapter I describe these "inside" efforts and argue that the antiwar movement demonstrated significant political impact in both pressuring Congress to establish limits on the US presence in Iraq and in helping to elect members of Congress and a president committed to ending the war. I begin the chapter with an overview of the typology of social movements and the factors that influence their ebb and flow, including the choice of whether to protest or participate in conventional politics. I discuss the frustrations of engaging in the 2004 Democratic presidential primaries, activist involvement in the 2006 congressional elections that helped the Democrats win control of Congress, the emergence of a formidable antiwar lobby that convinced Congress to demand the withdrawal of troops, and the essential role of the movement in the historic electoral victory of Obama. I conclude with thoughts on the ambiguities of Obama's troop withdrawal process and the limitations of conventional politics.

Outside and Inside

Organizers and social scientists alike measure the scale of a social movement on the basis of the number of people protesting in the streets. The most significant movements are those that generate the largest crowds. When we remember the Vietnam antiwar movement, we think of the major protests that shook the political establishment: the 1967 March on the Pentagon; the Vietnam Moratorium and Mobilization march in the fall of 1969; the upsurge after the Cambodia invasion and killings at Kent State; and the massive protests and civil disobedience actions in Washington of the spring of 1971. Our assessment of the Iraq movement is similar, emphasizing the iconic global protests of February 15, 2003, and the many other mass demonstrations that occurred. Large protests are important for increasing the salience of issues and raising political demands that established institutions tend to ignore. For scholars, the number of people who participate in demonstrations is a key indicator of importance. It is an objective figure that can be measured, or at least estimated given the limitations of crowd-counting methodology. Crowd size can form the basis for measuring trends of growth or decline in a movement, and for comparative analysis of one movement with another.

Erica Chenoweth and other scholars of civil resistance also focus on crowd size as a measure of impact. They define civil resistance as "non-institutional actions" that operate outside the political establishment and do not function though political parties, the courts, or electoral and legislative systems.[6] Working in political campaigns, registering and mobilizing voters, lobbying and advocating for policy change—these and other actions within the political system are not normally considered part of the repertoire of civil resistance. Chenoweth and her colleagues find that mass participation is the most important factor in accounting for the success of civil resistance campaigns, but they also argue that street protest is not the only or necessarily most effective form of resistance. Successful civil resistance campaigns use other methods of action as well, including boycotts and strikes. At times they combine both institutional and non-institutional forms of action.

Crowd size can tell us much about the scale and significance of a movement, but it does not capture all the nuances and dimensions of a movement's political impact. In many cases, especially in countries with developed political institutions like the United States, the influence of a movement is mediated through political and legislative mechanisms. During the Iraq war many activists were pragmatic about their choice of methods, demonstrating in the streets but also engaging in electoral organizing and legislative lobbying. Sharp boundaries between street protest and conventional politics were rare. Many activists worked in their communities, engaging local officials and elected representatives to encourage support for resolutions against the war. Groups at the national and local level also engaged in media communications efforts, as discussed in Chapter Three. All of these forms of action contributed to the movement.

Movement Dynamics

Movements inevitably experience waves of ebb and flow. Occasionally, they grow to massive scale in response to particularly outrageous events or policies—the invasion of Iraq being a prime example—and they rise or fall in relation to events that affect that policy. Eventually all movements go through periods of decline and fade away. The process of forming and disbanding groups is an inherent part of movement organizing. Movements often change form as new challenges arise, and they tend to shift toward institutional forms of action as opportunities for political engagement materialize.

The degree to which activists emphasize street protest or institutional engagement depends on multiple variables. Scholars emphasize the importance of political opportunity structures, which can be defined as the presence (or absence) of avenues for mobilizing audiences and engaging politically.[7] One of those opportunities is access to the established political system. If there are viable legislative options for ending or constraining war, or if there are electable candidates who are committed to working for peace, activists will be encouraged by these opportunities and will devote more of their time, energy, and money to working within the system and engaging in conventional forms of political action.[8] On the other hand, if options for legislative or electoral approaches are closed or absent, people will participate in street actions and protest demonstrations. They will join the "party in the streets" and demand change from the outside. Often both forms of action will occur during the same period.

Perceptions of success can influence these choices. In the latter stages of the Iraq antiwar movement, as public discontent with the war deepened, some opponents of the war saw the political odds shifting in their favor and devoted more of their time and energy to lobbying and electoral work rather than marching and protesting in the streets. As opportunities emerged for electing members of Congress and a president committed to withdrawing troops, their activism shifted toward electoral campaigns and lobbying.

Once Obama was elected, many activists believed their goals had been accomplished. They no longer felt the urgency of protesting to end the war and shifted their attention to other issues, many helping to support the administration's healthcare reform.[9] The leaders of United for Peace and Justice and ANSWER continued to call for protest and organized further demonstrations, but the crowds were minimal. Only highly committed peace activists turned up. With participation levels greatly lowered, the movement could no longer achieve critical mass.[10] In that sense, the movement in the streets did indeed diminish and fade away.

The organizations that emerged during the Iraq antiwar movement continued after the fading of large-scale protest. Win Without War, Code Pink, and other groups carried on public education and advocacy, and they remain active today. The existence of these groups is important for addressing peace policy issues, but their presence should not be confused with a social movement. Advocacy organizations may emerge from movements and are often strengthened by them, and they can help to build a movement when political opportunities are ripe, but on their own they do not constitute a social movement. The latter is a distinct phenomenon, a relatively rare and uniquely situated upsurge of public mobilization in response to particular circumstances.

Even after activists began devoting their time and attention to electoral work, protest actions and demonstrations continued.

Demonstration against the Republican National Convention, New York, August 2004. GARRIE ROUSE/GBASE GALLERIES.

In their surveys of participants at antiwar rallies, Heaney and Rojas found that many activists were involved in both protest and political activities. A person who volunteered or contributed to political campaigns in 2004 might also participate in a UFPJ demonstration in 2005. The last major Iraq antiwar protest took place in January 2007, when an estimated 100,000 people gathered in Washington DC to demand that the new Congress take action to withdraw troops from Iraq. Many in the crowd no doubt had worked in the 2006 elections to help elect antiwar candidates they were now seeking to lobby.

Protesters often heed political and electoral dynamics in planning their demonstrations. One of the largest protests against the war took place in New York in August 2004 at the Republican National Convention. Despite fabricated threats of terrorism and the refusal of city officials to grant a permit for demonstrating in Central Park, hundreds of thousands of protesters descended on the city to condemn the war and Bush administration policies. The labor movement played a major role in organizing the demonstration, which also addressed issues of social justice. It was the largest protest in the history of American political conventions, according to Hayden, with 1,800 arrested, three times more than during the historic protests at the Chicago Democratic Convention in 1968.[11] Movement leaders chose not to organize protests outside the Democratic Party convention that year, despite the fact that Democratic nominee John Kerry had voted for the war in 2002 and was not committed to withdrawing troops. Activists knew that the Democratic Party, despite the limitations of its leadership, represented their best hope as a potential political vehicle for ending the war.

To the Ballot Box

The movement's first foray into electoral politics emerged in June 2003 when former Vermont Governor Howard Dean raised a stir during a meeting of the Democratic National Committee by asking party officials why they had not taken a position opposing the invasion of Iraq. Dean had no organizational connection to the antiwar movement, but he understood the political salience of the Iraq issue and urged Democrats to take advantage of it. His question was an uncomfortable one for party leaders who had voted for the 2002 resolution authorizing the use of force in Iraq.

Until that time Dean's plan to enter the Democratic Party primaries in 2004 seemed a quixotic and forlorn cause. As soon as he raised the Iraq question, however, his campaign came to life and was flooded with volunteers and contributions. On a single day, June 27, 2003, donors sent half a million dollars in contributions. Dean ultimately raised $50 million from 600,000 supporters. His Meetup.com site grew from 432 to 190,000 members.[12] Dean suddenly rose to number one in the presidential polls, although he did relatively poorly in the Iowa caucus and New Hampshire primary, and his campaign quickly faded.

The force driving this sudden surge of support for Dean and interest in the 2004 election was MoveOn, which was and still is closely aligned with the Democratic Party, and which also grew into an internet powerhouse through its opposition to the war and leadership of Win Without War. Many MoveOn activists wanted the party to run on a platform of demanding the withdrawal of troops and an end to the occupation. They pointed to the Dean campaign as an early indication of the potential for the antiwar issue to mobilize support within the Democratic Party.

A similar pattern of activists backing an unlikely presidential contender occurred during the Vietnam antiwar movement. In 1968, Senator Eugene McCarthy ran as an antiwar candidate in the New Hampshire primary. The previously unknown challenger polled 42 percent of the vote, compared to a write-in vote of 49.5 percent for the incumbent President Lyndon Johnson—a result that historian Charles DeBenedetti termed "an astonishing psychological victory" that stunned Johnson and the political establishment in Washington.[13] This opened the door to the candidacy of a more electable candidate, Senator Robert Kennedy, and convinced Johnson to withdraw from the race. Johnson announced a temporary bombing halt and the beginning of peace talks and refused the Pentagon's request for 200,000 additional troops. This was a major turning point in the conduct of the war, although it took several more years to end the US role in the conflict.

Democratic Party activists were bitterly frustrated that year by a closed electoral system in which political bosses gave the nomination to war supporter Hubert Humphrey despite strong voter preference for antiwar candidates McCarthy and Kennedy.[14] In the wake of the 1968 election loss, Democrats organized a reform process led by Senator George McGovern, an outspoken opponent of the war. The McGovern commission made significant structural changes in the primary election system, giving greater voice and influence to voters in primary elections and caucuses. Those reforms diminished the influence of "old boy" power networks and increased public participation in the process of selecting delegates. As Hayden observed, the post-1968 reforms created wider space for activism and made the boundaries between inside and outside organizing more porous than before.[15] Antiwar forces helped to create institutional changes that exerted far-reaching political impact long after the movement that sparked them was over.

The 2004 presidential campaign of John Kerry was a grave disappointment for antiwar Democrats. Kerry's 2002 Senate vote to authorize force in Iraq haunted him at every turn, and it continues to dull his reputation among progressives even now, twenty years later. He was critical of Bush's handling of the war but did not campaign as an antiwar candidate or advocate the withdrawal of troops as activists wanted. As late as August 2004, Kerry said that he stood by his vote on the war. The next month, he sharply criticized Bush's Iraq policy,[16] but he was unable to convince voters that his position differed much from that of the president. Kerry had little understanding of the fervor and intensity of antiwar feelings among many voters. His campaign did not attract the wave of grassroots enthusiasm and internet activism that greeted Howard Dean's short-lived primary campaign, and that would later emerge as a significant force in the 2006 and 2008 election cycles. Kerry's ambivalent stance on the war was like an albatross that dragged down and ultimately doomed his candidacy.

Kerry was attacked during the campaign from the right, ironically not because of his position on the Iraq War but because of his opposition to the war in Vietnam more than thirty years earlier. In April 1971 Kerry, then a leader of Vietnam Veterans Against the War and a former swift boat commander in Vietnam, testified before the Senate Foreign Relations Committee, famously posing the question, "how do you ask a man to be the last man to die for a mistake?" In his remarks, he recounted the evidence of atrocities committed by American forces in Vietnam, drawing from testimony a few months before by recently returned veterans at the Winter Soldier Hearing in Detroit.[17] Kerry received favorable news coverage for his Senate testimony, and many veterans applauded his antiwar stance, but a handful objected and said the stories of war crimes were fabricated, although evidence of atrocities in Vietnam was fully documented by veterans and others.[18]

Thirty-three years later some of the same right-wing veterans renewed their attack. They gave themselves the disingenuous name Swift Boat Veterans for Truth, and they launched personal attacks against Kerry by spreading false claims about his service in the Navy.[19] The group spent more than $19 million on television advertising in 2004, with $5.1 million devoted to Ohio alone. A survey conducted after the election by GOP pollsters found that 75 percent of voters in twelve battleground states had seen or heard of the group's ads and their allegations.[20] The impact of the swift boat attacks is uncertain, but in the end Bush defeated Kerry by a narrow margin. Meanwhile the term "swift boat" entered the lexicon as a verb to denote strategic disinformation campaigns aimed at slandering and discrediting a political opponent.

Turning Congress

The 2004 presidential election generated disillusionment among antiwar activists. Many had supported Kerry despite his weaknesses on the war issue, hoping that the defeat of Bush would make it possible to organize politically for the withdrawal of US troops. For MoveOn, the shock of Bush's reelection was a wake-up call. The organization decided to double down on its commitment to political engagement and began preparing for expanded electoral mobilization and legislative lobbying efforts. They hired Tom Matzzie, an experienced campaign organizer who had worked previously with the AFL-CIO, to serve as Washington director and political manager. Working closely with Fenton Communications

and other media professionals, Matzzie and his team tested different issues and messages to determine their effectiveness in motivating voters. The results showed clearly that the Iraq issue had the
strongest influence in motivating a political commitment from
MoveOn supporters and, more importantly, from likely voters.[21]

Political activists began to apply pressure on the leadership of
the Democratic Party. Hayden pleaded with then–party chairman
Howard Dean to end the party's "silent consent" to Bush's Iraq war
policies. He and others demanded that the Democratic Party take
an unequivocal stand in favor of withdrawing the troops and ending the occupation.

Although some on the left warned against electoral engagement and argued that only independent mass action could end the
conflict, most activists saw the coming congressional elections as
an opportunity to turn the tide against the war. As Hayden put it,
this was not about ideology but how to "register a blow to the war-
makers in the White House." The result was an "intense flow of
antiwar energy during the 2006 electoral season," as the congressional elections became an antiwar battleground.[22]

The goal of turning the Democratic Party against the war was
a tough sell as long as hawks like Connecticut Senator Joe Lieberman played a prominent role in the party and in Congress. Activists began to consider the option of challenging Lieberman in the
2006 Democratic primary. The idea gained life when Matzzie was
invited to speak at Yale University and was asked if MoveOn would
support a challenge to Lieberman. Matzzie said the organization
would consider it if local voters were supportive. That became front-
page news the next day in the *New Haven Register* and soon afterwards in the *New York Times*. When antiwar critic and Connecticut
business executive Ned Lamont announced his decision to challenge Lieberman, MoveOn and local activists rallied to his side.

Lamont scored an upset victory in the early August vote. As
the *New York Times* reported, Lamont "soared from nowhere on a

fierce antiwar message [and] won a narrow but decisive victory."[23] The outcome in Connecticut sent shockwaves through Washington and showed Democratic candidates across the country the power of the antiwar message in motivating voters. Although Lieberman held on to his seat in the November election by running as an Independent and winning significant Republican support, the lesson of the Lamont campaign was clear. Democratic candidates could win on an antiwar message.

Activists were heavily involved in many local races that year and played a significant role in the election of dozens of candidates who were committed to withdrawing troops from Iraq. MoveOn launched a nationwide independent expenditure campaign which targeted fifty-five House campaigns and twelve Senate races, focusing on vulnerable Republicans in suburban districts. The organization spent more than $40 million on the campaign, making it one of the top three organizations in the Democratic Party during that election cycle. Campaign activities included raising money for candidates, polling voters in local districts, conducting research on political opponents, tracking and exposing hawkish statements by Republican candidates, producing and placing hundreds of television ads, sponsoring millions of robocalls to local voters, and hiring dozens of local organizers to work in targeted districts to mobilize thousands of campaign volunteers for voter education and turnout.

Republicans became increasingly alarmed. They recognized the war as a political liability and tried to distance themselves from Bush's policy. As the November vote neared, Republican Senate leader Mitch McConnell went to the White House for a private meeting with Bush. "Mr. President, your unpopularity is going to cost us control of the Congress," McConnell said. Bush later described the session in his memoir, admitting that "Mitch had a point."[24] When he asked McConnell what he should do about it, the senator said, "bring some troops home from Iraq." The day before McConnell had publicly excoriated Democrats for wanting to pull troops out of Iraq. Now he was urging the president to do just that.[25] Bush refused McConnell's advice and remained adamant in pursuing the war, even at the cost of his own party's political defeat.

The November vote was a decisive victory for the Democratic Party and a turning point in the politics of the war. Democrats picked up thirty-one seats in the House of Representatives and six in the US Senate. Republicans failed to win any seats held by Democrats in either the Senate or the House.[26] For the first time in twelve years, the Democrats controlled both houses of Congress, a result widely seen as swayed by antiwar sentiment.[27] Other issues also influenced the vote that fall, especially the mobilization within the Latino community against harsh anti-immigrant measures introduced by Rep. James Sensenbrenner and other Republican legislators, but the dominant concern was Iraq.[28] Democrats were able to take advantage of widespread voter dissatisfaction with Bush's conduct of the war.[29] Their candidates ran Iraq-related television spots in six of eight contested Senate races and seventeen of thirty-five tight House races. A *New York Times*/CBS poll a month before the election found two-thirds of voters surveyed disapproving of Bush's handling of the war and agreeing that the war was going badly, with 45 percent saying the Democrats were more likely to make the right decision on Iraq, compared to 34 percent for Republicans.[30]

Gallup polls prior to the election showed "the war in Iraq" as the most important issue for likely voters, selected as the top government priority by 61 percent of Democrats and 52 percent of Independents. Editorial page punditry and exit-poll surveys agreed, "Iraq was the Archimedean lever" that shifted independent voters massively toward the Democrats.[31] Public discontent with Bush's conduct of the war drove many voters to support Democratic candidates. The results of the 2006 election sent a clear message

US Voter Priorities, August 2006.

Policy Priority	Democrats	%	Independents	%	Republicans	%
1	War in Iraq	61	War in Iraq	52	War in Iraq	38
2	Economy	19	Economy	18	Fuel prices	20
3	Healthcare & fuel prices	18	Healthcare & fuel prices	14	Immigration	19
4	Energy crisis	10	Energy crisis	13	Terrorism	18
5	Disaster relief	10	Immigration	9	National security	12

Source: Gallup Poll 28–31 August 2006, cited in Davis, "The Democrats After November."

that antiwar activists were a force to be reckoned with in the Democratic Party—a message not lost on the junior senator from Illinois.

The Antiwar Lobby

The Democratic victory in 2006 dramatically improved the prospects for legislative action to end the war. Antiwar lobbying efforts had begun a couple of years before, as MoveOn, Win Without War, and other groups urged Congress to cut funding and withdraw the troops, and an Out-of-Iraq caucus emerged within the House of Representatives.[32] These initial legislative efforts were unsuccessful in the Republican-controlled Congress, but the situation changed in 2007.

Initially the new Democratic congressional leaders, Speaker of the House Nancy Pelosi and Senate Majority Leader Harry Reid, proposed a legislative agenda that ignored Iraq. Grassroots activists were furious, Hayden wrote, and delivered a focused "paralyzing email barrage" to Reid's office.[33] Pelosi also faced pressure from her constituents, as Code Pink members camped out in front of her home in San Francisco, calling on the speaker to declare herself and lead the legislative charge for military withdrawal.[34] Within days, the Democratic leadership changed their tune and offered assurances they had heard the voters and would develop plans for ending the war. MoveOn, Win Without War, and other groups kept up the pressure and worked directly with the new leadership. Matzzie and others met regularly with Pelosi and Reid and mobilized local supporters in key districts. Win Without War Director Tom Andrews used his legislative experience and connections on Capitol Hill to help coordinate grassroots pressure and support media efforts nationally and in local districts.

The strategic goal of the antiwar lobbying effort was to win congressional support for the withdrawal of troops and prevent the creation of permanent US bases in Iraq, with attention focused on amendments establishing a timetable for withdrawal. As pressure on Congress intensified, a debate ensued on the use of the word "withdrawal." Some members of Congress were uncomfortable with the term and did not want to be seen as weak on defense or unwilling to support the troops. Antiwar legislators and activist groups were conscious of these concerns and were careful to differentiate their opposition to the war from their support for the safety and well-being of US troops. To win over moderate members of Congress, legislative leaders substituted the word "redeployment" for "withdrawal." Redeployment meant the same as withdrawal in requiring the removal of troops from Iraq, but it indicated a willingness to accept the use of military force in other places.

Many activists were decidedly cool to the redeployment stratagem, with some wondering, as Hayden wrote, whether they were succeeding or being co-opted.[35] Grassroots groups within UFPJ and ANSWER demanded "out now," not gradual withdrawal. Indeed, most activists were opposed to all US military interventions, not just in Iraq. Some members of sectarian groups were opposed ideologically to working with the Democratic Party or in mainstream politics generally. Despite these doubts and divisions within the movement, many activists supported the lobbying effort and demanded that their elected representatives take action against the war.

Uniting Against Escalation

The task of unifying Democrats and activists against the war became more urgent when Bush escalated the war in January 2007. Defying the message of voter dissatisfaction with Iraq expressed in the 2006 elections, Bush doubled down on the war by ordering a "surge" of additional troops to Iraq. Once again, the obdurate president was ignoring public opinion. Activists were infuriated, as were many Democratic Party officials. The House of Representatives voted 246-182 for a nonbinding resolution opposing the surge.[36] A majority in the Senate also disapproved, but Bush pushed ahead.

In response to Bush's policy, MoveOn brought together SEIU, Win Without War and other organizations in a new coalition, Americans Against Escalation in Iraq (AAEI). The purpose of the new grouping was to mobilize political opposition to the war through a focused legislative campaign for the withdrawal of troops. The AAEI campaign, a continuation of the political mobilizing effort led by MoveOn in the 2006 congressional elections, focused on the districts of forty potentially vulnerable Republicans in a dozen states. Among the targets was Senator McConnell of Kentucky.[37] The mobilization of pressure in local districts was closely coordinated with legislative efforts on Capitol Hill.

A centerpiece of the AAEI action plan was "Iraq Summer," an intensive effort to mobilize antiwar action in the home districts of the targeted legislators. The coalition recruited and trained 150 organizers to work in specific local districts that were important for winning passage of congressional legislation and were also potential battleground areas for the 2008 presidential elections.

The political mobilizing effort targeted swing districts in locations such as Columbus, Ohio; the suburbs of Louisville, Kentucky; Des Moines, Iowa; and Erie and suburban Philadelphia in Pennsylvania. The campaign organized hundreds of local events and meetings with legislators. One of the most notable actions was a rally of 800 people who marched in Louisville to protest McConnell's support for the war, the largest antiwar protest in Kentucky since the Vietnam era.[38]

The movement's political engagement strategy in Washington was integrated with grassroots activism. It was an example of combining outside protest action with inside legislative strategy. As MoveOn, Win Without War, and other groups were attempting to forge a consensus for withdrawal in the halls of Congress, Code Pink, Peace Action, and other groups were active in the streets. The Iraq Summer campaign used the mobilization of social action in local districts as the means of generating press coverage and applying pressure from local voters on specific decision makers.

AAEI training session, summer 2007. TOM MATZZIE/MOVE ON.

As noted in Chapter Four, research indicates that members of Congress are more likely to be responsive to protests that are within their local district.[39] By mobilizing antiwar action among the constituents of key legislators, Iraq Summer applied focused pressure to demand congressional action.

One of the tactics used by AAEI activists was to organize town hall meetings. Fifty such meetings took place in late August 2007 in communities across the country. Local activists invited their elected representatives to come and explain their stand on the war. Most of the targeted Republican legislators refused to show up, as expected, so organizers placed an empty chair prominently at the center of the stage to symbolize the missing representative. In some cases, activists even created cardboard cutouts of the local politician. These actions attracted significant press coverage in local media and reinforced the message that local voters opposed escalation and were frustrated by the continuation of the war. They also delivered a strong message to political leaders: start the process of withdrawal. A former Bush administration official later described the movement and MoveOn's role in AAEI as "a vigorous and well-funded public relations campaign against the Administration and the Iraq war."[40]

To fund the continuation of war, the Bush administration introduced an emergency appropriations bill in early 2007. Congressional opponents of the war targeted the legislation and added language establishing a timeline for troop withdrawal. The language also prohibited the use of funds to establish permanent US military installations in Iraq or to exercise control over the country's oil revenues. The opposition scored an important success when the House of Representatives voted 218-212 to approve the measure, and the Senate followed suit.[41] The victory was short-lived, however, as President Bush exercised his presidential veto in May to kill the measure. It was only the second veto in Bush's six years in the White House. Lacking the votes to override the presidential veto, Congress settled for a watered-down version of the legislation that did not include the timeline provisions.[42]

Congressional attempts to force the withdrawal of troops continued. In July, the House voted again to set a timeline for withdrawal, this time by a slightly wider margin, 223-201.[43] The measure called for most US troops to be out of Iraq by April 2008. Opinion polls at the time showed strong support for the proposal. Pew and CBS/*New York Times* surveys showed 61 percent of respondents favoring a timetable for withdrawal, with another 8 percent favoring a cutoff of all funding for the war.[44] In the fall, congressional leaders introduced a new bill, the Orderly and Responsible Iraq Redeployment Appropriations Act, directing the president to commence an immediate redeployment of troops from Iraq. In November, the House of Representatives approved the Redeployment Act by a vote of 218 to 203. The Senate voted in favor by a 53 to 45 margin in December. Under filibuster voting rules in force at the time, however, sixty votes were needed in the Senate for passage, and the measure failed.[45] Despite majority backing from both houses of Congress, the bill did not become law. The one measure to make it through the congressional labyrinth to be signed into law was a prohibition on the establishment of permanent military bases in Iraq. It was a remarkable run of favorable votes for antiwar leaders in Congress, but in the end, they came up short.

Approval of the withdrawal bills in the House and Senate was nonetheless a substantial political achievement. It reflected a congressional consensus against the occupation and in favor of a timetable for withdrawal. It signaled widespread political opposition to the administration's handling of the war. It also reflected the growing impact of lobbying efforts by supporters of MoveOn, Win Without War, and other antiwar groups, as antiwar activists applied pressure on their elected representatives to bring the troops home. The movement did not succeed in legislating an end to the war, but it prepared the ground for engagement in the forthcoming presidential primaries.

These pressures also created an opening for Bush to start a partial withdrawal of troops. As attacks against US troops declined in 2007–08 following the awakening movement among Sunni insurgents,[46] Bush entered into negotiations with the government of Prime Minister Nouri al-Maliki in Baghdad to reduce US troop levels. The initial White House proposal called for maintaining American forces in Iraq for an extended period, but political leaders in Baghdad rejected that as an occupation agreement and insisted on a timeline for complete US withdrawal. The administration tried to keep the troops in Iraq until 2015, but al-Malaki refused. In July 2008, Bush agreed to Iraqi demands, and after further haggling the two sides signed a security agreement in November for complete US withdrawal by the end of 2011.[47]

Electing a President

From the very beginning of the presidential race, Barack Obama won the support of many antiwar activists. The principal distinction of his candidacy was his forthright stance against the war. Obama writes in his memoir that the Iraq war was the biggest issue for his campaign.[48] Hilary Clinton was heavily favored going into the Democratic primaries, with substantial financial backing and the support of many Democratic Party leaders, but she waffled on ending the war and was burdened by her Senate vote in 2002. Obama by contrast had spoken against the invasion at an October 2002 antiwar rally in Chicago, and he remained unequivocally opposed to the war, vowing to end it. His campaign expressed "an unapologetic antiwar boldness," writes journalist Spencer Ackerman.[49] The Obama candidacy was a political opportunity for the movement, and many activists embraced it. When MoveOn conducted an internal poll of its online members to determine which candidate the organization should support in the primaries, 70 percent of respondents endorsed Obama.[50] This brought with it a massive wave of volunteer and financial support from antiwar activists.

Obama's electoral strategy played to the strengths of this activist constituency. His campaign created an extensive field presence in dozens of states, built on the foundations of already existing activist networks—principally the antiwar movement, but also labor, women's, environmentalist, African American, Latino, and other established organizing networks. Obama's victories were concentrated in caucus states, where success is determined by the strength of local activist support rather than big name endorsements and large television advertising budgets. In the state of Washington, for example, Obama won two-thirds of the caucus delegates but only 51 percent of the popular vote and came away with two-thirds of the state's delegates. In Texas, Clinton won the popular vote, but Obama won more of the caucuses and ended up with the majority of the state's delegates. The national popular vote was extremely close, but Obama held a significant margin in the thirteen caucus contests, enough to win the nomination. Obama's victory was the result of his superior ability to mobilize tens of thousands of strongly committed loyalists from the antiwar movement and other activist networks.[51]

That activist support base also propelled Obama to victory in the general election. According to David Karpf, during the course of the 2008 election, MoveOn channeled almost $100 million in campaign contributions and one million volunteers to the Obama campaign.[52] It was one of the most influential organizations supporting the Democratic Party in the election that year. The Obama campaign pioneered the use of social media to harness volunteer and donor support, building a network of 13 million people on its various email and Facebook lists. Many of these names were drawn from the MoveOn list (which had grown to 5 million) and other pre-existing activist networks. With 8 million visitors a month, the Obama website was used to create 35,000 volunteer groups and organize 200,000 offline events. The campaign had 3 million online donors and received a total of 6.5 million contributions, with an average gift size of $80. Obama raised twice as much money as Republican candidate John McCain, a record $750 million, two-thirds of which came from small contributions.[53]

Many activists supported Obama because of his opposition to the war, but they had few illusions about his views on other foreign policy issues. In his 2002 speech at the antiwar rally in Chicago, he declared, "I don't oppose all wars. What I am opposed to is a dumb war."[54] During his 2008 campaign, he reiterated his commitment to withdraw troops from Iraq, but he was equally clear in pledging to increase military involvement in Afghanistan. He vowed to use force wherever he deemed necessary to counter terrorist threats. As president he ordered a surge of troops to Afghanistan and launched hundreds of drone strikes in Pakistan, much to the chagrin of many antiwar activists who supported him. He launched airstrikes against Libya in 2011, leading to the collapse of the state, civil war, and widespread regional destabilization, a decision he later regretted.[55] Yet on the issue that mattered most, withdrawing troops and ending the occupation of Iraq, Obama fulfilled his promise to voters. The pressure and support of the antiwar movement helped to make that possible.

In July 2008, after winning the Democratic nomination, Obama visited the troops in Iraq. He was under pressure from diplomats and many in the Pentagon to maintain a sizable troop presence in Iraq. Commanding general David Petraeus hosted Obama's visit and tried to convince him against setting a deadline for withdrawal and in favor of maintaining a residual force in Iraq. Obama listened respectfully but disagreed with the general, as he recounts in his memoir. He refused to back off on the commitment to withdraw US forces.[56]

Soon after taking office, Obama established a schedule for the withdrawal of troops. The original plan was to complete the process in sixteen months, but this was later extended to match the timeline established in the US-Iraq security agreement negotiated by Bush. The Pentagon and many military analysts had expected that a residual force of American troops would remain beyond that time.[57] Military analyst Tom Ricks argued for keeping 30,000 to 50,000 troops in Iraq indefinitely.[58] Administration officials floated proposals for a residual force of up to 10,000 troops, but the Iraqi government and parliament refused.[59] In December 2011, the White House announced that the last troops had left the country. Obama's decision was made easier by the fact that he was following the timeline originally established by the Bush administration.

The results of the antiwar movement's electoral and lobbying efforts were a disappointment for many activists. The movement was successful in the 2006 elections and won major congressional votes in favor of withdrawing troops in 2007, but those measures did not become law, and the war continued. Opponents of the war played a role in helping Obama become president in 2008, but many were impatient with the slow pace of his withdrawal timeline and were frustrated by his hesitation and waffling. Activists sometimes conflate conventional politics and the role of social movements. They tend to project their own values and goals onto politicians and become disillusioned when their demands are not met in the manner they want. In the process, Hayden observed, they "run the danger of underestimating the impact they are actually achieving."[60] They fail to recognize incremental or limited policy changes as a sign of the movement's success.

There are limits to what a social movement can accomplish, even one as large and persistent as the Iraq campaign. Movements make specific demands on politicians—stop the war, withdraw the troops—and when they exert enough pressure the political system responds, although usually not in the manner activists would prefer. Politicians deny the influence of social movements even as they are adjusting policy in response to protests. The Iraq antiwar movement did not accomplish all that activists wanted, but it achieved political successes that are of historic importance, and that deserve to be acknowledged by activists, and by scholars.

Seven

Global Impacts

The millions of people who poured into the streets of London, Rome, and other cities in February 2003 shared the grief of their counterparts in the US when Bush and Blair ignored global opinion and pushed ahead with the invasion. Many were disappointed at their inability to stop the war and mourned at the prospect of so many people dying needlessly because of the arrogance of power. If the leaders of supposedly democratic countries could ignore the largest peace demonstrations in history, many wondered, what was the point of protest? Activists could not imagine at the time that their opposition in fact was shaping political decision-making. Just as the movement in the US was having unacknowledged success in constraining the war and creating pressure for military withdrawal, the global opposition undermined the legitimacy of the US mission and weakened the so-called coalition of the willing. The United States stood largely on its own to face the futility of an unwinnable war and was unable to achieve its strategic objectives. As I explore in this chapter, opponents of the war had more power than they realized.

I begin by examining the political consequences of antiwar opposition in several major countries, some of them longstanding US allies: Germany, where Chancellor Gerard Schröder won a national election by running against George Bush and the war; Spain, where war supporter Prime Minister José María Aznar was voted out of office; Canada, where a loyal neighbor refused to fight alongside its traditional US and British allies; Turkey, where a once pliant partner denied US basing rights for the invasion; and Great Britain, as Tony Blair's support for Bush's war led to his political downfall and public disgrace. I analyze the political and human costs to the US of its international isolation on Iraq and the ways in which global antiwar opposition weakened the war effort and contributed to US military failure. Global political opposition also led to the Security Council's refusal to authorize the use of military force, a historic rejection of US leadership that had a significant impact on the outcome of the war.

Reluctant Allies

Opposition to the war was especially broad in countries where the government supported the US-led war effort. In Great Britain, Spain, and Italy, citizens said no while their political leaders were saying yes. In Spain and Italy, opinion polls showed overwhelming public opposition to participation in the US-led war. In Poland, although there was little organized protest, more than 70 percent found the war unjustified and opposed Polish participation.[1]

In Germany, antiwar sentiment played a decisive role in swaying the outcome of national elections and denying German support for US policy. Social Democratic Chancellor Gerhard Schröder won a narrow, come-from-behind victory in the September 2002 elections by emphasizing his opposition to war in Iraq. For months, Schröder had lagged behind in the polls because of widespread misgivings about his economic policies. As public alarm about the

Antiwar protesters at the Brandenburg Gate in Berlin, February 15, 2003. SEAN GALLUP/GETTY IMAGES.

war spread, Schröder cobbled together a successful electoral strategy by consciously exploiting voters' antiwar sentiments and sharpening his criticism of US policy. Schröder made it clear that Germany would unite with other countries in the fight against international terrorism but would not support US military action in Iraq. "We're not available for adventures, and the time for cheque-book diplomacy is over."[2] The latter comment was in reference to Germany's refusal to pay any of the costs of the invasion, in contrast to its financial support for the US-led international effort to reverse Iraq's aggression in Kuwait in 1991.

After the election an international commentator quipped, "Schröder beats Bush in German election."[3] The vote not only kept a strongly antiwar Schröder in office but elevated the Green Party to new heights, further strengthening the position of Foreign Minister and Green Party leader Joschka Fischer. The election results enhanced the influence of environmental and peace forces in German domestic politics and reinforced international opposition to war because of Germany's seat at the time on the UN Security Council. Fischer used the occasion of a foreign ministers' meeting on counterterrorism policy at the Security Council in January 2003 to state that Germany was "greatly concerned that a military strike against the regime in Baghdad would involve considerable and unpredictable risks for the global fight against terrorism [and] . . . would have disastrous consequences."[4]

In Spain, national elections also turned on the Iraq issue. Public revulsion over Spain's participation in the war contributed to the victory of the Socialist Party in national elections in March 2004. The Socialists campaigned on an antiwar platform and vowed to withdraw the small contingent of Spanish troops the previous government had sent to Iraq as part of the US-led coalition. Three days before the vote, a terrorist bombing ripped through the main train station in Madrid, killing 200 people. The Aznar government initially blamed the Basque terrorist group ETA for the attack, although evidence pointed to Al Qaida terrorists. The mishandling of the reaction to the terrorist bombing added to public discontent over Aznar's disregard of public opinion on the war. The day after the Socialists' election victory, incoming Prime Minister José Luis Rodríguez Zapatero vowed to act immediately to withdraw Spain's 1,400 troops, declaring that Spain's participation in the war was "a total error" based on "lies."[5] A few weeks later the troops were gone. The victory of Zapatero and the Socialists demonstrated the value of the antiwar message for winning elections. It also weakened the coalition of states the Bush administration had cobbled together to support the occupation.

Canada's unwillingness to support or join the US in Iraq was a major blow to Bush's claims of international support for the war. It was difficult for Prime Minister Jean Chrétien to turn aside entreaties from Bush and Blair, commenting later that it was the first time when US and British forces were committed to war that Canadians did not join them.[6] Canadian public opinion was solidly against the war, however, which made his decision easier. An Ipsos-Reid poll found 36 percent of Canadians against the war altogether and another 46 percent supporting war only with UN backing.[7] The intensity of antiwar opinion was growing and was reflected in the massive demonstrations that took place in Montreal and other cities in the months prior to the invasion and in the days before the prime minister made his historic announcement to Parliament that Canada would not support the war. Chrétien and his UN ambassador Paul Heinbecker were deeply skeptical of US intelligence claims. They shared their views with Security Council member states Mexico and Chile, who joined the majority in rejecting US attempts to win support for the use of force. This undermined Bush's war diplomacy and raised the ire of Washington. Chrétien and his ministers were able to parry US entreaties because they had broad support for their antiwar stance among Canadian citizens and in Parliament.

A remarkable manifestation of antiwar sentiment also occurred in Turkey, where a popularly elected Parliament refused the Bush administration's request to use the country as a base and transit corridor for US invasion forces. The *Washington Post* called Turkey's rejection "a stunning setback" to the Bush administration's war plans.[8] Ankara's decision went against a decades-long tradition of close military cooperation between Turkey and the United States. Turkish leaders also turned aside a huge package of financial inducements offered by Washington, including $6 billion in direct grants and up to $20 billion in loan guarantees.[9] The Turkish decision had direct military impact. The United States had planned to deploy more than 60,000 troops in Turkey, including a strike force from the Fourth Infantry Division. The battle plan against Iraq called for a two-pronged attack from both north and south. US officials were so confident of Turkish cooperation that more than thirty military transport ships were on their way or already deployed off Turkey's Mediterranean coast as the decision was being made. Several hundred US support troops were in Turkey renovating bases and ports in preparation for the invasion force. Parliament's last-minute rejection forced Pentagon planners to redeploy the Fourth Division and other troops to the south, creating a more complicated invasion scenario.

The Turkish rejection of war came from a government that at the time was pursuing a democratic, moderate Islamist approach to governing—precisely the kind of regime US officials claimed to want for Iraq and other Middle Eastern countries. The problem for US officials was that democratic expression meant rejection of American policy. Turkey's Justice and Development Party had won the November 2002 elections in part by appealing to popular opposition to US war plans. A March 2003 poll by the Pew Research Center measured antiwar opposition in Turkey at 86 percent. Only 13 percent of the population supported letting US troops launch the invasion from Turkey. More than 50,000 people demonstrated outside Parliament as the vote on the US request began on March 1. The legislators were under enormous pressure, pulled by a powerful ally to provide military cooperation, pushed by an energized domestic constituency to represent the overwhelmingly popular rejection of war. It was a critically important moment for the young Justice and Development Party, which was trying to create a more democratic, yet Islamist, tradition in Turkish politics. When the parliamentary votes were tallied, the resolution to approve the US request failed by four votes.[10] Officials in Washington immediately demanded a revote, but Turkish leaders refused, fearing that an attempt to overturn the vote would bring down the government. The Turkish people and their elected representatives had spoken. The answer was no.

There were many other global antiwar expressions. In Australia, the Senate voted to censure Conservative Prime Minister John Howard for agreeing to deploy troops to Iraq without parliamentary approval. It was the first no-confidence vote in the chamber's 102-year history. Australian opinion polls showed 76 percent of the public against participation in a war without UN backing.[11] In 2007, Howard suffered an embarrassing electoral defeat at the hands of Labor Party leader Kevin Rudd, a setback partly attributed to the country's participation in the Iraq war.[12] Rudd immediately announced an end to Australia's military involvement and a reduction in troop levels. In Italy, Parliament allowed troops to go to Iraq in 2003 but only for "humanitarian" purposes. Prime Minister Silvio Berlusconi later claimed that he tried repeatedly to dissuade Bush from going to war.[13] Following the election of 2006, Romano Prodi took office and immediately announced the withdrawal of Italian troops. In his first speech to Parliament, the new prime minister denounced the war as a "grave error."[14]

In South Korea, Roh Moo-Hyun won the presidency in December 2002, in part by riding a tide of anti-American sentiment. In his political campaign, Roh vowed to continue the conciliatory "sunshine" policy toward North Korea of his predecessor, Kim Dai-Jung, rather than the confrontational approach favored by the Bush administration and Korean conservatives. Roh's electoral victory was another example of governments of long-term American allies winning elections on the basis of popular rejection of US foreign policy. Roh was opposed to war in Iraq, as were most of his voters and parliamentary supporters, but he faced enormous pressure from the Bush administration to send troops to Iraq at a time when he needed Washington's backing for his diplomatic overtures with Pyongyang. He adopted a compromise strategy of deploying a limited number of medics and construction specialists for noncombat service.[15] The South Korean contingent eventually numbered more than 3,000, but Roh started withdrawing the troops in 2006, and they were gone by 2008. South Korea's military role in Iraq was minimal, far short of the significant role it played in the Vietnam War, which Bush administration officials were trying unsuccessfully to emulate.

In Pakistan, the October 2002 elections showed a significant gain for pro-Taliban, anti-American religious parties. A group of six hardline parties, campaigning on a platform that included sharp criticism of US policy, won a higher-than-expected number of seats in Pakistan's national assembly and a majority of seats from the North-West Frontier Province near the Afghanistan border.[16] The election results were more anti-American than antiwar, but they were another sign of deepening political opposition to the United States around the world.

The Iraq issue undermined the political career of British Prime Minister Tony Blair. Under his leadership the Labor Party won three straight national elections, in 1997, 2001, and 2005, an unprecedented feat, but Blair's decision to support the war without UN approval was deeply unpopular and ruined his political reputation. The deceptive and arrogant manner in which Blair argued for the war and his unseemly subservience to Bush fatally weakened him within the Labor Party and ultimately forced him from office.

Blair was able to cobble together a parliamentary majority in favor of going to war in March 2003 with the support of the Conservatives, but 139 members of his own party defected and refused to support the resolution. It was one of the largest parliamentary rebellions in British history, much larger than that which forced Neville Chamberlain's resignation in 1940. In the preliminary vote in February to back Blair's policy, a third of the House of Commons voted no, the biggest parliamentary revolt of Blair's premiership.[17] Because of his support for the war, the once triumphant political leader became a "great tragic figure," wrote journalist Geoffrey Wheatcroft.[18] Evidence that his pre-war justifications for war were false added to the ignominy. In the May 2005 national elections Labor retained its majority but suffered a sharper than expected loss of seats, a result partially attributed to voter disaffection with the war.[19] A Pew survey in Britain at the time found 53 percent of respondents agreeing that the government made the wrong decision in sending military forces to Iraq.[20] Blair clung to office for another year amidst the growing unpopularity of the war before finally handing the reigns of office to his rival Gordon Brown.[21] Blair bet his political career on the war and lost.

The Costs of Isolation

The significance of the pervasive international rejection of the US-led war can scarcely be exaggerated. Global antiwar consciousness prevented Washington from winning UN support for its planned invasion of Iraq and undermined international confidence in US leadership. The international opposition curtailed the military involvement of a number of states, depriving the United States of military allies. The Bush administration squandered the international empathy and support that flowed to the United States in the wake of the terrorist attacks of September 2001. Former president Jimmy Carter wrote in 2003, "The heartfelt sympathy and friendship offered to America after the 9/11 attacks, even from formerly antagonistic regimes, has been largely dissipated; increasingly unilateral and domineering policies have brought international trust in our country to its lowest level in memory."[22] Washington was defeated in its attempt to win authorization for the use of force at the UN Security Council, and it was forced to bear the burden of the war and military occupation mostly on its own, with only Britain offering meaningful support.

Nor was Washington successful in gaining substantial financial support for Iraq's reconstruction. Secretary of Defense Donald Rumsfeld and others claimed that the costs of the war and the reconstruction of Iraq would be paid by Iraq and the international community,[23] but the war cost the US Treasury nearly 2 trillion dollars, financed through debt and by American taxpayers.[24] Having pushed ahead with the invasion against the advice of virtually the entire world, Washington was left largely on its own to pay the price and deal with the violent and chaotic aftermath.

The international coalition assembled by the Bush administration was a threadbare arrangement that provided Washington with little actual help. The so-called Multi-National Force gave the appearance of a partnership, but the heavy lifting of the war fell to American troops.[25] The US Army's official history of the war states that the coalition had "political and diplomatic value" but was "largely unsuccessful" at the operational level.[26] The Bush administration spoke of a coalition of the willing, but very few states were actually willing to offer meaningful help. In fact, the coalition was a diplomatic attempt to cloak US aggression, creating a façade of international support to hide Washington's diplomatic isolation. It diverted attention from the huge and ever-rising burden American troops faced in policing the occupation and fighting the insurgency that arose in response.

The coalition forces never amounted to much militarily even at their high point, with most of the participating states sending only a few hundred and in some cases a few dozen troops. Withdrawals from the coalition were many, starting with Spain in 2004, followed by Portugal, the Netherlands, and others in 2005 and Italy in 2006. Even Britain announced its plan to start withdrawing troops in early 2007. Few of the partners in Bush's coalition came to the defense of American troops in their battles with Sunni insurgents and Shiite militias. American troops did most of the actual fighting in the war and suffered 93 percent of the casualties: 4,504 killed, compared to 179 fatalities among British troops and 139 among all other participating forces.[27]

The UN Stands Firm

Opponents of the war were successful in pressuring the White House to seek authorization from the UN Security Council. This was a victory for the advocates of diplomacy and the rule of international law. Hard-liners in the administration would have preferred bypassing the Security Council and proceeding directly to military action, but the administration needed at least to appear to be seeking UN involvement to gain political legitimacy in Congress and elsewhere. Colin Powell argued that working through the UN to resume weapons inspections was necessary to build international support for administration policy.[28]

As the UN debate began in October 2002, France, Russia, and other members of the Security Council were successful in forcing substantial changes in the draft resolution submitted by the US and UK. Their initial draft demanded that Iraq submit to UN disarmament and allow renewed weapons inspections, but it also included language authorizing "all necessary means" if Iraq refused. Other members of the council demurred and offered alternative language that accepted the demand for disarmament and renewed inspections but made no reference to the use of force. The result-ing Security Council Resolution 1441 in November lacked the explicit authorization for military action that Washington and London had sought.[29] The absence of UN authority solidified pub-lic opposition to the war.

The White House claimed it had all the authority it needed to attack Iraq, but Blair insisted during a January meeting with Bush that a second UN resolution was necessary to give explicit backing for military action.[30] In mid-January, Blair's senior legal adviser, former Attorney General Lord Peter Goldsmith, sent a legal advi-sory to Downing Street that war without explicit Security Council authorization might not hold up under international legal chal-lenge.[31] Goldsmith was responding to a request from British mili-tary leaders for legal assurances that their participation in military action in Iraq would be permissible under international law. Blair needed a UN authorization vote to assure domestic political sup-port for the use of force, and he pressured a reluctant Bush to seek a new resolution. Bush grudgingly agreed and told the press he would welcome Security Council action if it came quickly.

When the United States and Britain returned to the Security Council in February and March for a second resolution seeking authority for war, they were decisively rebuffed. Not only France, Germany, and Russia, but six nonpermanent members—Chile, Mexico, Cameroon, Guinea, Angola, and Pakistan—refused to sup-port the US proposal. The opposition of the nonpermanent mem-bers was especially significant, given their political and economic dependence on the United States. Washington made determined efforts to twist their arms but to no avail.[32] Bush made personal calls to the leaders of several countries, including President Vicente Fox of Mexico, where antiwar sentiment ran as high as 83 percent, and President Ricardo Lagos of Chile.[33] Lagos told Bush that pub-lic opinion against war in Chile made him "reluctant to support the resolution."[34] At the end of its lobbying effort, the United States

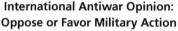

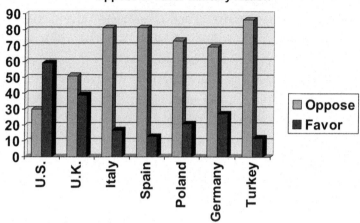

Source: Pew Global Attitudes Project, "America's Image Further Erodes, Europeans Want Weaker Ties" (questionnaire), 18 March 2003, www.pewresearch.org.

could only count on the votes of Britain, Bulgaria, and Spain. Rather than face the humiliation of such a meager showing, the White House withdrew the proposed resolution. This was a major victory for the global antiwar movement.

The cumulative impact of worldwide political opposition prevented the Bush administration from gaining Security Council support for its planned invasion and forced the administration to abandon efforts to win UN endorsement.[35] As a result, the United States and Britain stood practically alone in their drive for war. The importance of the Security Council rebuff to the United States is enormous. It was, according to scholar Immanuel Wallerstein, "the first time since the United Nations was founded that the United States, on an issue that mattered to it, could not get a majority on the Security Council."[36] The result was widely recognized as a humiliating political defeat for the supposed lone superpower. It represented a decisive loss of legitimacy and a fundamental weakening of US power and global standing. Many peace activists welcomed this outcome and hoped it might lead to greater military restraint in US policy for the future.

The interplay between the antiwar movement and the United Nations deserves special comment. Most UN officials and Security Council members were opposed to the war but were powerless to stop it. The UN Security Council by its very design is a captive of the permanent powers, and when its most powerful member is bent on military aggression, the UN has no capacity to prevent it. The most important power of the Security Council is its authority to confer international legitimacy. When it withholds consent, as it did in Iraq, it denies legitimacy. It was able to do so because of the worldwide antiwar movement. The lack of UN authority limited Washington's ability to forge a meaningful coalition for its occupation policy. Many nations as a matter of policy do not deploy troops abroad unless they are acting under a UN Security Council mandate. The council's highly visible refusal to grant that authority added to the illegitimacy of the war and diminished Bush's ability to assemble allies to carry out the mission.

A creative dialectic developed between the Security Council and global civil society. The public opposition to war hinged on the lack of UN authorization. The objection of the UN in turn depended on the strength of antiwar opposition. The stronger the antiwar movement in Germany, France, Mexico, and numerous other countries, the greater the determination of UN diplomats to resist US pressures. The stronger the objections at the UN, the greater the legitimacy and political impact of the antiwar movement.[37] It was a unique and unprecedented form of global political synergy. By defending the UN, despite its many shortcomings, and insisting upon international authorization for the use of force, the peace movement helped to build civil society opposition to war and strengthened respect for international law. Bush administration officials decried the United Nations for "failing its responsibilities" in Iraq, but for many in the antiwar movement the Security

Council's refusal to authorize the invasion was a shining moment for the organization. By standing up to Washington, the council displayed rare political courage and integrity and attempted to fulfill the mission for which it was created, to prevent war. It was one of the United Nations' finest hours.

This is not to suggest that the UN Security Council was blameless in its policies toward Iraq. The comprehensive trade sanctions imposed on Iraq during the 1990s at the behest of Washington and London caused vast suffering for innocent people and led to rising infant mortality and many preventable deaths among children and other vulnerable Iraqis.[38] Some activists and former UN officials blamed this disaster on the UN as an institution, but the United States and Britain were responsible for blocking efforts by other council members to lift or ease the sanctions.[39] It is also important to note that the Security Council allowed itself to become complicit in the occupation of Iraq when it agreed in Resolution 1483 (May 2003) to establish a UN mandate for supporting the "reconstruction" of Iraq and the creation of a new government, explicitly referring to the US and the UK as "occupying powers."[40]

If the US invasion of Iraq was an act of disregard for the war-prevention authority of the UN, the global civil society movement against the war was a dramatic affirmation of that authority. The UN Charter begins with the words "We the peoples," although the functioning of the organization depends on the action of states, particularly the permanent members of the Security Council. The framers of the organization hoped that it would grow to serve people in all nations and save them from the "scourge of war." During the Iraq War debate, peoples around the world cried out against war as never before and in so doing were voicing support for the organization's mission of peace.

There is a pattern here and a lesson for the future of the United Nations, one that is evident not only in matters of war and peace but in a wide range of issues related to human rights and development. The emergence of global civil society movements in recent decades has created new possibilities for advancing the principles of the UN Charter and the prospects for international cooperation. Activist networks and civil society groups have become prime movers in some of the most important and innovative efforts to address global challenges. They have articulated moral principles and political demands that in some cases have crystallized into policy. The cumulative effect of civil society activism has been to legitimize and build political support for peace, human rights, and international development.[41]

In the weeks before the invasion of Iraq, some wondered why Bush seemed to be in such a hurry to start the war. Why the indecent haste to attack when UN inspectors had just resumed their work and were gaining open access to Iraqi weapons sites? What motivated White House decisions to dismiss warnings from senior commanders and diplomatic advisers on the need for more troops and the likely steep costs of occupying the country? In the concluding chapter, I pursue these questions in order to both assess the costs and consequences of the administration's refusal to listen to the worldwide warning against war, and to evaluate the overall impact of the antiwar movement. I also highlight major lessons and findings from the movement and their implications for scholarship and future activism.

Eight

Evaluating the Antiwar Movement

Despite the unprecedented scale and scope of the antiwar movement—the largest antiwar demonstrations in history in a campaign of global dimensions—Bush ignored the pervasive opposition to war and rolled ahead with his preplanned invasion. Given the administration's determination to attack Saddam Hussein, the movement had little chance of halting the march to war. Nor was there much time available to organize the resistance in the United States. When United for Peace and Justice and Win Without War were launched in the fall of 2002, war was only a few months away. That the movement was able to do so much in such a short time was testament to the intensity and breadth of popular opposition. As UFPJ coordinator Leslie Cagan observed, people were shocked and outraged and feeling they had to register their dissent—and the movement gave them the opportunity. That's what happens during a genuine mass movement. People come forward in unexpectedly large numbers, giving of their time, money, and effort. They break out of their isolation and connect with others in an emotionally charged recognition of mutual concern and commitment. The Iraq movement was an exhilarating, powerful example of this social phenomenon. The vast antiwar outpouring was not sufficient to dissuade the unlistening White House, but it nonetheless persisted for years and had significant political impact.

In this final chapter I review how antiwar opposition shaped strategic decision making and contributed to the failures of US policy. I analyze the ways in which the rapid timetable for invasion was shaped by domestic political calculations and mounting public doubts about the war. I consider the implications of the US and British decisions to justify military action on the basis of false claims about weapons of mass destruction. I explore the significance of the Bush administration's decision to reject the advice of senior military commanders that more troops would be needed in Iraq, and the reasons for the administration's failure to plan for the postwar occupation.

It's easy to chalk up the appalling blunders of the White House to arrogance and delusional thinking, but it's also important to look at the political considerations that drove those fateful choices. Decisions to shortchange the military and downplay postwar planning served domestic political considerations and were a core element of the deception that was necessary to counter antiwar critics. To gain acceptance from a skeptical public, the Bush administration denied the likely costs of war. American troops and the Iraqi people paid with their lives for that subterfuge.

Why the Rush?

The White House launched its public relations campaign against Iraq in September 2002, just a couple months before the congressional midterm elections, part of a political strategy for Republican candidates to rally around the flag and win control of Congress, while distracting attention from criticisms of the administration's domestic policies. Scheduling the vote for the authorization to use force right before the November elections put Democrats in a quandary. If they voted against the authorization to use force, they would be accused of accommodating Saddam Hussein and being weak on defense. Members of Congress were coaxed into voting yes by assurances, subsequently proven false, that the president had not yet made up his mind on going to war. It was a cunning act of political manipulation to gain support for the use of military force.

The administration wanted to launch the invasion quickly so that the war would be over before the 2004 election, allowing Bush to campaign for reelection as a conquering war hero. His "mission accomplished" speech and triumphant swagger in the aftermath of the invasion helped to build his image, but the imagined benefits of overthrowing Saddam Hussein proved premature and short-lived, as the Iraq insurgency emerged and US casualties began to rise. Bush won a close vote for reelection, but the war issue was no help and actually cost him votes in some states.[1]

The president's haste in starting the war was also driven by concerns that the tide of public opinion was shifting against him. An August 2002 CNN/USA Today survey conducted by Gallup found public support for a ground invasion of Iraq declining steadily, down to just 53 percent, compared to 74 percent in November 2001 and 63 percent as recently as July 2002. Only 41 percent expressed support for military action that might have to last longer than a year. As Michael Mazarr writes, the window of opportunity in public opinion was closing.[2] Bush was under pressure to move quickly and promote the fiction of a short, low-cost war.

The president was also frustrated by the lack of international support. This was evident in a conversation between Bush and Condoleezza Rice in early January 2003, later recounted by Bob Woodward. The pressure campaign against Iraq "isn't holding together," the President lamented. The November consensus that produced Security Council Resolution 1441 "was beginning to fray." The attempt to use aggressive UN inspections against Saddam

Hussein was not working. Bush was infuriated by press reports of Iraqis opening up buildings for inspectors and saying "see, there's nothing here." He spoke as if the Iraqi leader was trying to trick him. "How is this happening?" Bush asked. "Saddam is going to get stronger." The president was clearly exasperated. "How long does he think I can do this? A year? I can't. The United States can't stay in this position while Saddam plays games with the inspectors." The Iraqi leader was "getting more confident, not less," he complained. "He can manipulate the international system again. We are not winning." He told Rice, "time is not on our side here."[3]

The longer Bush waited to start the war, the weaker he became politically. In his conversation with Rice, he noted that "the antiwar protests in European cities and in US would fortify Saddam and make them think the US would never invade." Bush recognized the political dilemma. The strategy and core message of the movement all along had been to argue for inspections, not war. The strategy was working, and UN monitors were returning to Iraq. Demanding more time for inspectors to verify and complete the disarmament process was the principal goal of opponents of the war in the streets and in the diplomatic corridors at the UN.

In a meeting with Blair and the prime ministers of Spain and Portugal on the eve of the invasion, Bush reiterated his concern about eroding public opinion and the timing of the war. He insisted there would be no further delay and said military action would start in a matter of days. If we wait longer, Bush warned, "public opinion won't get better, and it will get worse in some countries like America."[4]

The February 15 antiwar rallies around the world were indisputable evidence of that widespread public opposition and a significant blow to the case for war. The administration had already made its best argument for military action—the president's State of the Union address in January and Secretary of State Powell's presentation at the UN in early February—which produced a slight bump in the polls, but Gallup polling in late February showed support for military action drifting downward again.[5] Opinion surveys showed majorities in favor of giving UN inspections more time and opposed to an invasion without Security Council approval.[6] Activist groups were becoming stronger. Plans were underway for organizing additional rallies, concerts, and media campaigns. Opposition forces were gaining momentum.

Unable to win the argument for war, the administration had to cut off the public debate. The way to short-circuit dissent was to launch the bombers and send in the troops. Bush's answer to those who wanted to stop the war was to start the war. Moot the question. Rob the movement of its *raison d'être*.

Bypassing the UN

The White House timetable for war ran into obstacles at the UN. Bush and his inner circle were skeptical of seeking Security Council authority, but the administration needed UN involvement to gain political legitimacy in Congress and in the UK. UN backing was especially critical for Blair, who had to contend with many in the Labor Party who opposed the use of force and demanded working through the UN. Bush's decision in September 2002 to seek a new Security Council resolution was a direct response to that concern.[7]

To the surprise of many, and to the chagrin of war enthusiasts in Washington,[8] Baghdad immediately accepted the terms of Resolution 1441, at least partially, and opened its doors to UN weapons monitors. Inspectors from the UN Monitoring, Verification and Inspection Commission (UNMOVIC) and the International Atomic Energy Agency (IAEA) poured into the country and quickly began extensive operations to search for WMDs. On February 14, UNMOVIC and the IAEA publicly reported to the Security Council that their inspectors had received access to weapons sites in Iraq and so far had found no WMDs. UNMOVIC Executive Chairman Hans Blix stated, "So far, UNMOVIC has not found any such weapons."[9] He later wrote that UN technical experts conducted some 700 inspections of 500 different sites in the months before the war and reported no finds of WMDs.[10] Sitting next to Blix at the council meeting was IAEA Director General Mohamed ElBaradei, who gave a similar report: "We have to date found no evidence of ongoing prohibited nuclear or nuclear-related activities in Iraq."[11] Widely reported by the international press, the testimony of Blix and ElBaradei blew a gaping hole in Bush's claim of an imminent WMD threat, further complicating White House efforts to justify the use of force.[12]

Meanwhile, feverish diplomatic efforts were underway at the UN in search of a workable compromise to avoid war. Diplomats from France and Russia among other countries were close to brokering an agreement that would have allowed more time for inspections and diplomacy. A draft Security Council resolution emerged in March to establish specific disarmament benchmarks and a thirty-day timeline for Iraqi compliance. The proposal had the support of ten Security Council members and could have passed, but the Bush administration refused to consider it and brusquely swept aside all further diplomatic efforts.[13] The White House offered a one-week extension of its self-imposed deadline for war and then launched the invasion.

The WMD Gambit

There were many reasons the Bush administration offered for why it was necessary to use force in Iraq: Saddam Hussein's brutal repression of his people, the threat he posed to neighboring states, the supposed link between Baghdad and Al Qaida, the goal of creating a democratic Middle East. The overriding objective, however, was to "disarm the dictator." The emphasis on WMDs was a carefully calculated strategy to win political support for armed regime change. It was chosen not because it was the most imminent or plausible threat but because it conjured up an extreme danger. However baseless in fact, the claim of a WMD threat in Iraq was a powerful way of arousing public anxiety and mobilizing political support for the use of force, especially when the threat was amped up by linking it to Al Qaida. A steady stream of disinformation—uranium from Niger, aluminum tubes, defector reports—underlined the WMD danger, as did the indelible image of the mushroom cloud as a smoking gun. All were part of an appeal to fear, an elaborate deception designed to scare people into supporting extreme measures.

The political basis of the decision to focus on WMD was revealed publicly a few weeks after the invasion in a rare moment of unscripted candor from Deputy Defense Secretary Paul Wolfowitz. During an interview with *Vanity Fair* magazine, Wolfowitz acknowledged that the focus on weapons of mass destruction was a conscious decision: "The truth is that for reasons that have a lot to do with US government bureaucracy, we settled on the one issue that everyone could agree on, which was weapons of mass destruction as the core reason."[14] Wolfowitz's comment suggested that the administration was not fully confident of its ability to win the case for invasion on its merits. Rather than making a reasoned argument for the overthrow of a brutal tyrant, as Wolfowitz would have preferred, the administration appealed to base instinct, inciting the fear of nuclear-armed terrorism to mobilize political support. The tactic was successful in the short term, convincing many that Saddam Hussein had deadly weapons poised to use and hand off to Al Qaida. But the strategy backfired when White House claims were exposed as false.

A similar decision to focus on WMD issues unfolded in the UK, although there the government attempted to frame the argument in a moral context. In the face of the huge February protest in

London, Blair felt the need to intensify his efforts to win public support. The prime minister admitted to being "a bit worried" by the scale of the opposition, and his foreign minister, Jack Straw, later testified that he was "profoundly concerned" about the march. The London demonstration occurred on the very day of Blair's speech at the annual Labor Party conference in Glasgow, where the prime minister faced a cool reception from party members as he tried to make the case for war. Blair was relentless in the weeks leading up to the invasion, saturating the airwaves and newspaper pages with his "moral appeal," arguing that the WMD threat necessitated the use of force. He led five major House of Commons debates and constantly addressed the issue in weekly "question time" sessions. On many days leading up to the invasion, a senior editor of *The Times* remarked, Blair did "virtually nothing else but speak" about the threat from Iraq.[15]

Blair was able to win the vote in Parliament, but he never gained a public majority in support of waging a war without UN backing. The problem for Blair, scholar James Strong wrote, was that attempting to justify unprovoked armed invasion on ethical and legal grounds was "logically impossible."[16] Because viable alternatives to the use of force were underway, with new diplomatic measures in preparation at the Security Council, the use of force was not a last resort. The subsequent official British inquiry known as the Chilcot Report concluded, "at the time of the Parliamentary vote of 18 March, diplomatic options had not been exhausted. The point had not been reached where military action was the last resort."[17]

As Bush and Blair tried to make the case for military action, a steady drumbeat of contrary arguments and warnings of impending disaster came from opponents of the invasion. When the WMD threat was disproved after the invasion, the foundation of the case for war collapsed. Blair admitted in his political memoir that the absence of WMD "seemed to disintegrate the *casus belli*."[18]

In the view of respected analysts, the decision to wage war without Security Council approval was a violation of ethical and legal standards for the use of force.[19] The International Commission of Jurists issued a statement in March 2003 condemning the invasion as an illegal "war of aggression."[20] A 2010 Dutch Inquiry Report argued that the decision to use force in Iraq "had no basis in international law" and contravened the UN Charter.[21] Article 2 and Chapter VII of the Charter prohibit states from using force against another sovereign state except when necessary for self-defense against an attack or when authorized by the Security Council. Neither condition applied in the case of Iraq. UN Secretary General Kofi Annan stated in 2004 that the US and British use of force without Security Council approval was "not in conformity with the UN Charter. From our point of view and from the Charter point of view it was illegal."[22]

Explaining Defeat

The disingenuous political arguments for going to war were partly responsible for the disastrous outcome of the conflict. By focusing constantly on the WMD issue, Bush avoided the realities of regime change and refused to plan for the likely scale of the war and its aftermath. He and Secretary of Defense Rumsfeld ignored warnings from senior military leaders and diplomats about the enormous challenge of trying to take over and control Iraq. Rumsfeld admits in his memoir that US commanding general Tommy Franks requested a force of 450,000 troops, but the secretary ordered a force one third that size.[23] Franks was frustrated and angry. After a call, in which Rumsfeld demanded an even smaller invasion force, Franks hung up the phone and "sputtered a few expletives," according to journalist Robert Draper.[24] Other senior commanders were also upset, including former Marine Corps commandant General James L. Jones.[25] Rumsfeld refused to listen to the generals and repeatedly questioned, delayed, and deleted their requests for additional troops.

Army Chief of Staff General Eric Shinseki went public on the eve of the invasion, testifying to the Senate Armed Services Committee that "several hundred thousand troops would be needed in Iraq." Shinseki was castigated for telling the truth and was publicly rebuked by Wolfowitz, who told reporters the general's remarks were "wildly off the mark."[26] Shinseki was marginalized by the White House during his remaining months of service, but he was later vindicated when Obama appointed him to his cabinet as secretary of veterans affairs.

Administration efforts to lowball the war effort and underplay the likely risks were the result of several factors, including hubris and a belief that the Iraq operation would be as swift and relatively effortless as the military takeover of Afghanistan, but the underestimation of required sacrifice also had a political purpose. Just as Bush dissembled about having an open mind on the war to convince members of Congress to authorize the use of force, Rumsfeld shortchanged the military, saying the war would be quick and easy in order to quiet dissent. In the face of persistent questions and rising domestic and international opposition, the administration rushed ahead with the invasion and promoted the fiction of a war that would be won easily at low cost.

A similar purpose motivated the administration's failure to plan for the aftermath of the invasion and the costs and difficulties of occupying Iraq. As many analysts have observed, postwar planning for Iraq was atrociously flawed and incomplete. "In fact it was unconscionable," writes Brookings analyst Michael O'Hanlon. The reason for the failure was "the administration's desire to portray the Iraq war as a relatively easy undertaking in order to assure domestic and international support."[27] Draper makes a similar point in explaining why Bush ordered a delay in setting up a postwar planning office. He did so out of fear that leaks about its existence would undercut diplomatic efforts.[28] The political imperative of portraying the invasion as a short, simple operation contributed to decisions that undermined the mission.

The US Army's official history of the Iraq War determined that the war was a strategic defeat. In the conclusion to its 1,300-page two-volume study, the report acknowledges the "failure of the United States to attain its strategic objectives in Iraq."[29] The study confirms the conclusions of other military experts that the war was a fiasco and a historic loss for the United States.[30] The analysis identifies many reasons for this failure but singles out one factor above all, the lack of a sufficient number of troops.

It may seem like an excuse for military analysts to blame their loss on a lack of troops, but the concern about inadequate forces was registered in advance and raised often during official meetings before the war. The authors of the army report repeatedly hammer home the point. "Strategic defeat was almost assured by artificial constraints" of combat power and the "overall shortage of ground forces." Commanders had "too few troops to accomplish their military missions." At "no point in the war, even during the surge, did US commanders have enough forces at their disposal." The report takes direct aim at what it called a "short-war assumption," noting that US leaders "deluded themselves about the length of commitment required." The army analysis does not attempt to explain the reasons for the decision to limit the number of troops, but it traces the motivation to "domestic political considerations."[31]

Those considerations included the strategy of minimizing likely costs to win political support for the war. Overconfidence and self-deception were certainly factors, but these were fed by the political imperative of trying to win public support and counter widespread popular skepticism. To admit otherwise and acknowledge the required sacrifices would have empowered antiwar critics. A larger and longer war, as military advisers said was necessary, would have been harder to sell politically. Members of Congress might have been less willing to issue a blank check for military action. The public opposition to war would have been greater. To avoid further opposition and political resistance, the administration had to maintain the façade of a quick, low-cost mission. An American official who was involved in the planning for occupation explained this dynamic in an interview with George Packer for the *New Yorker*: "that's the political logic that works against advance planning."[32] To maintain the false assurances that were necessary to win political support for military action, the administration short-circuited preparations for the conduct of the war and its bloody aftermath.

Decisions made as a response to domestic antiwar pressures contributed to strategic defeat in Iraq. Failure was also the result of international opposition to the war and the resulting lack of meaningful military contributions from allies, as examined in Chapter Seven. Weak or nonexistent political support domestically and internationally limited military capabilities and significantly affected the outcome of the war.

The administration's deceit in justifying the invasion set the context for political opposition to the occupation. The antiwar movement's steady drumbeat of criticism about the lack of justification for war laid the groundwork for the Bush administration's subsequent political vulnerability. Postwar revelations of faulty intelligence and flawed assumptions undermined confidence in the administration's foreign policy. As the legitimacy and credibility of US assertions diminished, the administration's doctrine of military preemption suffered a well-deserved setback. Awareness that the White House had misled the country into war weakened the president's political standing and emboldened his opponents to demand the withdrawal of troops. This set the stage for Democratic Party victories in the 2006 congressional elections and the rise of the Obama candidacy. The peace movement played an important role in all of these developments.

Winners and Losers

War is never solely about military results, said Clausewitz. It is an extension of politics, a means of realizing specific political aims. For the Bush administration the war was intended to counter terrorism, validate its doctrine of unilateral preemption, and extend US domination over the oil-rich Middle East. In all these areas the war was a failure. It increased rather than decreased the terrorist threat. It demonstrated the folly of preemptive war fought without international support, and it grossly overburdened and weakened the US military. The political legitimacy of American leadership suffered major setbacks at the international level and domestically. The WMD deception and manipulation of public opinion created a further corrosive effect on government credibility, which was already tarnished from Vietnam and was now torn to shreds. The result was a weakening of the institutions of American democracy. The disregard for truth and reasoned debate now roiling American politics are the result of many developments, but the wholesale deceit of the Bush administration in waging an unjustified war in Iraq was surely a contributing factor.

Iraq itself suffered grievously from the war. Estimates of the number of war-related Iraqi deaths range from hundreds of thousands to more than a million.[33] In the fragile political structure that emerged in Baghdad under the US occupation, political power shifted decisively to the Shia majority and political parties and leaders closely aligned with Tehran. A gruesome civil war broke out, fomented by Washington's shortsighted emphasis on sectarian politics and the nihilist strategy of Al Qaida in Iraq. This was followed by the rise of ISIS, the intensification of sectarian violence, and the spread of war into Syria and beyond. The diversion of US resources to Iraq meanwhile undermined the prospects for success in Afghanistan and contributed to the US defeat there.

Ironically, the big winner of the Iraq War was Iran. Tehran gained a huge security advantage with the overthrow of its archenemy Saddam Hussein. Iranian officials developed and maintained widespread influence in Iraq through many social networks within the country's Shia power structure and religious and cultural institutions.[34] With its Iraq folly, the Bush administration ended up strengthening its declared enemy. The US Army study concluded by stating "Iran appears to be the only victor" in the war.[35]

The ways in which social movements influence policy are not always readily apparent. They often emerge in unanticipated form or have impacts far into the future. "It is always too early to calculate effect," Rebecca Solnit observed.[36] We can never know today how our actions may influence events tomorrow. Movements can win even as they appear to lose. While the antiwar movement did not succeed in preventing the invasion of Iraq, it helped set the terms of the debate and exerted decisive influence on public opinion. The Bush administration rammed through its war policy, but it was unable to win the larger and more important struggle for hearts and minds at home and abroad. The White House lost the war politically before it ever began militarily.

As noted in Chapter Six, social movements at times intertwine with institutional politics. The "party in the streets" can exert pressure and shape public opinion, but its influence on political decision making is often indirect and indeterminate. Movements engage in politics to help elect political leaders, but politicians rarely fulfill all their promises and often act in ways that frustrate those who support them. The antiwar movement helped to forge a Democratic Party consensus for withdrawal, but it had little say over how that goal was achieved, as the war continued and even expanded with Bush's surge policy. The withdrawal of troops dragged on for three years after Obama was elected. His policies of drone warfare and expanded military intervention in Afghanistan disappointed many peace activists. The movement made little or no progress on the larger agenda of creating a more peaceful US foreign policy.

The effects of social movements on political culture can be significant but are difficult to measure. The agony of the American military defeat in Southeast Asia led to the Vietnam syndrome, as Americans turned against war and foreign military intervention. In fact, Colin Powell enunciated principles derived from that experience for constraining when and how force could be used. These included having the support of the American people and broad international backing. These cautionary guidelines were cast aside in Bush's rush to war after 9/11. In the crucible of the political struggle over Iraq, however, a new syndrome emerged, an "Iraq syndrome," as Tom Hayden called it. Today we can perhaps speak of a broader Iraq-Afghanistan syndrome. After the fall of Kabul and the strategic defeat in Iraq, the policies of military intervention and nation building have lost political support and legitimacy.

The shadow of Iraq was manifest in the August 2013 British and US debate over air strikes against Syria following the use of chemical weapons by the Assad government. As the UK contemplated a possible military response, Prime Minister David Cameron asked for authorization from Parliament. In itself, this was unusual since there is no constitutional precedent or requirement for such action in Britain. Even more unexpected was the decision in the House of Commons to reject the use of force by a 295-272 vote. This was the first time a government request for parliamentary authority to use force overseas had been denied since 1782.[37] Labor leader David Miliband explained: "People are deeply concerned about the chemical weapons attacks in Syria, but they want us to learn the lessons of Iraq."[38] The ghost of Tony Blair loomed large over the debate. In Washington a stunned White House vowed initially to proceed with military action, but Obama decided at the last minute to seek a vote in Congress. With strong opposition emerging in the House of Representatives,[39] demonstrators marching in front of the White House, and polls showing Americans opposed to armed intervention,[40] the administration postponed the vote and deferred military action, negotiating with Russia an agreement to send UN monitors to verify and dismantle Syrian chemical weapons. This was the antiwar formula of "inspections not war" reappearing in a new context.[41]

The long struggle against the war in Iraq and US failures there and in Afghanistan reshaped the American political landscape. In the immediate aftermath of 9/11, the mood of the country was angry and vengeful. Politicians did not pay a price for being hawkish and advocating military action. On the contrary, liberals feared they would be the ones to suffer politically if they did not support Bush's open-ended authorization to use force. During the course of the war, however, as movement pressures continued, the fraudulent case for war was exposed, and military setbacks mounted, the political climate shifted. Military intervention and nation building became politically toxic. The meme to "end endless war" began as a MoveOn bumper sticker but gradually entered the political mainstream. Even Donald Trump for all his madness was a critic of the Iraq and Afghan wars and set a timetable for pulling US forces out of Afghanistan. President Biden's decision to withdraw troops followed Trump's script and was a decisive turning point in ending the war. Many criticized the abrupt and chaotic process of the final days in Kabul, but there was no significant political opposition to withdrawing US troops. Polls showed public approval of the decision to leave.[42]

In the final analysis, the arguments of the Iraq antiwar movement were proven correct: there was no evidence of WMDs, UN inspections and sanctions were working, and invading and occupying the country would lead to chaos and an increase in terrorist violence. Those of us who opposed the war were right in warning political leaders of the dangers ahead, especially the perils of acting without UN authorization or the support of allies. We were right in arguing that the war was a violation of ethical standards and had no basis in international law. They should have listened to us.

Tens of millions of people across the planet protested, communicated, and organized politically to register their opposition to war. People from every walk of life and occupation (even members of the military), of multiple nationalities and ethnic origins, expressing many faiths and moral values—all stood together in a vast mosaic of protest and political mobilization across the United States and the world, united in rejecting war. Reflecting distinct identities, speaking many languages, and employing diverse cultural symbols, opponents of the war formed a global "rainbow coalition." They were motivated by sometimes divergent and often conflicting political beliefs and interests, but the separate social sectors were able to unite on a common agenda for peace, agreeing to focus on the common menace of a reckless military adventure and its negative consequences. The movement was an expression of cosmopolitan consciousness and universal morality, of worldwide opposition to an unjustified war.

That Bush was able to defy world opinion and push ahead with the invasion is a sad commentary on the failures of democracy, especially on matters of war and peace. As long as the military–industrial system maintains its grip on political decision making in Washington, the dangers of war will persist. So will the need for social mobilization, resistance to war, and advocacy for more peaceful means of resolving conflicts and building human security. The experience of the Iraq antiwar movement holds many lessons that can inform that effort and motivate future peace campaigns. The movement mobilized and spread its message on a global scale and achieved unprecedented legitimacy. Opponents of the war generated political pressures that eventually ended the conflict, demonstrating the power of social action to shape the course of history. The challenge for the future is to build on and learn lessons from that experience and maintain persistent pressure and advocacy for more peaceful foreign policies.

Acknowledgments

This book is the collective enterprise of many individuals and institutions. My greatest debt is to the Fourth Freedom Forum, the private foundation I led for seventeen years and whose board of trustees I chair. The Forum supported the research on nuclear disarmament, cooperative nonmilitary security strategies, and sanctions and weapons inspections in Iraq that formed the basis of our opposition to the Bush administration's war policy. The Forum produced reports on alternatives to the use of force in Iraq and hosted consultations that led to the formation of Win Without War as a vehicle for expressing opposition to the war. Alistair Millar, the Forum's president, played a central role in these consultations and in the research and writing that led to the initial edition of this book, a 2004 special report produced by the Fourth Freedom Forum. Linda Gerber, chief operating officer of the Forum, provided research and editing support for that initial edition and assisted in the production of this volume. I am also indebted to Jennifer Glick, former publications director at the Forum, and Ruth Miller, former executive assistant, who assisted with production of that initial volume. I owe special gratitude to the Forum's founder and longtime chair, Howard S. Brembeck, a successful business executive and entrepreneur who used his wealth to create the Fourth Freedom Forum to fulfill FDR's vision of freedom from fear through the prevention of war and terrorism.

I am indebted to the University of Notre Dame's Kroc Institute for International Peace Studies in the Keough School of Global Affairs. George A. Lopez, the Institute's former director of policy studies and senior fellow, partnered with me in writing half a dozen books on UN Security Council sanctions and co-authoring the reports on nonmilitary security strategies in Iraq that led to the founding of Win Without War and the writing of this book. I am also grateful for the support of the Kroc Institute's current leadership and staff: Asher Kaufman, director; Erin Corcoran, executive director; Juan Flores Ramirez, assistant director for finance and administration; Hannah Heinzekehr, communications director; and staff colleagues Jeanine Dziak and Kristi Flaherty.

I benefitted enormously in this and all my work in recent decades from the encouragement and support of Scott Appleby, former director of the Kroc Institute and dean of the Keough School of Global Affairs.

I am grateful to Emeritus Professor Sidney Tarrow at Cornell University, distinguished scholar of contentious politics and social movements, for inviting me to a graduate student seminar on the initial edition of the book, and encouraging this project to update, expand and fully develop my analysis of the Iraq antiwar movement. I am thankful to sociologist David S. Meyer for writing the foreword for the book.

Many colleagues contributed ideas and comments in support of the research and writing of this volume: Tom Andrews and Stephen Miles, past and current directors of Win Without War; Leslie Cagan and Bill Fletcher, former co-chairs of United for Peace and Justice; Steve Cobble, former political director, and Jack Odell, former international affairs director, of the National Rainbow Coalition; Lynn Erskine, former coordinator of the Win Without War coalition; Van Gosse, professor of history at Franklin Marshall College and former organizing director of Peace Action; Eli Parser and Tom Matzzie, former campaigns directors of MoveOn; Gerard Powers, director of Catholic peacebuilding studies at the Kroc Institute; Susan Shaer, former executive director of Women's Action for New Directions and co-chair of Win Without War; Celeste Kennel Shank, former student activist at Goshen College; Duane Shank, former senior policy adviser at Sojourners; Maggie Shum, research associate, Keough School of Global Affairs; and Jim Wallis, co-founder and former president of Sojourners.

Also contributing to the work of producing this book were Amir Amirani, Medea Benjamin, Ron Carver, Gene Case, Melissa Daar Carvajal, Sylvia Rodriguez Case, Rory Fanning, David Fenton, Gary Ferdman, Robert Greenwald, Bill Hartung, Anne Hayner, Jonathan Hutto, Marilyn Katz, Ben Manski, Dana Moss, Laurel Quinn, Karl Shelly, Art Silverman, and Bill Zimmerman. I am grateful to all who were interviewed for the book and who agreed to share their recollections and insights about the movement. I benefitted greatly from their wisdom, but the responsibility for errors and misperceptions that undoubtedly exist in these pages is mine alone.

I offer heartfelt thanks to Elizabeth Rankin and Kristen Wall, each of whom meticulously reviewed and edited the manuscript and provided many editorial corrections and substantive suggestions that enormously improved the quality of the text and the coherence of the analysis. I am also thankful to Lynne Elizabeth, founding director of New Village Press, who agreed to publish the book and provided important guidance in bringing this project to fruition.

Most of all I am grateful to Karen Jacob, life partner and colleague in the struggle for peace, who provided constant support and encouragement throughout the long process of writing and producing this volume. Karen always inspires and gives me hope that peace is possible and that in concert with the many millions of others who share our vision we can build a more peaceful world.

Notes

Introduction

1. Estimates of the number of demonstrators at antiwar events
   mentioned here are drawn from the website of United for
   Peace and Justice, the largest grassroots peace coalition in the
   United States. The UFPJ web archive is available at the Library
   of Congress. Researchers for *We Are Many,* the documentary film
   about the Iraq war protests in 2003, found evidence of demon-
   strations in 789 cities in 72 countries and claims of more than
   30 million total demonstrators. See Amir Amirani, dir., *We Are
   Many,* 2014, Amirani Media, www.wearemany.com. For newspa-
   per accounts of the protests, see Angelique Chrisafis et al.,
   "Threat of War: Millions Worldwide Rally for Peace," *Guardian*
   (London), 17 February 2003, 6; Glenn Frankel, "Millions
   Worldwide Protest Iraq War," *Washington Post,* 16 February 2003,
   A1; Alan Lowell, "1.5 Million Demonstrators in Cities Across
   Europe Oppose a War in Iraq," *New York Times,* 16 Febru-
   ary 2003, A20. Crowd size estimates are often uncertain as
   noted in Chapter Two. The recently established Crowd
   Counting Consortium (CCC) has developed more objective,

academically consistent methodologies for estimating crowd sizes.

2. Barbara Epstein, "Notes on the Antiwar Movement," *Monthly Review* 55, no. 3 (July–August 2003): 109.

3. For a firsthand account, see Andrew Murray and Lindsey German, *Stop the War: The Story of Britain's Biggest Mass Movement* (London: Bookmarks Publications, 2005).

4. Mark LeVine, "The Peace Movement Plans for the Future," *Middle East Report Online*, 15 July 2003, https://merip.org.

5. Stephen Gill, *Power and Resistance in the New World Order* (London: Palgrave, 2003), 218.

6. Moisés Naim, *The End of Power: From Boardrooms to Battlefields and Churches to States, Why Being in Charge Isn't What It Used to Be* (New York: Basic Books, 2013).

7. David Cortright, *Soldiers in Revolt: GI Resistance during the Vietnam War* (Chicago: Haymarket Books, 2005); Ron Carver, David Cortright, and Barbara Doherty, eds., *Waging Peace in Vietnam: U.S. Soldiers and Veterans Who Opposed the War* (New York: New Village Press, 2019).

8. David Cortright, *Peace Works: The Citizen's Role in Ending the Cold War* (Boulder, CO: Westview Press, 1993).

9. Rebecca Solnit, "Acts of Hope: Challenging Empire on the World Stage," *Mother Jones*, 14 June 2005, www.motherjones.com.

10. Todd Gitlin, *The Whole World Is Watching: Mass Media in the Making and Unmaking of the New Left* (Berkeley: University of California Press, 2003).

11. Solnit, "Acts of Hope."

12. Kate Hudson, "Reflecting on the Recent Anti-War Movement," *Contemporary Politics* 13, no. 4 (December 2007), 380.

13. Michael Walzer, "The Right Way," *New York Review of Books*, 13 March 2003, https://nybooks.com.

14. Patrick E. Tyler, "Threats and Responses: News Analysis; A New Power in the Streets," *New York Times*, 17 February 2003, A1.

15. Jonathan Schell, "The Other Superpower," *The Nation*, 27 March 2003, www.thenation.com.
16. Geoffrey Nunberg, "As Google Goes, So Goes the Nation," *New York Times*, 18 May 2003, sec. 4, 4.
17. Schell, "The Other Superpower."
18. Colonel Joel D. Rayburn and Colonel Frank K. Sobchak, eds., *The U.S. Army in the Iraq War*, Volume 2: *Surge and Withdrawal* (Carlisle Barracks, PA: Strategic Studies Institute/U.S. Army War College Press, 2019).

Chapter One: A War Predetermined

1. Arthur M. Schlesinger Jr., *War and the American Presidency* (New York: W. W. Norton, 2004); and Ivan Eland, *War and the Rogue Presidency* (Oakland, CA: Independent Institute, 2019).
2. Michael T. Heaney and Fabio Rojas, *Party in the Street: The Antiwar Movement and the Democratic Party after 9/11* (New York: Cambridge University Press, 2015), 7.
3. Hannah Hartig and Carroll Doherty, "Two Decades Later, the Enduring Legacy of 9/11," Pew Research Center, 2 September 2021, www.pewresearch.org.
4. J. Bryan Hehir, "What Can Be Done? What Should Be Done?" *America*, 8 October 2001, www.americamagazine.org.
5. The United States Department of Justice, Civil Rights Division, *Combatting Post-9/11 Discriminatory Backlash: Enforcement and Outreach*, 6 August 2015, www.justice.gov.
6. Bob Wing, interview by author, 14 November 2003.
7. George Packer, "Smart-Mobbing the War," *New York Times Magazine*, 9 March 2003, 46.
8. Janet Thomas, *The Battle in Seattle: The Story Behind and Beyond the WTO Demonstrations* (Golden, CO: Fulcrum Publishing, 2000); Erica Chenoweth, *Civil Resistance: What Everyone Needs to Know* (New York: Oxford University Press, 2021), 142–43.

9. Leslie Cagan, interview by author, 26 August 2003.

10. Significant portions of the document were printed in the *New York Times* and the *Washington Post*. See Patrick E. Tyler, "U.S. Strategy Plan Calls for Insuring No Rivals Develop a One-Superpower World: Pentagon's Document Outlines Ways to Thwart Challenges to Primacy of America," *New York Times*, 8 March 1992, www.nytimes.com; and Barton Gellman, "Keeping the U.S. First; Pentagon Would Preclude a Rival Superpower," *Washington Post*, 11 March 1992, A1.

11. Steven R. Weisman, "A New Doctrine; Pre-emption: Idea with a Lineage Whose Time Has Come," *New York Times*, 23 March 2003, B1.

12. Project for a New American Century, "Letter to President Clinton on Iraq," 26 January 1998, https://www.noi.org/wp-content/uploads/2016/01/iraqclintonletter1998-01-26-Copy.pdf.

13. Bob Woodward, *Bush at War* (New York: Simon and Schuster, 2002), 99.

14. Joel Roberts, "Plans for Iraq Attack Began on 9/11," 4 September 2002, www.cbsnews.com.

15. Woodward, *Bush at War*, 49.

16. All quotations from Bruce Riedel, "9/11 and Iraq: The Making of a Tragedy," *Lawfare*, 11 September 2021, www.lawfareblog.com.

17. Bob Woodward, *Plan of Attack: The Definitive Account of the Decision to Invade Iraq* (New York: Simon & Schuster, 2004), 81.

18. PBS News Hour, "Text of Downing Street Memo," 16 June 2005, www.pbs.org.

19. Recounted in Michael J. Mazarr, *Leap of Faith: Hubris, Negligence, and America's Greatest Foreign Policy Tragedy* (New York: Public Affairs, 2019), 235–236.

20. Ole R. Holsti, *American Public Opinion on the Iraq War* (Ann Arbor: University of Michigan Press, 2011), 133.

21. Dean Acheson, *Present at the Creation: My Years in the State Department* (New York: W. W. Norton, 1969), 374–75.

22. See the Congressional Research Service report, *Congressional Restrictions on U.S. Military Operations in Vietnam, Cambodia, Laos, Somalia, and Kosovo: Funding and Non-Funding Approaches*, 16 January 2007, CRS-6, https://sgp.fas.org.

23. Public Law 105-235, 105th Cong., 2d sess. (14 August 1998) [*Iraqi Liberation Act of 1998*]; and Public Law 105-338, 105th Cong., 2d sess. (31 October 1998) [*Iraqi Breach of International Obligations*].

24. Miles A. Pomper, "Bush Hopes to Avoid Battle with Congress over Iraq," *Congressional Quarterly Weekly* 60, no. 33 (31 August 2002): 2252.

25. Miles A. Pomper, "Senate Democrats in Disarray After Gephardt's Deal on Iraq," *Congressional Quarterly Weekly* 60, no. 38 (5 October 2002): 2606–07.

26. Jim VandeHei and Juliet Eilperin, "Congress Passes Iraq Resolution," *Washington Post*, 11 October 2002, A1.

27. Andrew Taylor, "Though Neither Party is Crying 'Politics,' Election Year Puts War Vote on Fast Track," *Congressional Quarterly Weekly* 60, no. 34 (7 September 2002): 2317; and Gebe Martinez, "Democratic Group Finds Tough Sell in Go-Slow Approach to War," *Congressional Quarterly Weekly* 60, no. 37 (28 September 2002): 2500. Four-to-one constituent message statistic provided by Win Without War staffer Lynn Erskine, email message to author, 22 December 2003.

28. Jane Kellett Cramer, "Militarized Patriotism: Why the U.S. Marketplace of Ideas Failed Before the Iraq War," *Security Studies* 16, no. 3 (2007): 490–492, doi: 10.1080/09636410701547949.

29. Louis Fisher, "Deciding on War against Iraq: Institutional Failures," *Political Science Quarterly* 118, no. 3 (Fall 2003): 391.

30. PBS Frontline, "The 2002 Vote on Iraq," 12 October 2004, www.pbs.org.

31. Woodward, *Plan of Attack*, 100.

32. Mazarr, *Leap of Faith*, 398.

33. Brent Scowcroft, "Don't Attack Saddam," *Wall Street Journal*, 15 August 2002, www.wsj.com.

34. Col. Ann Wright (ret.) and Susan Dixon, *Dissent: Voices of Conscience* (Kihei, HI: Koa Books, 2008), 117.

35. Eric Boehlert, "'I'm not sure which planet they live on,'" *Salon*, 17 October 2002, www.salon.com.

36. General Anthony Zinni, "They've Screwed Up," *60 Minutes*, CBS, 21 May 2004, quoted in Wright, *Dissent*, 116.

37. Thomas E. Ricks, "Desert Caution," *Washington Post*, 28 January 2003, C1.

38. David Margolick, "The Night of the Generals," *Vanity Fair*, April 2007, https://archive.vanityfair.com; Robert Draper, *To Start a War: How the Bush Administration Took America into Iraq* (New York: Penguin Books, 2020), 188–190.

39. The ad appeared in the *New York Times* on 26 September 2002. Among the signers were John J. Mearsheimer and Robert Pape, University of Chicago; Robert Jervis, Columbia University; Stephen M. Walt, Harvard University; and Kenneth N. Waltz, Columbia University.

40. William J. Broad, "41 Nobel Laureates Sign Declaration Against a War Without International Support," *New York Times*, 28 January 2003, A12.

41. William J. Burns, "How We Tried to Slow the Rush to War in Iraq," *Politico*, 13 March 2019, www.politico.com.

Chapter Two: Building the Movement

1. Tom Hayden, *Ending the War in Iraq* (New York: Akashic Books, 2007), 117.

2. Todd Gitlin, "Who Will Lead?" *Mother Jones*, 14 October 2002, www.motherjones.com.

3. David Corn, "Behind the Placards: The Odd and Troubling Origins of Today's Antiwar Movement," *LA Weekly*, 1–7 November 2002.

4. Edith Kaplan, "A Hundred Peace Movements Bloom," *The Nation*, 6 January 2003, www.thenation.com.

5. Cited in Karin Simonson, "The Anti-war Movement: Waging Peace on the Brink of War," Programme on NGOs and Civil Society of the Centre for Applied Studies in International Negotiation, Geneva, March 2003, https://ethz.ch.

6. Michael Wilson, "Thousands at Central Park Rally Oppose an Iraq War," *New York Times*, 7 October 2002, www.nytimes.com.

7. Chris Hedges, "A Long-time Antiwar Activist, Escalating the Peace," *New York Times*, 4 February 2003, B2.

8. Cagan, interview.

9. Ibid.

10. Holsti, *Public Opinion*, 36

11. Van Gosse, "February 15, 2003 in New York: A Preliminary Assessment," 17 February 2003, www.historiansagainstwar.org /feb15van.html.

12. Cagan, interview.

13. Heaney and Rojas, *Party in the Street*, 134.

14. Heaney and Rojas, *Party in the Street*, 156.

15. Hayden, *Ending the War in Iraq*, 126–27.

16. There is an inherent tendency for activists to exaggerate and for the press and government sources to underestimate the size of crowds at antiwar protest rallies. Crowd counting methodology has advanced significantly in recent years, largely due to the work of the Crowd Counting Consortium established by Jeremy Pressman and Erica Chenoweth.

17. Crowd estimates based on Heaney and Rojas, *Party in the Street*, 252–256; Hayden, *Ending the War in Iraq*, 126.

18. Quoted in Brad Knickerbocker, "Whither All the War Protesters?", *Christian Science Monitor*, 19 January 2007, www.csmonitor .com.

19. Hayden, *Ending the War in Iraq*, 127.

20. George H.W. Bush, "Remarks to the American Legislative Exchange Council," 1 March 1991, *Public Papers of the President of the United States: George H. W. Bush, Book 1*, www.govinfo.gov.

21. Hayden, *Ending the War in Iraq*, 23–26.

22. Heaney and Rojas, *Party in the Street*, 156.

23. Bill Fletcher, interview by author, 16 December 2003.

24. Kevin Martin, interview by author, 4 December 2003.

25. Amirani, *We Are Many*.

26. Glenn Kessler and Mike Allen, "Bush Faces Increasingly Poor Image Overseas," *Washington Post*, 24 February 2003, A01; CNN, "Poll: U.S. More a Threat Than Iraq," 11 February 2003, http://edition.cnn.com/2003/WORLD/europe/02/11/british.survey/.

27. BBC, "Huge Antiwar Protest in Florence," BBC News, 9 November 2002, www.bbc.com.

28. Knickerbocker, "Whither All the War Protesters?"

29. Crowd estimates in this paragraph drawn from Bill Weinberg, "Antiwar Around the World," Global Movement Against War: Taking it to the Streets, *Nonviolent Activist* 20, no. 2 (March–April 2003): 5, 9. See also Norm Dixon, "The Largest Coordinated Antiwar Protest in History," Scoop [New Zealand] 20 February 2003, www.scoop.co.nz.

30. Hudson, "Reflecting," 379.

31. Steve Cobble, email message to author, 14 December 2003.

32. Hudson, "Reflecting," 385–86.

33. Dennis Ellam, "Protest Virgins," *Sunday Mirror*, 16 February 2003. www.mirror.co.uk.

34. Matthew Parris, "Forgotten, Ignored, Scared. And On the March Today," *The Times*, 15 February 2003, www.thetimes.co.uk.

35. James R. Strong, *Public Opinion, Legitimacy and Tony Blair's War in Iraq* (London: Routledge, 2017), 50, 126.

36. Strong, *Public Opinion*, 42–43.

37. James Tapper, "Proof that Blair Is Bush's 'Poodle' . . . President Calls Him 'My Boy,'" *The Daily Mail*, 22 July 2006, www.dailymail.co.uk.

38. James Naughtie, "How Tony Blair Came to Be So Unpopular," BBC News, 9 July 2016, www.bbc.com.

39. Guinness World Records, https://guinnessworldrecords.com.

40. Timothy Sayle, "But he has nothing on at all!", *Canadian Military History* 19, no. 4 (2010), Art. 2., 5–19.

41. For a portrait of MoveOn, see Michelle Goldberg, "MoveOn Moves Up," Salon, 1 December 2003, www.salon.com.

42. Heaney and Rojas, *Party in the Street*, 134.

43. Gary Ferdman, interview by author, 23 December 2003.

44. Melissa Daar, email message to author, 23 December 2003.

45. Based on personal conversations by author with the directors of the three organizations—Susan Shaer, Kevin Martin, and Bob Musil—September 2003.

46. Clicktivism should not be confused with the related term hacktivism, which uses internet tools to expose hidden or secret information and also to disrupt or damage data systems. There are now many forms of digital engagement. For a typology and analysis see Jordana J. George and Dorothy E. Leidner, "From Clicktivism to Hacktivism: Understanding Digital Activism," *Information and Organization* 29, no. 3 (2019): 1–45.

47. David Karpf, *The MoveOn Effect: The Unexpected Transformation of American Political Advocacy* (University of Oxford Press, 2012).

48. Heaney and Rojas, *Party in the Street*, 165.

49. Andrew Boyd, "The Web Rewires the Movement," *The Nation* 277, no. 4, 4–11 August 2003, 14.

50. Saul Alinsky, *Rules for Radicals: A Practical Primer for Realistic Radicals* (New York: Vintage Books, 1971), 113.

51. Peter Ackerman and Christopher Kruegler, *Strategic Nonviolent Conflict: The Dynamics of People Power in the 20th Century* (Westport, CT: Praeger, 1994), 26.

52. Chris Hayes, "MoveOn.Org is Not as Radical as Conservatives Think," *The Nation*, 16 July 2008, www.thenation.com.

53. Ken Butigan, "The Pledge of Resistance: Lessons from a Movement of Solidarity and Nonviolent Direct Action," in *Peace Movements Worldwide*, eds. Marc Pilisuk and Michael Nagler (Santa Barbara, CA: Praeger Publishers, 2011).

54. Sean D. Hamill and David Heinzmann, "Chicago Anti-War Demonstration Shuts Down City," *Chicago Tribune*, 21 March 2003, www.chicagotribune.com.

55. Joe Garofoli and Jim Herron Zamora, "San Francisco Police Play Catch Up; Protestors Roam," *San Francisco Chronicle*, 21 March 2003, www.sfgate.com.

56. CNN, "Hundreds of Thousands Protest War," 22 March 2003, www.cnn.com.

57. Knickerbocker, "Whither All the War Protesters?"

58. Barbara Deming, "On the Necessity to Liberate Minds," in *We Are All Part of One Another: A Barbara Deming Reader*, ed. Jane Meyerding (Philadelphia: New Society Publishers, 1984), 199.

59. Erica Chenoweth and Maria J. Stephan, *Why Civil Resistance Works: The Strategic Logic of Nonviolent Conflict* (New York: Colombia University Press, 2011).

60. James M. Lindsay, "Rally 'Round the Flag," Brookings, 25 March 2003, www.brookings.edu/opinions/rally-round-the-flag.

Chapter Three: Communicating for Peace

1. Todd Gitlin wrote, "as the war steadily lost popularity in the late Sixties, so did the antiwar movement." Todd Gitlin, *The Sixties: Years of Hope, Days of Rage* (New York: Bantam Press, 1987), 262.

2. Ian Taylor, *Media Relations of the Anti-War Movement: The Battle for Hearts and Minds* (New York: Routledge, 2017); Simon Cottle and Libby Lester, *Transnational Protests and the Media* (New York: Peter Lang, 2011).

3. Scott McClellan, *What Happened: Inside the Bush White House and Washington's Culture of Deception* (New York: Public Affairs, 2008), 134, 142, 144.

4. Elizabeth Bumiller, "Bush Aides Set Strategy to Sell Policy on Iraq," *New York Times*, 7 September 2002, www.nytimes.com.

5. Andrew Glass, "Bush Makes Case for War with Iraq, September 4, 2002," *Politico*, 4 September 2018, www.politico.com.

6. In 2006 *Mother Jones* magazine produced a timeline of the deceptions that led to war. Jonathan Stein and Tim Dickinson, "Lie by Lie: A Timeline of How We Got into Iraq," *Mother Jones*, September/October 2006, www.motherjones.com.

7. FAIR (Fairness and Accuracy in Reporting), "In Iraq Crisis, Networks Are Megaphones for Official Views," 18 March 2003, https://fair.org.

8. Steve Rendall and Tara Broughel, "Amplifying Officials, Squelching Dissent," FAIR (Fairness and Accuracy in Reporting), reposted in *Bulatlat* 3, no. 20, 22–28 June 2003 (Quezon City, Philippines), www.bulatlat.com/news/3-20/3-20-fair.html.

9. Taylor, *Media Relations*, 194.

10. Holsti, *Public Opinion*, 134.

11. Spencer Ackerman, *Reign of Terror: How the 9/11 Era Destabilized America and Produced Trump* (New York, Viking, 2021), 65

12. Victor Navasky and Christopher Cerf, "Who Said the War Would Pay for Itself? They Did!," *The Nation*, 13 March 2008, www.thenation.com.

13. Holsti, *Public Opinion*, 142–44.

14. For a vivid and detailed account of media manipulation during the Gulf War, see John R. MacArthur, *Second Front: Censorship and Propaganda in the Gulf War* (New York: Hill and Wang, 1992).

15. Richard L. Berke, "War in the Gulf: The Press: Pentagon Defends Coverage Rules, While Admitting Some Delays," *New York Times*, 21 February 1991, www.nytimes.com.

16. Charlotte Ryan, *Prime Time Activism* (Boston: South End Press, 1999), 31–35.

17. Elisa Shearer, "Social Media Outpaces Print Newspapers in the U.S. as a News Source," Pew Research Center, 10 December 2018, www.pewresearch.org.

18. See the classic studies Benjamin Page, Robert Shapiro, and Glenn Dempsey, "What Moves Public Opinion," *American Political Science Review* 81, no. 1 (1987): 23; and Roy Behr and

Shanto Iyengar, "Television News, Real-World Cues and Changes in Public Opinion," *Public Opinion Quarterly* 49, no. 1 (1985): 39.

19. Taylor, *Media Relations*, 197.

20. William Gamson, *The Strategy of Social Protest*, 2nd ed. (Belmont, CA: Wadsworth Publishing, 1990), 147.

21. The phrase was derived from the report by David Cortright, Alistair Millar, and George A. Lopez, *Winning Without War: Sensible Security Options for Dealing with Iraq*, October 2002, Policy Brief F5. www.fourthfreedomforum.org/wp-content /uploads/2020/06/2002-October-Cortright-Lopez-Millar -Winning-Without-War.pdf.

22. Cramer, "Militarized Patriotism," 521.

23. Steven Kull, Clay Ramsay and Evan Lewis, "Misperceptions, the Media, and the Iraq War," *Political Science Quarterly* Vol. 118, No. 4 (Winter, 2003/2004), 569.

24. Cramer, "Militarized Patriotism, 521.

25. Johanna Neuman, "Talk About War Reveals Stark Differences," *Los Angeles Times*, 2 March 2003, www.latimes.com; Kull, Ramsay, and Lewis, "Misperceptions," 570.

26. Lakoff quoted in Robert Salladay, "Peace Activism: A Matter of Language," *San Francisco Chronicle*, 7 April 2003, www.sfgate .com.

27. Cramer, "Militarized Patriotism," 490–492.

28. Martin Luther King Jr., "Why I am Opposed to the War in Vietnam," sermon, Ebenezer Baptist Church, Atlanta, GA, 16 April 1967, https://:wpblog.wyzant.com.

29. Salladay, "Peace Activism."

30. See the important study by Jerry Lembke, *The Spitting Image: Myth, Memory, and the Legacy of Vietnam* (New York: New York University Press, 1998).

31. "Bush: Move.On.Org Ad on Petraeus 'Disgusting,'" 18 September 2007, www.cnn.com.

32. Robert Greenwald, email message to author, 2 December 2003.

33. David Fenton, interview by author, 30 December 2003.

34. Ira Berkow, "Baseball: Hall of Fame President Acknowledges Mistake," *New York Times*, 12 April 2003, www.nytimes.com.

35. Tim Robbins, "A Chill Wind Is Blowing in This Nation" (speech, National Press Club, Washington, D.C., 15 April 2003), www .spiritofchange.org/tim-robbins-a-chill-wind-is-blowing-in-this -nation/.

36. Andrew Leahey, "Flashback: The Dixie Chicks Are Ashamed of the President . . . Again," *Rolling Stone*, 7 August 2014, www .rollingstone.com.

37. The Dixie Chicks Official Artist Club, "From the Dixie Chicks with Respect to Statements Being Reported in the British Media," 12 March 2003, www.theguardian.com/music/2003 /mar/19/artsfeatures.popandrock.

38. Quoted in Peter Blecha, *Taboo Tunes: A History of Banned Bands & Censored Songs* (San Francisco: Backbeat Books, 2004), 182.

Chapter Four: Faces of the Movement

1. Gerard F. Powers, "The U.S. Bishops and War since the Peace Pastoral," *U.S. Catholic Historian* 27, no. 2 (September 2009): 89–90.

2. United States Conference of Catholic Bishops, "Statement on Iraq, 2002," Washington, DC, 13 November 2002, www.usccb .org.

3. All quotes of religious groups from Pew Research Center, "Religious Groups Issue Statements on War in Iraq," compiled by Religion News Service, 19 March 2003, www.pewresearch.org /religion/2003/03/19/publicationpage-aspxid616/.

4. Ben Smietana, "Keeping Attention on Iraq's Recovery," *Washington Post*, 2 May 2003, www.washingtonpost.com/archive/local /2003/05/03/keeping-attention-on-iraqs-recovery/4e88d90d -9a38-4b40-95a0-524a0519216c/.

5. Francis Fukuyama, "After Neo-Conservatism," *New York Times Magazine*, 19 February 2006, 62.

6. Pew Research Center, "Views of a Changing World 2003; War with Iraq Further Divides Global Publics," Report, 3 June 2003 www.pewresearch.org.

7. Leander Schaerlaeckens, "Analysis: Arab-Americans oppose Iraq war," *Defense News*, 29 June 2007 www.upi.com.

8. BBC, "Pope Condemns War in Iraq," 13 January 2003, http://news.bbc.co.uk/1/hi/world/europe/2654109.stm.

9. CBC, "Pope Says War Threatens Humanity," 22 March 2003, www.cbc.ca/news/world/pope-says-war-threatens-humanity-1.395431.

10. BBC, "Pope Makes Plea for Peace," 25 December 2002, http://news.bbc.co.uk/2/hi/europe/2604729.stm.

11. Statement of Cardinal Joseph Ratzinger, 21 September 2002, https://digilander.libero.it/galatrorc4/terrorismo4/20020921_ratzinger_from11sept_to_iraq.htm.

12. Bob Edgar, interview by author, 27 August 2003.

13. LeVine, "Peace Movement Plans for the Future."

14. Solnit, "Acts of Hope."

15. The editors, "Guns and Butter Issues," *The Nation*, 8 May 2003, www.thenation.com.

16. AFL-CIO Executive Council, "Iraq," 27 February 2003, https://aflcio.org/about/leadership/statements/iraq.

17. John Bennett Sears, "Peace Work: The Antiwar Tradition in American Labor from the Cold War to the Iraq War," *Diplomatic History* 34, no. 4 (September 2010): 699.

18. David Bacon, "AFL-CIO Convention Calls for Troop Withdrawal from Iraq," 26 July 2005, http://dbacon.igc.org.

19. Mario Diani, "Promoting the Protest: The Organizational Embeddedness of the Demonstrators," in *The World Says No to War: Demonstrations Against the War on Iraq*, eds. Stefaan Walgrave and Dieter Rucht (Minneapolis: University of Minnesota Press, 2010), 203.

20. Leslie Wayne, "Union Spends Heavily for Obama in Primaries," *New York Times*, 26 February 2008, www.nytimes.com.

21. Amy Cortese, "Private Sector; An Antiwar Chief (and Proud of It)," *New York Times*, 6 April 2003, www.nytimes.com.

22. Allison Linn and Heather Draper, "Businesses Ponder Costs of Going to War Against Iraq," *Rocky Mountain News*, 18 October 2003.

23. Gary Ferdman, interview by author, 27 January 2022.

24. Epstein, "Notes on the Antiwar Movement," 111.

25. Polling Report, "Iraq (p. 4)," www.pollingreport.com/iraq18.htm

26. Heaney and Rojas, *Party in the Street*, 168–69.

27. Libero Della Piana, "War's Racial Edge," *ColorLines* (Spring 2003): 21.

28. Wing, interview.

29. Fletcher, interview.

30. Sarah Abruzzese, "Iraq War Brings Drop in Black Enlistees," *New York Times*, 22 August 2007, www.nytimes.com.

31. Anthony Arnove, *Iraq: The Logic of Withdrawal* (New York: The New Press, 2007), 93.

32. Ron Harris, "Black America's Opposition to the Iraq War," interview by Farai Chideya, NPR, 27 October 2005, www.npr.org.

33. Pew Research Center, "Survey of Latino Attitudes on A Possible War with Iraq," 18 February 2003, www.pewresearch.org.

34. Epstein, "Notes on the Antiwar Movement," 112.

35. Winona LaDuke, "The Case Against the War," *Indian Country Today*, 4 April 2003, https://indiancountrytoday.com/archive/laduke-the-case-against-the-war.

36. Tex Hall, "Healthy Communities, Strong Tribal Governance," National Congress of American Indians, 3 February 2005, www.ncai.org/resources/ncai-publications/2005_SOIN_Speech.pdf, 7.

37. Tomio Geron, "Racial Justice Groups Organize Against War," *War Times* 6, October 2002, http://id34109.securedata.net/war-times/issues/6art9.html.

38. Frances Beal and Ty dePass, "The Historical Black Presence in the Struggle for Peace," *The Black Scholar* 17, no. 1 (January/February 1986): 2.

39. Piana, "War's Racial Edge," 21.

40. Martin Luther King Jr., "A Time to Break Silence," 4 April 1967, in *A Testament of Hope: The Essential Writings and Speeches of Martin Luther King Jr.*, ed. James Melvin Washington (San Francisco, CA: HarperSanFrancisco, 1991), 233.

41. Jack O'Dell, interview by author, July 1986.

42. Malik Miah, "Black America and the Iraq War," *Against the Current* 104 (May–June 2003), https://againstthecurrent.org.

43. Chenoweth, *Civil Resistance*, 248; Larry Buchanan, Quoctrung Bui, and Jugal K. Patel, "Black Lives Matter May Be the Largest Movement in U.S. History, *New York Times*, 3 July 2020, www.nytimes.com.

44. Lisa Leitz and David S. Meyer, "Gendered Activism and Outcomes: Women in the Peace Movement," in *The Oxford Handbook of U. S. Women's Social Movement Activism*, eds., H. J. McCannon, V. Taylor, J. Reger, and R. L. Einwohner (New York: Oxford University Press, 2017), 708–728.

45. For a detailed social science analysis of this phenomenon, see Richard C. Eichenberg, "Gender Differences in Public Attitudes toward the Use of Force by the United States, 1990–2003," *International Security* 28, no. 1 (Summer 2003): 110–141; for evidence of the continuation of this pattern see Pew Research Center, "The Gender Gap: Three Decades Old, as Wide as Ever," Report, 29 March 2012, www.pewresearch.org.

46. Polling Report, "Iraq (p. 4)," www.pollingreport.com/iraq17.html.

47. "Aggregate Zogby America Pre War Support, 9/25/02 thru 3/17/03," Zogby International, special report to Fourth Freedom Forum, 26 August 2003.

48. Greenberg Quinlan Rosner Research Inc., "Public Supports Bush, Is More Divided Over Iraq: Report on the First WorldView Survey for VVAF," memorandum from Jeremy Rosner and William McInturff to Vietnam Veterans of America Foundation, 14 March 2003.

49. Stefaan Walgrave, Dieter Rucht and Peter van Aelst, "New Activists or Old Leftists: The Demographics of Protesters," in Walgrave and Rucht, *The World Says No to War*, 84–91.

50. Eleanor Smeal, interview by author, June 2003.

51. Quoted in Ann Moline, "'Code Pink' White House Vigil Continues," National Organization for Women, 29 December 2002, https://womensenews.org.

52. Liza Featherstone, "Mighty in Pink," *The Nation* (3 March 2003), www.thenation.com.

53. Leitz and Meyer, "Gendered Activism," 724.

54. Figures from the Lysistrata Project archive, http://lysistrataprojectarchive.com/lys/archive.html.

55. Daniel Q. Gillion, *The Political Power of Protest: Minority Activism and Shifts in Public Policy* (Cambridge University Press, 2013), 17, 58.

56. Heaney and Rojas, *Party in the Street*, 132.

57. Statement of Karen Dolan, Director, Cities for Peace, National Conference of the Rainbow/PUSH Coalition, 24 June 2003, Chicago, IL.

58. "San Francisco Ballot to Call for End to Iraq War," *Associated Press*, 1 July 2004, www.foxnews.com.

59. See the Wikipedia report of San Francisco's 2004 election results, https://en.wikipedia.org/wiki/November_2004_San _Francisco_general_election, accessed 22 July 2022.

60. "Wisconsin Votes for Troop Pullout," *Los Angeles Times*, 6 April 2006, www.latimes.com.

61. Peter Slavin, "Iraq Referendum Splits Wisconsin Voters," 19 March 2007, *The Boston Globe*, http//:Boston.com.

62. Alinsky, *Rules for Radicals*,127–28.

63. George A. Lopez, "Iraq and Just War Thinking," *Commonweal* 129, no. 16 (27 September 2002), 14–15.

64. Karen Jacob, interview by author, 28 December 2003.

65. David Fast, interview by author, 8 December 2003.

66. Amber Brockway, "Goshen Rally Opposes War with Iraq," *Goshen News*, 11 December 2002, A1.

67. Simonson, "Waging Peace on the Brink of War."

68. Bryan Long, "Students Pencil in Iraq Protest," CNN.Com, 5 March 2003, www.cnn.com.

Chapter Five: Dissent in the Ranks

1. Sources on the GI and veterans movement include Richard Moser, *The New Winter Soldiers: GI and Veteran Dissent during the Vietnam Era* (New Brunswick, NJ: Rutgers University Press, 1996); Richard Stacewicz, *Winter Soldiers: An Oral History of the Vietnam Veterans Against the War* (New York: Twayne Publishers, 1997); Andrew E. Hunt, *The Turning: A History of Vietnam Veterans Against the War* (New York: New York University Press, 1999); and David Cortright, *Soldiers in Revolt: GI Resistance during the Vietnam War*, 2nd edition (Chicago: Haymarket Books, 2005).

2. Richard Sisk, "Uneasy GIs Speak Their Peace," *Daily News* (New York), 16 March 2003, 4.

3. Oliver Burkeman, "War in the Gulf: One Killed, Twelve Injured by 'Resentful' Muslim GI," *The Guardian* (London), 24 March 2003, 6.

4. George Lepre, *Fragging: Why U.S. Soldiers Assaulted their Officers in Vietnam* (Lubbock, TX: Texas Tech University Press, 2011); Cortright, *Soldiers in Revolt*, 2005.

5. Paul Harris and Jonathan Franklin, "Bring Us Home: GIs Flood U.S. with War-Weary Emails," *The Guardian* (London), 10 August 2003, www.theguardian.com.

6. Michael Moore, "Letters the Troops Have Sent Me," 19 December 2003, http://www.labournet.net/other/0312/troops1.html.

7. Bootie Cosgrove-Mather, "Low-Morale Letters from Iraq," CBS News, 17 July 2003, www.cbsnews.com/.

8. Jeffrey Gettleman, "Anger Rises for Families of Troops in Iraq," *New York Times*, 4 July 2003, A1.

9. Wes Allison, "A Moment to Remember Fallen Comrades; In a Soldiers' Haven, Worry and Frustration Taking a Toll," *St. Petersburg Times*, 7 November 2003, 1A.

10. Robert Collier, "Pentagon Retaliates Against GIs who Spoke out on TV," *San Francisco Chronicle*, 18 July 2003, A1.

11. Dana Milbank, "Bush Courts Regional Media," *Washington Post*, 14 October 2003, A4.

12. Steve Liewer, "What Will Spell Success?" *Stars and Stripes*, 21 October 2003, 3; the investigation results and questionnaire findings were published in seven consecutive issues of *Stars and Stripes* beginning 15 October 2003.

13. David Josar, "From Weekend Warrior to Full-time Fighter," *Stars and Stripes*, 18 October 2003, 5.

14. Vernon Loeb, "Protests Grow Over Yearlong Army Tours," *Washington Post*, 20 September 2003, A13.

15. Steve Vogel, "Soldiers Miss Flights Back to Iraq," *Washington Post*, 21 October 2003, A20.

16. Associated Press, "A Region Inflamed: The Reserves; Reservist Faces Punishment After Questioning a Waiver," *New York Times*, November 29, 2003, www.nytimes.com.

17. Leonard Greene, "AWOL State of Mind: Calls from Soldiers Desperate to Leave Iraq Flood Hotline," *New York Post*, 5 October 2003, 12.

18. Arnove, *Logic of Withdrawal*, 95.

19. Quotations from Nan Levinson, *The New Antiwar Soldiers and the Movement They Built* (New Brunswick, NJ: Rutgers University Press, 2014), 128.

20. Camilo Mejía, *Road from ar Ramadi: The Private Rebellion of Staff Sergeant Camilo Mejía, An Iraq War Memoir* (Chicago: Haymarket Books, 2008), 126.

21. "Prisoner of Conscience—Staff Sergeant Camilo Mejia Castillo," National Campaign for a Peace Tax Fund, https://peacetaxfund .org/conscientious-objection/prisoner-of-conscience-staff -sergeant-camilo-mejia-castillo/.

22. Statement of Camilo Mejía, quoted in Wright and Dixon, *Dissent*, 144.

23. Joshua Key and Lawrence Hill, *The Deserter's Tale: The Story of an Ordinary Soldier Who Walked Away from the War in Iraq* (New York: Atlantic Monthly Press, 2007).

24. Peter Laufer, *Mission Rejected: U.S. Soldiers Who Say No to Iraq* (White River Junction, Vt.: Chelsea Green Publishing Company, 2006), 8–11.

25. Key and Hill, *The Deserter's Tale*, 229.

26. John Darrell Sherwood, *Black Sailor, White Navy: Racial Unrest in the Fleet During the Vietnam War Era* (New York: New York University Press, 2007). 1.

27. See Jonathan W. Hutto, Sr., *Antiwar Soldier: How to Dissent Within the Ranks of the Military* (New York: Nation Books, 2008), 33–60.

28. Wikipedia, s.v. "Appeal for Redress," last modified 9 May 2020, https://en.wikipedia.org.

29. Ann Scott Tyson, "Grass-Roots Group of Troops Petition Congress for Pullout from Iraq," *The Washington Post*, 25 October 2006, A13; CBS News, 60 Minutes, "GIs Petition Congress to End War," 22 February 2007, www.cbsnews.com /news/gis-petition-congress-to-end-iraq-war/.

30. Wright and Dixon, *Dissent*.

31. Lisa Leitz, *Fighting for Peace: Veterans and Military Families in the Anti–Iraq War Movement* (Minneapolis: University of Minnesota Press, 2014).

32. Nancy Lessin and Charlie Richardson, interview by author, 20 December 2003.

33. George W. Bush, *Decision Points* (New York: Crown Publisher, 2010), 358.

34. Maureen Dowd, "Why No Tea and Sympathy?" *New York Times*, 10 August 2005, www.nytimes.com.

35. Leitz, *Fighting for Peace*, 43.

36. The record of the original Winter Soldier investigation was published as Vietnam Veterans Against the War, *The Winter Soldier Investigation: An Inquiry into American War Crimes* (Boston: Beacon Press, 1972). A film of the event was also produced, *Winter Soldier*, by the Winterfilm Cooperative (1972).

37. Aaron Glantz and Iraq Veterans Against the War, *Winter Soldier: Iraq and Afghanistan: Eyewitness Accounts of the Occupations* (Chicago: Haymarket Books, 2008).

38. Alice Lynd and Staughton Lynd, *Moral Injury and Nonviolent Resistance: Breaking the Cycle of Violence in the Military and Behind Bars* (Oakland, CA: PM Press, 2017).

39. Andrew J. Bacevich, "I Lost My Son to a War I Oppose. We Were Both Doing Our Duty," *Washington Post*, 27 May 2007, B1.

40. For a detailed account of the coffeehouse movement, see David Parsons, *Dangerous Grounds: Antiwar Coffeehouse and Military Dissent in the Vietnam Era* (Chapel Hill: University of North Carolina Press, 2017).

41. Tod Ensign, "G.I. Joe: Lessons for the Coffeehouse Movement," *Win* magazine, Summer 2009, www.warresisters.org/win/.

42. Zogby Conducts First Poll of Iraq Troops," *PTSD Combat: Winning the War Within*, 28 February 2006, http://ptsdcombat .blogspot.com.

43. Lawrence Kapp and Charles A. Henning, "Recruiting and Retention: An Overview of FY2006 and FY2007 Results for Active and Reserve Component Enlisted Personnel," Congressional Research Service, 7 February 2008, 8, www.everycrsreport .com.

44. Carl Andrew Castro and Sara Kintzle, "Suicides in the Military: The Post-Modern Combat Veteran and the Hemingway Effect," *Current Psychiatry Reports* 16, no. 460 (June 2014), 2.

45. Meghann Myers, "Four Times as Many Troops and Vets Have Died by Suicide as in Combat, Study Finds," *Military Times*, 21 June 2021, www.militarytimes.com.

Chapter Six: Protest and Politics

1. Mike Davis, "The Democrats After November," *New Left Review* 43 (January–February 2007), 5–31.
2. Arnove, *Logic of Withdrawal*, 98.
3. Heaney and Rojas, *Party in the Street*, 229, 9
4. Hayden, *Ending the War in Iraq*, 17 and 119.
5. David S. Meyer and Catherine Corrigall-Brown, "Coalitions and Political Context: U.S. Movements Against Wars in Iraq, *Mobilization: An International Journal* 10, no. 3 (June 2005), 329.
6. Erica Chenoweth, *Civil Resistance*, 3–4.
7. Charles Tilly and Sidney G. Tarrow, *Contentious Politics* (New York: Oxford University Press, 2015).
8. McAdam, Doug, and Sidney G. Tarrow, "Ballots and Barricades: On the Reciprocal Relationship between Elections and Social Movements," *Perspectives on Politics* 8, no. 2 (2010): 529–542.
9. Dennis Chong, *Collective Action and the Civil Rights Movement* (Chicago: University of Chicago Press, 1991).
10. Heaney and Rojas, *Party in the Street*, 172.
11. Hayden, *Ending the War in Iraq*, 142.
12. Joe Trippi, *The Revolution Will Not Be Televised: Democracy, the Internet and the Overthrow of Everything* (Regan Books, 2004), 131, 86.
13. Charles DeBenedetti, *The Peace Reform in American History* (Bloomington, IN: Indiana University Press, 1980), 181–82.
14. Of the approximately 7.5 million votes cast in the primaries, McCarthy and Kennedy together polled 69 percent. See the Our Campaigns website, www.ourcampaigns.com/RaceDetail.html ?RaceID=47021, accessed 22 July 2022.
15. Hayden, *Ending the War in Iraq*, 118.
16. Jodi Wilgoren and Elisabeth Bumiller, "In Harshest Critique Yet, Kerry Attacks Bush Over War in Iraq," *New York Times*, 21 September 2004, www.nytimes.com.

17. "Transcript: Kerry Testifies Before Senate Panel, 1971," NPR, 25 April 2006, www.npr.org.

18. Bertrand Russell, *War Crimes in Vietnam* (New York: Monthly Review Press, 1967); for a later, more comprehensive treatment, see Nick Turse, *Kill Anything That Moves: The Real American War in Vietnam* (New York: Macmillan, 2013).

19. A detailed assessment at the time concluded that his accusers "failed to come up with sufficient evidence to prove" their charges. See Michael Dobbs, "Swift Boat Accounts Incomplete," *The Washington Post*, 22 August 2004, A1.

20. See Pamela Colloff, "Sunk," *Texas Monthly*, January 2005, www.texasmonthly.com.

21. Tom Matzzie, interview by author, 12 July 2021.

22. Hayden, *Ending the War in Iraq*, 147–48, 158–59.

23. Patrick Healy, "Lamont Defeats Lieberman in Primary," *New York Times*, 8 August 2006, www.nytimes.com

24. Bush, *Decision Points*, 354.

25. Peter Baker, *Days of Fire: Bush and Cheney in the White House* (New York: Anchor Books, 2014), 486–87.

26. Holsti, *Public Opinion*, 145.

27. Michael T. Heaney and Fabio Rojas, "The Partisan Dynamics of Contention: Demobilization of the Antiwar Movement in the United States, 2007–2009," *Mobilization: An International Journal* 16, no. 1 (2011): 45–64. See also Michael Grunwald, "Opposition to War Buoys Democrats," *The Washington Post*, 8 November 2006, A31.

28. Mark Engler and Paul Engler, *This Is an Uprising: How Nonviolent Revolt is Shaping the Twenty-First Century* (New York: Nation Books, 2017), 217.

29. Jeff Zeleny and Megan Thee, "Democrats Captured Key Group in Center," *New York Times*, 8 November 2006, www.nytimes.com/2006/11/08/world/americas/08iht-exit.3455582.html?searchResultPosition=7.

30. Adam Nagourney and Jim Rutenberg, "Tables Turned on the GOP Over Iraq Issue," *New York Times*, 19 October 19, 2006, www.nytimes.com.

31. Davis, "The Democrats After November."

32. Heaney and Rojas, *Party in the Street*, 175.

33. Hayden, *Ending the War in Iraq*, 166.

34. Jesse McKinley, "Home in San Francisco, Pelosi Gets the Crawford Treatment," *New York Times*, 13 March 2007, www.nytimes.com.

35. Hayden, *Ending the War in Iraq*, 158.

36. Baker, *Days of Fire*, 542.

37. Michael Crowley, "Can Lobbyists Stop the War?" *New York Times Magazine*, 9 September 2007, 654.

38. "McConnell Assailed Over Iraq: Hundreds Attend Rally and March," *Louisville Courier-Journal*, 28 August 2007.

39. Gillion, *Political Power of Protest*, 17, 58.

40. Quote from an unnamed source in Holsti, *Public Opinion*, 148.

41. Martha Angle, "Defying Bush, House Passes New Deadline for Withdrawal from Iraq," *New York Times*, 12 July 2007, www.nytimes.com.

42. Jennifer K. Elsea, Michael John Garcia, and Thomas J. Nicola, CRS Report to Congress, "Congressional Authority to Limit U.S. Military Operations in Iraq," Congressional Research Service, updated 27 February 2008, RL 33837, https://sgp.fas.org.

43. Angle, "Defying Bush."

44. Holsti, *Public Opinion*, 64–65.

45. Elsea, Garcia, and Nicola, CRS Report to Congress.

46. For a detailed assessment of the factors associated with the decline in Iraqi attacks, see Stephen Biddle, Jeffrey A. Friedman, and Jacob N. Shapiro, "Testing the Surge: Why Did Violence Decline in Iraq in 2007," *International Security* 37, no. 1 (Summer 2012): 7–40.

47. Baker, *Days of Fire*, 601, 619–20.

48. Barack Obama, *A Promised Land* (New York: Penguin Random House, 2020), 158.

49. Ackerman, *Reign of Terror*, 114.

50. Hayes, "MoveOn.Org is Not as Radical as Conservatives Think."

51. "2008 Democratic Primary Election Results," http:// uselectionatlas.org; see also Jeralyn, "Caucuses vs. Primaries: A Report," Talk Left, 27 May 2008, www.talkleft.com.

52. Karpf, *The MoveOn Effect*, 29.

53. Martin Walker, "The Year of the Insurgents: The 2008 US Presidential Campaign," *International Affairs* 84 (2008): 1095–1107. See also Jose Antonio Vargas, "Obama Raised Half a Billion Online," *The Washington Post*, 20 November 2008, http://voices .washingtonpost.com/44/2008/11/20/obama_raised_half_a _billion_on.html; see also list of candidate fundraising at "2008 Presidential Election," www.opensecrets.org; and Monte Lutz, "The Social Pulpit: Barack Obama's Social Media Toolkit," (Washington, DC: Edelman.com 2009).

54. Barack Obama, *A Promised Land*, 47.

55. Dominic Tierney, "The Legacy of Obama's 'Worse Mistake,'" *The Atlantic*, 15 April 2016, www.theatlantic.com.

56. Barack Obama, *A Promised Land*, 157–159.

57. Arnove, *Logic of Withdrawal*, 87–88.

58. Thomas E. Ricks, "Extending Our Stay in Iraq," *New York Times*, 23 February 2010, www.nytimes.com; see also Thomas E. Ricks, *The Gamble: General David Petraeus and the American Military Adventure in Iraq, 2006–2008* (New York: Penguin Press, 2009).

59. Colin H. Kahl, "No, Obama Didn't Lose Iraq," *Politico Magazine*, 15 June 2014, www.politico.com.

60. Hayden, *Ending the War in Iraq*, 170–71.

Chapter Seven: Global Impacts

1. Draper, *To Start a War*, 310.

2. John Hooper, "German Leader Says No to Iraq War," *The Guardian*, 5 August 2002, www.theguardian.com.

3. Tekla Szymanski, "Schröder Beats Bush in German Election," *World Press Review*, 26 September 2002, www.worldpress.org.

4. Karen DeYoung, *Soldier: The Life of Colin Powell* (New York: Vintage, 2007), 432–33.

5. Sonni Efron and Bruce Wallace, "Spanish Victor Says Iraq War Based on 'Lies,'" *Los Angeles Times*, 16 March 2004, www.latimes.com/archives/la-xpm-2004-mar-16-fg-spain16-story.html.

6. Sunny Freeman, "Canada's 'No' To Iraq War a Defining Moment for Prime Minister, Even 10 Years Later," *Huffington Post*, 19 March 2013, www.huffpost.com/archive/ca/entry/canada-iraq-war_n_2902305.

7. "Pro-Canadian, Anti-American or Anti-War? Canadian Public Opinion on the Eve of the War," *Policy Options*, Institute for Research on Public Policy, Montreal, April 2003, https://policyoptions.irpp.org.

8. Philip P. Pan, "Turkey Rejects U.S. Use of Bases," *Washington Post*, 2 March 2003, A1.

9. CNN, "NATO Approves Planning for Turkey's Defense," 16 February 2003, http://edition.cnn.com/2003/WORLD/meast/02/16/sprj.irq.nato.belg/index.html.

10. Draper, *To Start a War*, 332–34.

11. BBC, "Australian PM Censured over Iraq," 5 February 2003, www.bbc.com.

12. "Howard's Reign in Australia Ends," *The Guardian*, 24 November 2007, www.theguardian.com.

13. "Berlusconi Says He Tried to Talk Bush Out of War," *New York Times*, 30 October 2005, www.nytimes.com; Roxanne Roberts, "The Italian Connection," *Washington Post*, 20 May 2004, C1.

14. "Prodi to Speed up Troop Withdrawal," *Spiegel International*, 18 May 2006, www.spiegel.de.

15. Howard W. French, "Despite Protests Seoul to Send Troops to Iraq for Reconstruction," *New York Times*, 2 April 2003, www.nytimes.com;

16. *Guardian* (London), "Boost for Religious Parties in Pakistan Elections," 11 October 2002, www.theguardian.com.

17. Matthew Tempest, "Labour MPs Revolt over Iraq," *The Guardian*, 26 February 2003, www.theguardian.com.

18. Geoffrey Wheatcroft, "The Tragedy of Tony Blair," *The Atlantic*, June 2004,

19. Michael White and Alan Travis, "Labour's Majority Slides Away," *The Guardian*, 5 May 2007, www.theguardian.com.

20. Holsti, *Public Opinion*, 40.

21. Alan Cowell, "Blair to Give Up Post as Premier Within One Year," *New York Times*, 8 September 2006, www.nytimes.com.

22. Jimmy Carter, "Just War—or a Just War?," *New York Times*, 9 March 2003, sec. 4, 13.

23. Navasky and Cerf, "Who Said the War Would Pay for Itself?"

24. Neta Crawford, "The Iraq War Has Cost the U.S. Nearly $2 Trillion," *Military Times*, 6 February 2020, www.militarytimes .com.

25. Andrew Bacevich, *After the Apocalypse: America's Role in a World Transformed* (New York: Metropolitan Books, 2021), 44–45.

26. Rayburn and Sobchak, *Surge and Withdrawal*, 616.

27. Figures derived from the iCasualties site for the years 2003 through 2011, http://icasualties.org/.

28. Draper, *To Start a War*, 245.

29. United Nations Security Council, S/Res/1441 (2002), 8 November 2002.

30. "Blair 'Absolutely' for Second Resolution," *The Guardian*, 31 January 2003, www.theguardian.com.

31. DeYoung, *Life of Colin Powell*, 454. Goldsmith later altered his legal opinion on the eve of the invasion following meetings in Washington with Bush administration legal advisers. See "Lord Goldsmith's Legal Warning to Tony Blair that Iraq War Would Be Illegal," *Evening Standard*, 30 June 2010, www .standard.co.uk.

32. The pressure campaign included a memo from a senior figure in the National Security Administration to its British equivalent, GCHQ, requesting the monitoring of private communications of UN delegates for information, personal or otherwise, that could be used to "give the US an edge" in leveraging support for the use of force resolution. The memo was leaked to the *Observer* by whistleblower Katherine Gunn, as portrayed in the 2019 film *Official Secrets*.

33. Draper, *To Start a War*, 345–46.

34. Bush, *Decision Points*, 246.

35. Phyllis Bennis, "Bush Isolated, Launches Terrifying Attack," *War Times* 9, April 2003, http://id34109.securedata.net/war-times /issues/9art1.html.

36. Immanuel Wallerstein, "U.S. Weakness and the Struggle for Hegemony," *Monthly Review* 55, no. 3 (July–August 2003): 28.

37. I am indebted for this insight to Jack O'Dell, interview by author, 17 December 2003.

38. David Cortright and George A. Lopez, "Are Sanctions Just? The Problematic Case of Iraq," *Journal of International Affairs* 52, no. 2 (Spring 1999): 735–755.

39. Hans C. von Sponeck, *A Different Kind of War: The UN Sanctions Regime in Iraq* (New York: Berghahn Books, 2006).

40. See the discussion in Hilary Charlesworth, "Think Pieces: Law After War," *Melbourne Journal of International Law* 8 (2007), www .anu.edu.au/.

41. These themes are developed in *Civil Society, Peace and Power*, eds. David Cortright, Melanie Greenberg, and Laurel Stone (Lanham, MD: Roman & Littlefield, 2016).

Chapter Eight: Evaluating the Antiwar Movement

1. David Karol and Edward Miguel, "The Electoral Cost of War: Iraq Casualties and the 2004 U.S. Presidential Election," *Journal of Politics* 69, no. 3 (August 2007): 633–648.

2. Mazarr, *Leap of Faith*, 224; David W. Moore, "Majority of Americans Favor Attacking Iraq to Oust Saddam Hussein," Gallup News Service, 23 August 2002, gallup.com.

3. Woodward, *Plan of Attack*, 253–54.

4. Ibid., 357.

5. David W. Moore and Frank Newport, "Powell 'Bounce' Fades, But Majority of Americans Still Open to War with Iraq," Gallup News Service, 21 February 2003, gallup.com.

6. Kull, Ramsay, and Lewis, "Misperceptions," 569–570.

7. Woodward, *Plan of Attack*, 177–78.

8. As Mazarr writes, the reaction to Iraq's acceptance of renewed inspections in some Pentagon offices "was one of horror. This was the beginning of precisely what they had feared," a UN process on renewing and evaluating UN weapons inspections. Mazarr, *Leap of Faith*, 255.

9. "Hans Blix's Briefing to the Security Council," full text, *The Guardian*, 14 February 2003, www.theguardian.com.

10. Hans Blix, "Inspections or Invasions, Lessons from Iraq," in *Lessons from Iraq: Avoiding the Next War*, eds. Miriam Pemberton and William D. Hartung (Boulder, CO: Paradigm Publishers, 2008), 88.

11. Mohamed ElBaradei, International Atomic Energy Agency, "The Status of Nuclear Inspections in Iraq: 14 February 2003 Update," 14 February 2003, www.iaea.org.

12. Draper, *To Start a War*, 309.

13. See the analysis by James P. Rubin, "Stumbling into War," *Foreign Affairs* 82, no. 5 (September/October 2003): 56.

14. See the transcript of the Wolfowitz interview: Sam Tanenhaus, "Bush's Brain Trust," *Vanity Fair*, July 2003, https://archive.vanityfair.com.

15. Strong, *Public Opinion*, 126, 61.

16. Ibid., 7.

17. "Chilcot Report: Key Points from the Iraq Inquiry," *The Guardian*, 6 July 2016, www.theguardian.com.

18. Tony Blair, *A Journey* (London: Hutchinson, 2010), 374.

19. See the analysis of Michael Walzer, "The Right Way."

20. International Commission of Jurists, "Iraq–ICJ Deplores Moves toward a War of Aggression on Iraq," Statement of 18 March 2003, https://web.archive.org/web/20030407232423/http:/www.icj.org/news.php3?id_article=2770.

21. Afua Hirsch, "Iraq War Was Illegal, Dutch Panel Rules," *The Guardian*, 12 January 2010, www.theguardian.com.

22. Ewen MacAskill and Julian Borger, "Iraq War Was Illegal and Breached UN Charter, Says Annan," *The Guardian*, 15 September 2004, www.theguardian.com.

23. Donald Rumsfeld, *Known and Unknown: A Memoir* (New York: Sentinel, 2012), 438.

24. Draper, *To Start a War*, 74.

25. Joseph P. Hoar, "Why Aren't There Enough Troops in Iraq?" *New York Times*, 2 April 2003, www.nytimes.com.

26. Nicolaus Mills, "Punished for Telling Truth About Iraq War," *CNN Opinion*, 20 March 2013, www.cnn.com.

27. Michael O'Hanlon, "Iraq Without a Plan," 1 January 2005, Brookings Institution, www.brookings.edu.

28. Draper, *To Start a War*, 315.

29. Rayburn and Sobchak, *Surge and Withdrawal*, 639, 641.

30. Thomas Ricks, *Fiasco: The American Military Adventure in Iraq* (New York: Penguin, 2006); Daniel Bolger, *Why We Lost: A General's Insider Account of the Iraq and Afghanistan Wars* (New York: Mariner Books, 2015).

31. Rayburn and Sobchak, *Surge and Withdrawal*, 619. 622, 627.

32. George Packer, "War After the War," *New Yorker*, 24 November 2003, 64.

33. John Tirman, *The Deaths of Others: The Fate of Civilians in America's Wars* (New York: Oxford University Press, 2011), 229, 240, 242, 326–334.

34. Ray Takeyh, "Iran's New Iraq." *Middle East Journal*, vol. 62, no. 1 (Middle East Institute, 2008), 13–30.

35. Rayburn and Sobchak, *Surge and Withdrawal*, 639.

36. Solnit, "Acts of Hope."

37. Strong, *Public Opinion*, 176, 2.

38. BBC, "Syria Crisis: Cameron Loses Commons Vote on Syria Action," 30 August 2013, www.bbc.com.

39. Paul Singer, "Opposition to Syria Attack Emerges in Congress," *USA Today*, 2 September 2013, www.usatoday.com.

40. Pew Research Center, "Opposition to Syrian Airstrikes Surges," 9 September 2013, www.pewresearch.org.

41. The resulting UN Organization for the Prohibition of Chemical Weapons joint mission completed the task of removing substantial quantities of chemical weapons from Syria in 2014, but chemical attacks by the Syrian government continued, and the U.S. France and the UK launched a combined air strike against three Syrian chemical facilities in April 2018. See Arms Control Association, "Timeline of Syrian Chemical Weapons Activity, 2012–2021," May 2021, www.armscontrol.org.

42. Ariel Edwards-Levy, "Most Americans Favor Afghanistan Withdrawal But Say It Was Poorly Handled," CNN, 23 August 2021, www.cnn.com.

Bibliography

Ackerman, Spencer. *Reign of Terror: How the 9/11 Era Destabilized America and Produced Trump*. New York: Viking, 2021.

Arnove, Anthony. *Iraq: The Logic of Withdrawal*. New York: The New Press, 2007.

Bacevich, Andrew. *After the Apocalypse: America's Role in a World Transformed*. New York: Metropolitan Books, 2021.

Baker, Peter. *Days of Fire: Bush and Cheney in the White House*. New York: Anchor Books, 2014.

Castro, Carl Andrew, and Sara Kintzle. "Suicides in the Military: The Post-Modern Combat Veteran and the Hemingway Effect." *Current Psychiatry Reports* 16, no. 460 (June 2014): 1–9. doi: 10.1007/s11920-014-0460-1.

Cramer, Jane Kellett. "Militarized Patriotism: Why the U.S. Marketplace of Ideas Failed Before the Iraq War." *Security Studies* 16, no. 3 (2007): 489–524. doi: 10.1080/09636410701547949.

Davis, Mike. "The Democrats After November" *New Left Review* 43 (January–February 2007): 5–31.

Draper, Robert. *To Start a War: How the Bush Administration Took America into Iraq*. New York: Penguin Books, 2020.

Epstein, Barbara. "Notes on the Antiwar Movement." *Monthly Review* 55, no. 3 (July–August 2003).

Fisher, Louis. "Deciding on War against Iraq: Institutional Failures." *Political Science Quarterly* 118, no. 3 (Fall 2003): 389–410.

Glantz, Aaron, and Iraq Veterans Against the War. *Winter Soldier: Iraq and Afghanistan: Eyewitness Accounts of the Occupations*. Chicago: Haymarket Books, 2008.

Gitlin, Todd. "Who Will Lead?" *Mother Jones*, 14 October 2002, www .motherjones.com.

Hayden, Tom. *Ending the War in Iraq*. New York: Akashic Books, 2007.

Heaney, Michael T., and Fabio Rojas. *Party in the Street: The Antiwar Movement and the Democratic Party after 9/11*. New York: Cambridge University Press, 2015.

Holsti, Ole R. *American Public Opinion on the Iraq War*. Ann Arbor: University of Michigan Press, 2011.

Hudson, Kate. "Reflecting on the Recent Anti-War Movement." *Contemporary Politics* 13, no. 4 (December 2007); 379–88.

Hutto, Jonathan W. Sr. *Antiwar Soldier: How to Dissent Within the Ranks of the Military*. New York: Nation Books, 2008.

Kaplan, Edith. "A Hundred Peace Movements Bloom." *The Nation*, 6 January 2003, www.thenation.com.

Karol, David, and Edward Miguel. "The Electoral Cost of War: Iraq Casualties and the 2004 U.S. Presidential Election." *Journal of Politics* 69, no. 3 (August 2007): 633–648.

Karpf, David. *The MoveOn Effect: The Unexpected Transformation of American Political Advocacy*. Oxford, UK: University of Oxford Press, 2012.

Key, Joshua, and Lawrence Hill. *The Deserter's Tale: The Story of an Ordinary Soldier Who Walked Away from the War in Iraq*. New York: Atlantic Monthly Press, 2007.

Kull, Steven, Clay Ramsay, and Evan Lewis. "Misperceptions, the Media, and the Iraq War." *Political Science Quarterly* 118, no. 4 (Winter 2003/04): 569–598.

Leitz, Lisa. *Fighting for Peace: Veterans and Military Families in the Anti-Iraq War Movement*. Minneapolis: University of Minnesota Press, 2014.

Levine, Mark. "The Peace Movement Plans for the Future." *Middle East Report Online* (15 July 2003), https://merip.org.

Lopez, George A. "Iraq and Just War Thinking." *Commonweal* 129, no. 16 (27 September 2002): 14–15.

Mazarr, Michael J. *Leap of Faith: Hubris, Negligence, and America's Greatest Foreign Policy Tragedy*. New York: Public Affairs, 2019.

Mejía, Camilo. *Road from ar Ramadi: The Private Rebellion of Staff Sergeant Camilo Mejía, An Iraq War Memoir*. Chicago: Haymarket Books, 2008.

Meyer, David S., and Catherine Corrigall-Brown. "Coalitions and Political Context: U.S. Movements Against Wars in Iraq." *Mobilization: An International Journal* 10, no. 3 (June 2005): 327–346.

Miah, Malik. "Black America and the Iraq War." *Against the Current* 104 (May–June 2003), https://againstthecurrent.org.

Murray, Andrew, and Lindsey German, *Stop the War: The Story of Britain's Biggest Mass Movement*. London: Bookmarks Publications, 2005.

Pemberton, Miriam, and William D. Hartung, eds. *Lessons from Iraq: Avoiding the Next War*. Boulder, CO: Paradigm Publishers, 2008.

Rayburn, Colonel Joel D., and Colonel Frank K. Sobchak, eds. *The U.S. Army in the Iraq War, Volume 2: Surge and Withdrawal*. Carlisle Barracks, PA: Strategic Studies Institute/U.S. Army War College Press, 2019.

Rubin, James P. "Stumbling into War." *Foreign Affairs* 82, no. 5 (September/October 2003): 46–66.

Schell, Jonathan. "The Other Superpower." *The Nation*, 27 March 2003, www.thenation.com.

Sears, John Bennett. "Peace Work: The Antiwar Tradition in American Labor from the Cold War to the Iraq War." *Diplomatic History* 34, no. 4 (September 2010): 699–720.

Solnit, Rebecca. "Acts of Hope: Challenging Empire on the World Stage." *Mother Jones,*14 June 2005.

Strong, James R. *Public Opinion, Legitimacy and Tony Blair's War in Iraq.* London: Routledge, 2017.

Taylor, Ian. *Media Relations of the Anti-War Movement: The Battle for Hearts and Minds.* New York: Routledge, 2017.

Walgrave, Stefaan, and Dieter Rucht, eds. *The World Says No to War: Demonstrations Against the War in Iraq.* Minneapolis: University of Minnesota Press, 2010.

Wallerstein, Immanuel. "U.S. Weakness and the Struggle for Hegemony," *Monthly Review* 55, no. 3 (July-August 2003). doi: 10.14452/MR-055-03-2003-07_3.

Walzer, Michael. "The Right Way." *New York Review of Books,* March 13, 2003.

Wheatcroft, Geoffrey. "The Tragedy of Tony Blair." *The Atlantic,* June 2004.

Woodward, Bob. *Bush at War.* New York: Simon and Schuster, 2002.

———. *Plan of Attack: The Definitive Account of the Decision to Invade Iraq.* New York: Simon & Schuster, 2004.

Wright, Col. Ann (ret.), and Susan Dixon. *Dissent: Voices of Conscience.* Kihei, HI: Koa Books, 2008.

Index

About the Author

David Cortright is professor emeritus at the University of Notre Dame's Kroc Institute for International Peace Studies in the Keough School of Global Affairs. Cortright is the author or editor of more than twenty books, including *Waging Peace in Vietnam* (New Village Press, 2019), *Governance for Peace* (Cambridge University Press, 2017), *Gandhi and Beyond* (Paradigm, 2009) and *Peace: A History of Movements and Ideas* (Cambridge University Press, 2008).

Cortright has a long history of public advocacy for disarmament and the prevention of war. He spoke out against the Vietnam War while serving as an active-duty soldier and examined the history and impact of antiwar resistance in the military in his 1975 book, *Soldiers in Revolt*, republished in 2005. In 1978, Cortright was named executive director of SANE, the Committee for a Sane Nuclear Policy, which under his leadership grew from 4,000 to 150,000 members and became the largest disarmament organization in the United States. In November 2002, he helped create Win Without War, an organization that opposed the invasion of Iraq and continues to work today for progressive US security policies.